Better Homes and Gardens

MEAT COOK BOOK

MEREDITH PRESS
NEW YORK   DES MOINES

CONTENTS

MEAT MAKES THE MEAL

All-American beef 6
Flavorful, young, tender veal 24
Palate tempting pork 32
Ham for all occasions 44
Lamb puts spring into mealtime 52
Ever-popular ground meat served plain or fancy 62
Variety meats to select .72
Add quick-cooking fish and seafood to the menu 78
New ways with poultry .88
Carving is the difference 104
Brighten the budget with careful buying and storing .108

MEALS MADE WITH EASE

Spark mealtimes with sausages and frankfurters 116
Meats ready to serve 124
Color menus with planned-overs 126

SALADS AND SANDWICHES

Imagination makes for savory sandwiches 134
Plan a meal around hearty salads 138

FOOD FUN WITH ACTION-MEALS

Clambake for everyone 144
Barbecue is hot coals and sizzling juices 146
Fish fry over a blazing campfire 150
Chuck wagon full of western favorites 152
American-style luau 154
Evening appetizer buffet 156
Index 158

On the cover: Beef Rib Supreme is a mouth-watering special for a large party. Carving at the table adds drama to the meal.

At left: Tropical Ham Sauce is a duet—a glaze and a sauce. During baking, glaze ham, then add fruit to serve as a sauce.

Our seal assures you that every recipe in the MEAT COOK BOOK is tested and endorsed by the Better Homes and Gardens Test Kitchen. Each recipe is tested until it measures up to high standards of family appeal, practicality, and deliciousness!

MEAT MAKES THE MEAL

If meat jargon has you befuddled, check the section on terms for an answer. It is essential to be able to identify, buy, and store various meat cuts to save pennies. Included are charts and tips that will help. Scan the pages for meat recipes of all kinds to star in the meal, from large roasts, to ground meats and variety meats. Also look here for fish and seafood recipes, poultry and game recipes, and of course, how to make gravy and season meat. Want to carve like an expert? Just follow the step-by-step drawings and directions included.

Here's a chance to fix meat with the same cook-at-the-table showmanship of a skilled maitre d'. Feature Steak Diane with fluted mushroom trim.

All-American beef

BEEF RIB SUPREME*

Have meatman cut one 4- to 6-pound roast as for Delmonico or rib eye roast, but with 3-inch length ribs still attached. Place roast, fat side up, on rack in shallow roasting pan. Insert meat thermometer. Roast, uncovered, according to Beef Roasting Chart. To serve, trim with cherry tomatoes and watercress. Allow 2 or 3 servings per pound of meat.

As shown on the cover.

ROLLED ROASTS AU JUS

Select a boned and rolled rib *or* rump roast. (Only top grades of rump should be roasted.) Place meat, fat side up, on rack in shallow roasting pan; season with salt and pepper. Insert meat thermometer; roast, uncovered, according to Beef Roasting Chart. Serve Au Jus. Allow 3 or 4 servings per pound.

Au Jus: Remove roast from pan. Skim off excess fat from meat juices. Add a little water to juices in pan. Simmer about 3 minutes, stirring to remove crusty bits. Strain.

Insert meat thermometer into center of meat so bulb rests in thickest part of lean meat and does not touch bone or fat.

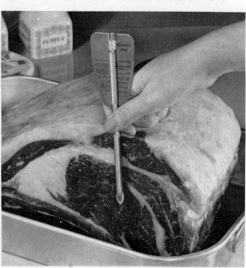

STANDING RIB ROAST

Place standing rib roast, fat side up, in shallow roasting pan. Season with salt and pepper. Insert meat thermometer into center of roast; roast, uncovered, according to Beef Roasting Chart. Serves 2 or 3 per pound.

ROAST BEEF TENDERLOIN

Remove surface fat and connective tissue from one 4- to 6-pound whole beef tenderloin. Place on rack in shallow roasting pan; season with salt and pepper. Tuck under small end; insert meat thermometer. Brush meat with salad oil. Roast, uncovered, according to Beef Roasting Chart. Serves 2 or 3 per pound.

CHATEAUBRIAND

1   1½- to 2-pound center-cut beef tenderloin
2   tablespoons butter, melted
    Bearnaise Sauce

Place meat on rack of broiler pan. Brush with butter. Broil 4 inches from heat, 12 to 15 minutes; season with salt. Turn; brush again. Broil 12 to 15 minutes more; season second side. Outside will be browned, inside, rare. Serve with Bearnaise Sauce. Serves 2.

Bearnaise Sauce: In saucepan, blend 3 tablespoons tarragon vinegar, 1 teaspoon finely chopped shallots *or* green onion, 4 black peppercorns, crushed, and a Bouquet Garni of dried tarragon and chervil leaves. Simmer till liquid is reduced to half. Strain; add 1 tablespoon cold water to liquid.

Beat 4 egg yolks in top of double boiler (not over water). Slowly add herb liquid. Soften ½ cup butter; add a few tablespoons to yolks. Place over *hot, not boiling,* water; cook and stir till butter melts and sauce starts to thicken. Slowly add remaining butter, stirring till sauce resembles thick cream. Remove from heat. Salt to taste; add 1 teaspoon snipped fresh tarragon *or* ¼ teaspoon dried tarragon, crushed. Makes 1 cup.

TENDERLOIN DELUXE

1   2-pound beef tenderloin
2   tablespoons butter or margarine,
    softened

    • • •

¼   cup chopped green onion
2   tablespoons butter or margarine
2   tablespoons soy sauce
1   teaspoon Dijon-style mustard
    Dash freshly ground pepper
¾   cup sherry

Remove surface fat and connective tissue from meat; spread with 2 tablespoons butter. Place on rack in shallow roasting pan. Insert meat thermometer. Roast according to Beef Roasting Chart for 20 minutes.

Meanwhile, in small saucepan, cook green onion in 2 tablespoons butter or margarine till tender but not brown. Add soy sauce, mustard, and pepper. Stir in wine; heat just to boiling. Remove roast from oven; pour wine sauce over tenderloin. Return roast to oven; continue roasting according to Beef Roasting Chart. Baste frequently with sauce. Pass remaining wine sauce with meat. Allow 3 or 4 servings per pound of meat.

SIRLOIN TIP ROAST

1   3- to 4-pound sirloin tip roast
2   tablespoons all-purpose flour
2   tablespoons shortening
½   cup pineapple juice
1   tablespoon instant minced onion
1   tablespoon lemon juice
1   teaspoon Italian salad
    dressing mix
1   teaspoon Worcestershire sauce

Sprinkle meat lightly with flour; brown slowly on all sides in hot shortening in roasting pan. Season with 2 teaspoons salt. Combine remaining ingredients and ⅛ teaspoon pepper; pour over meat. Cover; roast at 325° for 2 to 2¾ hours or till meat is tender. Remove to serving platter. Allow 3 or 4 servings per pound of meat.

To prepare gravy, pour pan juices into large measuring cup. Skim off excess fat; return 1½ cups juices to pan. Combine ½ cup cold water and ¼ cup all-purpose flour in shaker; shake well. Stir into juices; cook, stirring constantly, till gravy is thickened and bubbly. If desired, add kitchen bouquet for color. Makes 2 cups gravy.

BEEF ROASTING CHART

Cut	Approximate Weight (Pounds)	Internal Temp. on Removal from Oven	Approximate Cooking Time (Total Time)
Roast meat at constant oven temperature of 325° unless otherwise indicated.			
Standing Rib	4 to 6	140° (rare) 160° (medium) 170° (well done)	2¼ to 2¾ hrs. 2¾ to 3¼ hrs. 3¼ to 3½ hrs.
Standing Rib	6 to 8	140° (rare) 160° (medium) 170° (well done)	2¾ to 3 hrs. 3 to 3½ hrs. 3¾ to 4 hrs.
Rolled Rib	5 to 7	140° (rare) 160° (medium) 170° (well done)	3¼ to 3½ hrs. 3¾ to 4 hrs. 4½ to 4¾ hrs.
Rolled Rump	4 to 6	150° to 170°	2 to 2½ hrs.
Sirloin Tip	3½ to 4	150° to 170°	2 to 2¾ hrs.
Rib Eye or Delmonico (Roast at 350°)	4 to 6	140° (rare) 160° (medium) 170° (well done)	1½ to 1¾ hrs. 1¾ hrs. 2 hrs.
Tenderloin, whole (Roast at 425°)	4 to 6	140° (rare)	45 min. to 1 hr.
Tenderloin, half (Roast at 425°)	2 to 3	140° (rare)	45 to 50 min.

Beef cuts

For Basic Bone Identification Chart and How Much Meat to Serve, see Index.

1. *Standing Rib Roast*—from the rib section of the loin, contains the rib bones and the backbone. The predominant muscle is the rib eye. A thin muscle called the cap is often between the rib eye and the outer layer of fat. If the backbone is loosened for ease of carving, the roast should be tied. Roast this cut. *Rib Eye Roast*—a boneless cut, is also called a Delmonico Roast. The only muscle is the rib eye as the cap muscle has been removed. Roast this cut. *Rolled Rib Roast*—is a boned, rolled, and tied Standing Rib Roast. It will include the rib eye and the cap muscles. Roast this cut.

2. *Flank Steak*—comes from the flank section which is below the center loin and sirloin section. It is a boneless cut consisting of many long muscle fibers. It is oval in shape and has a small amount of fat. High-quality steak can be broiled and is often used for a London Broil. Braise Flank Steak of lower quality. *Rolled Flank Steak*—is often stuffed. Braise this cut. *Flank Steak Fillets (pinwheels)*—are cut from the Rolled Flank Steak. They are secured with a wooden skewer. A cube of suet is in the center for flavor and juiciness. Broil high-quality fillets; otherwise braise Flank Steak Fillets.

3. *Corned Beef Brisket*—is cut from the brisket section located immediately under the shoulder and to the right of the arm. All bones and extra fat have been removed. It is then cured in salt brine (pickled). Unless pre-tendered, cook this cut in liquid. *Cross Cut Shanks*—can be identified by the round shank bone. They are cut 1 to 1½ inches thick. Braise or cook this cut in liquid for soup. *Short Ribs*—are cut from the ribs immediately below the rib section. This cut contains a cross section of the rib bone and has alternating layers of lean and fat. Braise or cook the short ribs in liquid.

1. *Rib Roast: Standing*, upper left, *Rib Eye*, lower left, *Rolled*, upper right.

2. *Flank Steak*, left; *Rolled Flank Steak*, right; *Flank Steak Fillets*, bottom.

3. *Corned Beef Brisket*, upper left; *Cross Cut Shanks*, lower left; *Short Ribs*, right.

4. *Pot Roast: Boneless Chuck*, upper left, *Blade*, lower left, *Arm*, right.

5. *Sirloin Tip Roast*, top; *Round Steak: Bottom and Eye*, left, *Top*, right.

6. *Standing Rump Roast*, lower left; *Rolled Rump Roast*, upper right.

4. *Boneless Chuck Pot Roast*—is cut from the shoulder (chuck). It is boned, rolled, and tied and has fat interspersed between the muscles. Braise this pot roast. *Blade Pot Roast*—cut from the shoulder next to the rib section, can be identified by the blade bone, sometimes referred to as the 7-bone. The backbone and rib bone can also be included in this cut. Braise this pot roast. *Arm Pot Roast*—can be identified by the round arm bone (front leg). A cross section of rib bones may also be present. Braise this pot roast.

5. *Sirloin Tip Roast*—is cut from the leg (round section) and has a small portion from the lower sirloin section. The only bone in the cut is usually removed. If cut is high quality, roast, otherwise braise. *Round Steak*—is oval in shape and can be identified by the round leg bone. It consists of four muscles which are often sold separately: sirloin tip, top round, bottom round, and the eye of the round. Often round steak will have one end cut off parallel to the leg bone. This muscle which surrounds the leg bone and is often removed is called the sirloin tip. *Top Round Steak*—is cut from the inside of the leg. It's the largest muscle and is considered the most tender. Roast high quality, otherwise braise. *Bottom Round Steak* —often contains both the bottom muscle and the eye of the round. These two muscles are separated by white connective tissue. The bottom round is less tender than the top and should be braised. *Eye of the Round*—is the smallest muscle and is egg shaped. If thinly sliced and of high quality, panfry, otherwise braise.

6. *Standing Rump Roast*—triangular in shape, is cut from the top part of the leg. It contains the pelvic bone and may or may not contain a portion of the backbone. It consists of many different muscles including part of top and bottom of the round and part of the sirloin. Braise this cut, or for high quality, roast. *Rolled Rump Roast*—is a boned, rolled, and tied Standing Rump Roast. Its many layers of muscles are interspersed with fat and the roast is covered with a thin layer of fat. Braise this cut; if high-quality meat is purchased, it may be roasted.

BEEF STEAK IDENTIFICATION

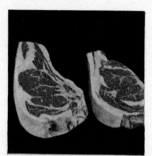

Rib Steak (*left*) identified by the rib bone, is cut from the rib section of the loin. The large muscle is the rib eye. The cap muscle may be present if cut close to the shoulder (chuck).

Rib Eye Steak (*right*) is also called the Delmonico Steak. Cut from the rib section of the loin, the only muscle present is the rib eye. The boneless steak will vary in thickness.

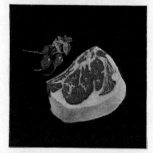

Club Steak (*left*) is the first steak cut from the center loin section. It may or may not contain the thirteenth rib. The large muscle is the loin eye.

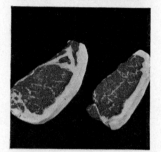

Top Loin Steak (*right*) cut from center loin section, has only the loin eye muscle. Strip Steak (left) has the finger of the T-bone present. Boneless Strip Steak (right) is also called the New York Cut or Kansas City Steak.

T-bone Steak (*left*) is cut from the center loin section. The finger of the T-bone separates the loin eye from the tenderloin muscle, the smaller muscle.

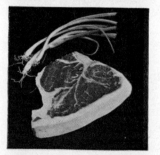

Porterhouse Steak (*right*) is also cut from the center loin section. The difference between this steak and the T-bone steak is that the tenderloin muscle in the Porterhouse is larger.

Chateaubriand (*left*) is the center cut from the tenderloin which has been removed from one side of the T-bone. It's a dining-out classic, listed on the menu "for two." The whole tenderloin may be sliced into Filet Mignons.

Pin Bone Sirloin Steak (*right*) is the first steak cut from the sirloin section of the loin. It can be identified by the pin shaped bone of the wedge bone.

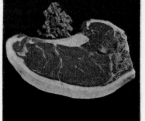

Flat Bone Sirloin Steak (*left*) is cut from the middle of the sirloin section of the loin. The identifying bone is the flat shaped bone of the hip bone, commonly known as the wedge bone.

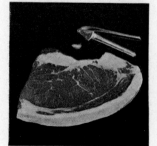

Wedge Bone Sirloin Steak (*right*) is cut from the section of the sirloin closest to the leg. The identifying bone for this steak is the wedge bone.

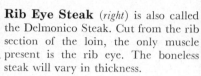
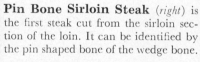
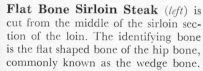

STEAK BROILING CHART			
Thickness of Steak	(Total Time In Minutes)		
	Rare	Medium	Well-done
1 inch	8 to 10	12 to 14	18 to 20
1½ inch	14 to 16	18 to 20	25 to 30
2 inch	20 to 25	30 to 35	40 to 45

BROILED BEEF STEAK

Have a beef porterhouse, T-bone, club, sirloin, or tenderloin (filet mignon) steak cut 1 to 2 inches thick.* Slash fat edge (not into meat) at 1-inch intervals.

Place steak on cold rack in broiler pan. Broil 1- to 1½-inch thick steaks so surface of meat is 3 inches from heat, thicker cuts 4 to 5 inches from heat. (Check broiler instruction booklet.) Broil about *half* of time indicated on Steak Broiling Chart; season. Turn with tongs; broil for remaining time. Season with salt and pepper.

*Or pre-tendered beef where available.

Doneness test: Make small slit in center of steak. Note inside color: red—rare; pink—medium; gray—well.

PANBROILED STEAK

Choose beef porterhouse, T-bone, club, sirloin, or tenderloin (filet mignon) steak cut 1 inch thick or less. Place in cold heavy skillet. *Do not add shortening* (unless very lean cuts are used). Brown both sides. Cook, uncovered, over medium-high heat, turning occasionally. Total cooking time is about 9 to 10 minutes for rare; 11 to 12 minutes for medium; 20 minutes for well-done. Season.

TENDERIZED STEAK

Choose beef round, chuck, or rump steak, cut 1 inch thick. Sprinkle meat with instant unseasoned meat tenderizer according to label directions. *Do not use additional salt.* Place steak on rack in broiler pan. Broil meat to desired degree of doneness according to Steak Broiling Chart (see above), *except* reduce broiling time slightly. Serve steak sizzling hot.

PLANKED STEAK

Broil 1½-inch thick beef steak according to Steak Broiling Chart, *except* reduce timing 7 minutes for second side. Place on seasoned plank (brush plank with oil; heat in 300° oven, 1 hour). Pipe or spoon border of Duchess Potatoes around edge of plank. Oil exposed wood. (If desired, make extra potato cups; fill with hot cooked vegetables just before serving.) Broil 4 inches from heat 5 to 7 minutes, or till potatoes brown and meat is cooked to desired degree of doneness.

Duchess Potatoes: Beat 1 tablespoon butter or margarine, 1 beaten egg, and salt and pepper to taste into 4 cups hot mashed potatoes. Using pastry bag with large star tip, pipe hot potatoes around partially broiled steak on wooden plank. Melt 2 tablespoons butter and drizzle over potatoes.

SESAME TOPPER

¼ cup butter, softened
Dash garlic salt
2 teaspoons sesame seed, toasted

Blend together butter, garlic salt, and sesame seed. Pass as topper for hot broiled steak.

To prevent steaks from curling during cooking, slit fat and membrane at 1-inch intervals. Do not cut into the lean meat.

BEEF FONDUE

        Salad oil
1½ pounds beef tenderloin, cut in
        ¾ -inch cubes
        Curry Sauce
        Basil Butter
        Tomato Sauce
        Hot Mustard Sauce

Pour salad oil in saucepan or beef fondue cooker to no more than ½ capacity or to depth of about 2 inches. Heat to 425° on range (don't let oil smoke). Transfer hot oil to cooker; place over alcohol burner or canned heat. Have beef cubes at room temperature in serving bowl.

Set out small bowls of several of the special butters and sauces. Each guest spears a beef cube with fondue fork, then holds it in the hot oil until cooked to desired doneness—it doesn't take long to learn the length of time. Then transfer the meat to a dinner fork and dip in a sauce on a plate. Makes 4 servings.

Curry Sauce: In saucepan, melt 3 tablespoons butter or margarine over low heat. Stir in 1 teaspoon curry powder; cook for 1 to 2 minutes. Blend in 2 tablespoons all-purpose flour, ½ teaspoon salt, and dash pepper. Add 1 cup milk all at once. Cook quickly, stirring constantly till mixture thickens and bubbles. Serve hot. Makes 1 cup sauce.

Basil Butter: Cream ½ cup softened butter till fluffy. Beat in 1 teaspoon lemon juice and ¾ teaspoon dried basil, crushed. Keep basil butter at room temperature for at least 1 hour to mellow before serving. Makes ½ cup.

Tomato Sauce: Combine ½ cup dairy sour cream, 2 tablespoons chili sauce, ½ teaspoon prepared horseradish, ¼ teaspoon salt, and dash freshly ground pepper. Chill mixture until serving time. Makes ⅔ cup.

Hot Mustard Sauce: In a jar, mix together ½ cup dry mustard and ½ cup vinegar. Cover and let stand overnight. In saucepan, beat 1 egg; stir in ¼ cup sugar, dash salt, and mustard mixture. Cook, stirring constantly, over low heat till mixture thickens slightly and coats spoon. Cool. Blend 1 cup mayonnaise or salad dressing into cooled mustard mixture. Makes about 2 cups sauce.

STUFFED FLANK STEAK

⅓ cup chopped onion
2 tablespoons butter or margarine
2 hard-cooked eggs, chopped
2 cups herb-seasoned stuffing
   croutons
1 cup dairy sour cream
1 beaten egg
1 pound beef flank steak
   Meat tenderizer
2 tablespoons shortening

Cook onion in butter till tender. Stir in chopped eggs, croutons, ¼ *cup* of the sour cream, beaten egg, and ½ cup hot water. Pound steak to thin rectangle. Use tenderizer following label directions. Spread stuffing over meat; roll up from long side. Skewer securely. Brown in hot shortening. Add ½ cup water. Cover; simmer about 1½ hours. Remove meat; add water to drippings to make ½ cup; stir in remaining sour cream. Heat just to boiling; pass sauce. Serves 4.

DEVILED FLANK ROLLS

Pound thick end of one 1½-pound beef flank steak to flatten slightly. Use meat tenderizer following label directions. Spread surface with one 2¼-ounce can deviled ham. Roll up from long side; skewer securely. Cut meat into 1-inch slices. Combine ⅓ cup catsup, 1 tablespoon salad oil, and 1 teaspoon kitchen bouquet. Brush both sides of meat with sauce. Place on rack in broiler pan. Broil 4 inches from heat for 5 minutes; turn. Brush with sauce; broil 5 minutes. Serves 2 or 3.

LONDON BROIL

Score one 1½-pound top-quality beef flank steak. Place in shallow pan. Combine 1 cup salad oil, 1 tablespoon vinegar, and 1 small clove garlic, minced; pour over steak. Cover; let stand at room temperature 2 to 3 hours; turn several times.

Place steak on cold rack in broiler pan. Broil 3 inches from heat about 5 minutes; season with salt and pepper. Turn. Broil 5 minutes more for medium rare. Season. To serve, carve in *very thin* slices diagonally across grain. Serves 4 or 5.

SAUCY TENDERLOIN TIPS

Cook 1 cup sliced fresh mushrooms in 2 tablespoons butter or margarine till tender. Stir in 1 tablespoon all-purpose flour. Add 1 cup beef broth and 1 bay leaf. Cook and stir till thickened and bubbly; reduce heat and simmer, uncovered, for 2 minutes. Remove bay leaf. Cut 1 pound beef tenderloin tips *or* sirloin steak into thin bias strips. Brown on all sides in 2 tablespoons hot shortening. Reduce heat and add ½ cup green pepper cut in thin strips; cook 1 to 2 minutes more. Add to broth mixture; mix well. Heat through and serve immediately. Makes 4 or 5 servings.

BEEF STROGANOFF

Cut 1 pound beef sirloin into ¼-inch strips. Coat meat with mixture of 1 tablespoon all-purpose flour and ½ teaspoon salt. Heat blazer pan of chafing dish over direct flame or heat skillet, then add 2 tablespoons butter. When melted, add sirloin strips and brown quickly on both sides. Add one 3-ounce can sliced mushrooms, drained, ½ cup chopped onion, and 1 clove garlic, minced. Cook 3 or 4 minutes or till onion is crisp-tender. Remove meat and mushrooms from pan.

Add 2 tablespoons butter to pan drippings; blend in 3 tablespoons all-purpose flour. Add 1 tablespoon tomato paste. Stir in 1¼ cups cold beef stock *or* one 10½-ounce can condensed beef broth. Cook and stir over medium-high heat till thickened and bubbly.

Return meat and mushrooms to blazer pan or skillet. Stir in 1 cup dairy sour cream and 2 tablespoons dry white wine; cook slowly till heated through. Do not boil. Keep warm over hot water. Serve over hot buttered noodles. Makes 4 or 5 servings.

BEEF TERIYAKI

Combine ⅔ cup soy sauce, ¼ cup dry sherry, 2 tablespoons sugar, 1 teaspoon ground ginger, and 1 clove garlic, minced. Cut 2 pounds beef sirloin steak, ½ inch thick, in serving-size pieces. Marinate in soy sauce mixture at room temperature about 30 minutes. Broil 3 inches from heat for 5 to 7 minutes on *each* side, basting with marinade 2 or 3 times while cooking. Serves 6 to 8.

Pounding meat with metal or wooden meat mallet breaks up tough fibers and works flour into the meat for coating.

STEAK DIANE

> 4 beef sirloin strip steaks, cut ½ inch thick
> 1 teaspoon dry mustard
> 4 tablespoons butter or margarine
> 3 tablespoons lemon juice
> 2 teaspoons snipped chives
> 1 teaspoon Worcestershire sauce

With meat mallet, pound steaks to ⅓ inch thickness. Sprinkle one side of each steak with salt, freshly ground black pepper, and ⅛ *teaspoon* of the dry mustard; pound into meat. Repeat with other side of meat. Heat blazer pan of chafing dish over direct flame or heat skillet, then add butter or margarine. When melted, add 2 steaks and cook 2 minutes on each side. Transfer meat to hot serving plate. Repeat, cooking remaining meat. To blazer pan or skillet, add lemon juice, chives, and Worcestershire sauce; bring to boiling. Return meat to chafing dish. Spoon a little sauce over meat. Garnish with cooked, fluted mushrooms, if desired. Serves 4.

14

Serve Savory Pepper Steak over rice as a
meal-on-a-platter. Round steak strips are
cooked slowly in a rich tomato sauce.

Plain or fancy round steak

COOKING ROUND STEAK

Beef round steak contains 3 muscles. Top round, the tenderest muscle, can be broiled when high quality or tenderized; braise lower quality. Bottom round, not as tender, is always braised. Eye of the round, if cut thin and of high quality, can be panbroiled; braise lower quality and thicker cuts.

SAVORY PEPPER STEAK

Cut 1½ pounds beef round steak, cut ½ inch thick, in strips. Coat with mixture of ¼ cup all-purpose flour, ½ teaspoon salt, and ⅛ teaspoon pepper. In large skillet, brown strips in ¼ cup hot shortening.

Drain one 8-ounce can tomatoes, reserving liquid. Add reserved liquid, 1¾ cups water, ½ cup chopped onion, 1 small clove garlic, minced, and 1 tablespoon beef-flavored gravy base to meat. Cover; simmer 1¼ hours or till meat is tender. Uncover; stir in 1½ teaspoons Worcestershire sauce. Cut 2 large green peppers in strips and add to meat. Cover; simmer meat and green peppers for 5 minutes.

If gravy is too thin, combine 1 to 2 tablespoons all-purpose flour with an equal amount of cold water; stir into sauce. Cook and stir till thickened and bubbly. Add drained tomatoes, cut up; cook 5 minutes more. Serve over hot cooked rice. Makes 6 servings.

BEEF ROLL-UPS

Cut 2 pounds beef round steak, ¼ inch thick, in 8 rectangular pieces; spread all with 3 tablespoons prepared mustard to within ½ inch of edge. Sprinkle all with ¼ cup finely minced onion. Cut 1 large dill pickle in 8 lengthwise strips. Halve 4 slices bacon. Top *each* steak with pickle strip and half slice bacon. Roll up jelly-roll fashion, tucking in edges. Tie with heavy cord or skewer securely.

Coat meat with mixture of 2 tablespoons all-purpose flour, 1½ teaspoons salt, and ⅛ teaspoon pepper. In large skillet, brown meat slowly in 3 tablespoons hot shortening.

Combine one 8-ounce can tomato sauce, 1 teaspoon Worcestershire sauce, 1 teaspoon beef-flavored gravy base, 1 cup hot water, and 1 teaspoon brown sugar; pour over meat. Cover and simmer for 1¼ hours. Remove meat from sauce; remove cord or skewers. If sauce is too thin, combine 1 to 2 tablespoons all-purpose flour with an equal amount of cold water; stir into sauce. Cook and stir till thickened and bubbly. Serve meat over hot buttered noodles; top with sauce. Serves 8.

SHORT RIB STEW

Brown slowly 2 to 3 pounds beef short ribs on all sides in Dutch oven; drain off excess fat. Season with salt and pepper; add water to almost cover meat. Cover; simmer for 2 to 2½ hours or till meat is tender.

Add 2 medium onions, quartered, 2 medium potatoes, pared and cubed, 1 medium rutabaga, pared and cubed, 4 medium carrots, pared and cut in 1-inch pieces, 2 teaspoons Worcestershire sauce, and 1 bay leaf. Season with salt and pepper. Cover; simmer 20 to 30 minutes or till tender. Remove meat and vegetables to serving dish. Discard bay leaf.

Skim excess fat from pan juices. Combine ½ cup cold water with ¼ cup all-purpose flour; stir into juices. Cook, stirring till thick and bubbly. Serve atop stew. Serves 6.

BARBECUED SHORT RIBS

Trim excess fat from 4 pounds beef short ribs. Season with salt and pepper. Place ribs in Dutch oven; add water to cover. Cover; simmer till tender, about 2 hours. Drain; place ribs on rack of broiler pan.

Combine ⅓ cup catsup, 2 tablespoons molasses, 1 tablespoon lemon juice, 2 teaspoons dry mustard, ¼ teaspoon chili powder, and dash garlic powder; brush over ribs. Broil 4 to 5 inches from heat for 15 minutes, turning often and brushing with sauce. Serves 4.

ITALIAN STUFFED STEAK

Remove bone and excess fat from 2 pounds round steak, cut ½ inch thick; cut into serving pieces. Blend ½ teaspoon *each* salt, dried basil, crushed, dried oregano, crushed, and ¼ teaspoon pepper; sprinkle seasonings and 2 ounces salami, chopped (about ⅔ cup) over meat. Roll each steak as for jelly roll; tie.

In 10-inch skillet, brown meat rolls in 2 tablespoons hot shortening; add ½ cup tomato juice. Cover; simmer for 1 hour, or till tender. Remove meat rolls to platter.

Pour pan juices into large measuring cup; skim off excess fat. Return ½ cup juices to skillet. Combine 1 tablespoon all-purpose flour with ½ cup cold water; add to juices. Cook and stir till thickened and bubbly. Serve over meat. Makes 4 to 6 servings.

Try Braised Short Ribs, a medley of beef, vegetables, and rice for a flavorful meal-in-one dish served from the oven.

BRAISED SHORT RIBS

    3 pounds beef short ribs, cut in
      serving-size pieces
    ¾ cup uncooked long-grain rice
    ½ cup chopped onion
    ½ cup chopped celery
    ¼ cup chopped green pepper
    2 teaspoons beef-flavored gravy
      base
    1 teaspoon Worcestershire sauce
    ¼ teaspoon dried thyme, crushed

Brown ribs, 25 to 30 minutes, on all sides in skillet. Season with salt. Place in 3-quart casserole. Cover; bake at 325° for 1 hour. Using same skillet, combine rice and vegetables; cook till rice is lightly browned. Remove ribs from oven after baking for 1 hour; drain. Remove ribs from casserole. Place rice mixture in casserole; top with ribs. Combine remaining ingredients, 2¼ cups water, 2 teaspoons salt, and ⅛ teaspoon pepper in saucepan; bring to boil. Pour over ribs. Cover; bake 1 hour more. Serves 4 to 6.

BEEF MINUTE STEAKS

Lightly grease hot skillet. Cook minute steaks over high heat, 1 minute per side; season with salt and pepper. Remove steaks. Swirl a *little* water in pan; pour over steaks.

SKILLET PIZZA STEAK

    6 minute steaks
    2 tablespoons shortening
    6 slices mozzarella cheese
    1 8-ounce can tomato sauce
    1 clove garlic, minced
    1 teaspoon dried oregano, crushed
    ½ teaspoon dried basil, crushed

Brown 2 or 3 steaks at a time in hot shortening, in skillet, for 1 to 1½ minutes. Turn; top each with cheese slice; brown second side. Remove to platter. Add remaining ingredients, ¾ cup water, and dash pepper to skillet. Boil 1 to 2 minutes. Top meat with some sauce; pass remaining. Serves 6.

MINUTE STEAK SUKIYAKI

Cut 4 minute steaks in strips; in skillet, brown quickly in 2 tablespoons hot salad oil. Stir in one 10¾-ounce can beef gravy and 2 tablespoons soy sauce. Add ½ pound fresh spinach, stems removed, 1½ cups 1-inch bias-cut celery slices, ¼ cup 1-inch bias-cut green onion slices, and one 6-ounce can chopped mushrooms, drained. Cook, stirring gently, about 5 to 7 minutes or till vegetables are crisp-tender. Serve over hot cooked rice. Pass additional soy sauce. Serves 4.

STEAK AND BEAN POT

    4 minute steaks
    ¼ cup chopped onion
    2 tablespoons butter or margarine
    2 21-ounce cans pork and beans in
      tomato sauce
    1 small clove garlic, minced
    ¼ teaspoon chili powder
    ⅛ teaspoon dried oregano, crushed
    6 slices tomato
    ¼ cup shredded sharp process
      American cheese

Cut steaks in 3x1-inch strips; brown quickly with onion in melted butter in skillet. Add beans, garlic, and seasonings. Turn into 2-quart casserole. Bake, uncovered, at 350° for 30 minutes. Remove from oven; stir. Top with tomato; bake 15 minutes more. Top with cheese; heat till cheese melts. Serves 6.

SPICY RUMP ROAST

    1 3- to 4-pound beef rump roast
    2 tablespoons shortening
    ½ teaspoon dried marjoram, crushed
    1 8-ounce can tomatoes
    ½ cup dry red wine
    ½ cup chopped onion
    ¼ cup chopped green pepper
    1 clove garlic, crushed
    1 tablespoon sugar
    ⅛ teaspoon ground cinnamon
      Dash ground cloves
    ¼ cup all-purpose flour

In Dutch oven, slowly brown roast in hot shortening. Season with 1 teaspoon salt and marjoram. Add remaining ingredients except flour. Cover tightly; cook slowly for 2¼ to 2½ hours or till tender. Remove to platter.

To make gravy, pour pan juices into large measuring cup; skim off excess fat. Return 1½ cups juices to pan. Blend ½ cup cold water with flour; add to juices. Cook, stirring till thickened and bubbly. Makes 8 servings.

HAWAIIAN RUMP ROAST

    1 4-pound rolled beef rump roast
    2 tablespoons shortening
    1 medium onion, sliced
    3 tablespoons soy sauce
    ¼ teaspoon ground ginger
    ⅛ teaspoon pepper
    1 8¾-ounce can pineapple
      tidbits, drained
    ¼ cup sliced celery
    ¼ cup all-purpose flour

In Dutch oven, slowly brown roast on all sides in hot shortening. Add onion, soy sauce, ginger, pepper, and ¼ cup water. Cover tightly; simmer for 2½ hours or till tender. Add pineapple and celery. Continue cooking, covered, 20 minutes, or till celery is tender. Remove meat to platter. Drain pineapple and celery, reserving juices; set aside.

Skim excess fat from pan juices. Return 1½ cups juices to pan. Blend ½ cup cold water with flour; stir into juices. Cook, stirring constantly, till thickened and bubbly; cook 1 minute more. Season with salt and pepper. Add reserved pineapple and celery. Serve with meat. Makes 6 to 8 servings.

SWISS STEAK

¼ cup all-purpose flour
2 pounds beef round steak, 1 inch thick
3 tablespoons shortening
½ cup chopped onion
1 16-ounce can tomatoes, cut up
2 tablespoons chopped green pepper

Combine flour, 1 teaspoon salt, and ¼ teaspoon pepper; pound into meat. In large skillet, brown meat on both sides in hot shortening*. Top with onion and tomatoes. Cover; cook over low heat 1½ hours or till tender. Add green pepper; cook 15 minutes more. Skim off excess fat. Thicken juices, if desired. Season to taste. Makes 6 to 8 servings.

*To oven bake, transfer browned meat to 12x7½x2-inch baking dish. Top with onion and tomatoes. Bake, covered, at 350° for 1½ hours. Uncover; add green pepper and bake 15 minutes, basting meat occasionally.

BEEF BURGUNDY

2 to 2½ pounds beef round steak, ¼ inch thick
¼ cup all-purpose flour
¼ cup butter or margarine
½ cup coarsely chopped onion
1 tablespoon finely snipped parsley
1 medium clove garlic, crushed
1 bay leaf
1 teaspoon salt
Dash freshly ground black pepper
1 6-ounce can whole mushrooms, drained
1 cup Burgundy
Hot cooked rice

Cut steak into bite-size pieces; coat with flour. In 12-inch skillet, quickly brown *half* the steak on both sides in melted butter; remove meat. Brown remaining meat. Remove from heat; return all meat to skillet. Add onion and next 5 ingredients. Stir in mushrooms, wine, and ½ cup water. Bring to boiling; reduce heat and simmer, covered, about 1 hour or till tender. Add more water during cooking if necessary. Remove bay leaf. Serve over fluffy hot cooked rice. Makes 8 servings.

PIZZA SWISS STEAK

Cut 2 pounds beef round steak, 1 inch thick, into 6 serving-size pieces. Combine 2 tablespoons all-purpose flour, 2 teaspoons salt, and ¼ teaspoon pepper; pound into steak. In skillet, brown meat slowly on both sides in 3 tablespoons hot shortening or hot salad oil. Transfer to 12x7½x2-inch baking dish.

Combine one 8-ounce can tomato sauce, one 8-ounce can pizza sauce, ½ cup water, ½ teaspoon dried oregano, crushed, and ½ teaspoon sugar. Pour sauce mixture over meat. Top with 1 medium onion, sliced. Cover; bake at 350° for 1 hour. Uncover; bake 30 minutes more or till tender. Serves 6 to 8.

STEAK AND ONIONS

1½ to 2 pounds beef round steak, cut in serving-size pieces
2 tablespoons shortening
1 10½-ounce can condensed cream of mushroom soup
¼ cup water
1 3½-ounce jar cocktail onions
1 tablespoon snipped parsley

In skillet, brown meat slowly on both sides in hot shortening. Drain off excess fat. Combine soup, water, and onions with liquid; pour over meat. Simmer, covered, for 1½ hours or till tender. Sprinkle with parsley. Serves 6.

ROUND STEAK DINNER

Cut 2 pounds beef round steak, ½ to ¾ inch thick, into serving-size pieces. Combine 3 tablespoons all-purpose flour, 1 teaspoon salt, and dash pepper; pound into meat. In large skillet, brown meat in ¼ cup hot shortening. Transfer to 3-quart casserole. Dissolve 1 beef bouillon cube in 1 cup boiling water. Stir into one 10¾-ounce can condensed tomato soup; pour over meat. Add 1 bay leaf. Cover; bake at 350° for 45 minutes. Remove bay leaf.

Arrange 3 large potatoes, pared and quartered, and 2 medium onions, sliced, around edge of casserole; season with salt and pepper. Spoon tomato sauce over vegetables. Cover; bake 45 minutes longer. Add two 16-ounce cans French-style green beans, drained, in center. Cover; bake 15 minutes. Serves 6 to 8

BEEF POT ROAST

Coat one 3- to 4-pound beef pot roast with flour. In Dutch oven, large skillet, or roasting pan, brown slowly on all sides in 2 tablespoons hot shortening or salad oil. Season with salt and pepper. Remove from heat; add ½ cup water*. Cover tightly and simmer slowly 2½ hours or till tender. Add water if needed.

If desired, add small potatoes, pared and halved, small whole onions, and medium carrots, pared and cut in 1-inch pieces, the last 45 to 60 minutes. Using pan juices, prepare Pot Roast Gravy (see Index). Serves 6 to 8.

*If desired, tomato juice or beef broth can be substituted for the water.

CRANBERRY POT ROAST

Combine 2 tablespoons all-purpose flour, 1 teaspoon salt, 1 teaspoon onion salt, and ¼ teaspoon pepper. Rub one 3- to 4-pound beef pot roast with flour mixture (use all of mixture). In Dutch oven, slowly brown meat on both sides in 2 tablespoons hot shortening or salad oil. Remove from heat; add 4 whole cloves, 2 inches stick cinnamon, and ¼ cup water. Cover tightly and simmer about 2½ hours or till tender. Add water if necessary.

Pour off excess fat. Add one 16-ounce can (2 cups) whole cranberry sauce, 2 tablespoons water, and 1 tablespoon vinegar. Cover and cook 10 to 15 minutes longer. Pass sauce with meat. Makes 6 to 8 servings.

SAUERBRATEN

In large bowl or crock, combine 2 medium onions, sliced, ½ lemon, sliced, 2½ cups water, 1½ cups red wine vinegar, 12 whole cloves, 6 bay leaves, 6 whole black peppercorns, 1 tablespoon sugar, 1 tablespoon salt, and ¼ teaspoon ground ginger. Add one 4-pound beef rump roast, turning to coat. Cover and refrigerate about 36 hours; turn meat occasionally. Remove meat; wipe dry. Strain marinade and reserve. In Dutch oven, brown meat on all sides in 2 tablespoons hot shortening; add strained marinade. Cover; cook slowly 2 hours. Remove meat. For each cup gravy: Combine ¾ cup meat juices and ¼ cup water; add ⅓ cup broken gingersnaps. Cook and stir till thick. Makes 10 servings.

POLYNESIAN BEEF ROAST

1 3- to 4-pound beef chuck roast
1 large onion, sliced
1 cup pineapple juice
¼ cup soy sauce
1½ teaspoons ground ginger
1 cup diagonally sliced celery
4 carrots, cut in 3- to 4-inch strips
½ pound spinach, cleaned and stems removed *or* one 10-ounce package frozen spinach, thawed
1 pint fresh mushrooms, sliced
2 tablespoons cornstarch

In shallow baking dish, cover meat with onion rings. Combine pineapple juice, soy sauce, ginger, and ¼ teaspoon salt. Pour over meat. Let stand in pineapple mixture 1 hour at room temperature, turning meat once.

Place meat and onions in Dutch oven. Pour pineapple mixture over; cover and simmer 2 to 2½ hours or till meat is tender. Add celery and carrots. Sprinkle vegetables with salt; bring to boiling, then simmer 20 minutes. Arrange spinach and mushrooms on top of meat. Simmer 10 minutes or till spinach is wilted and other vegetables are crisp-tender. Remove meat and vegetables to heated platter; keep hot. Skim fat from meat juices. Blend together ¼ cup cold water and cornstarch. Stir into juices; cook and stir till thickened and bubbly. Makes 6 to 8 servings.

BEEF POT ROAST IN BEER

Coat one 3- to 4-pound beef rump roast with 2 tablespoons all-purpose flour. In Dutch oven or large skillet, brown slowly on all sides in 2 tablespoons hot shortening. Season with 1 teaspoon salt and dash pepper. Add ½ cup beer and 2 bay leaves. Cover tightly; simmer 1½ hours. Remove bay leaves.

Add 6 small whole onions and 4 medium carrots, pared and cut in 1-inch pieces. Cook 1 hour or till meat and vegetables are tender. Remove to heated platter. Skim fat from meat juices. Add enough beer to juices to make 1½ cups. Put ½ cup cold water in shaker with ¼ cup all-purpose flour. Shake well. Stir into juices with 2 tablespoons catsup. Cook, stirring till thickened and bubbly. Season. Cook and stir 2 to 3 minutes longer. Serves 6 to 8.

Spark up the popular pot roast by adding
mixed dried fruit and red Burgundy to
create this colorful Fruited Pot Roast.

Pot roasts perfect for company

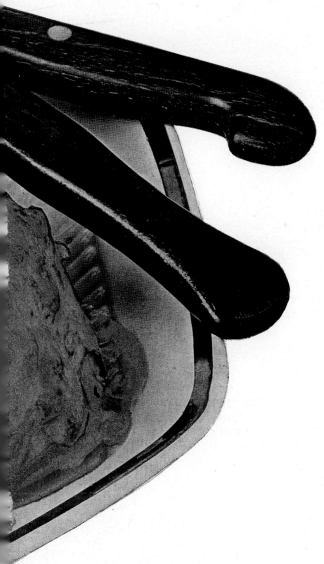

FRUITED POT ROAST

  1 3- to 4-pound beef arm or
    blade pot roast
  2 tablespoons shortening
  ½ cup finely chopped onion
  ⅓ cup finely chopped carrot
  ¼ cup red Burgundy
  1 clove garlic, minced
  1 11-ounce package mixed dried
    fruit (1¾ cups)
  3 tablespoons all-purpose flour

In Dutch oven, brown meat on both sides in hot shortening. Add onion, carrot, wine, garlic, 1½ teaspoons salt, and ¼ teaspoon pepper. Cover; simmer for 2 hours.

Pour 1½ cups hot water over fruit; let stand 1 hour. Drain, reserving liquid. Place fruit atop meat. Cover and cook 45 minutes to 1 hour or till meat is tender. Remove meat and fruit to warm platter.

Pour pan juices and fat into large measuring cup; skim off fat. Add reserved liquid to pan juices to make 1½ cups. Return to Dutch oven. Blend together flour and ½ cup cold water; stir into pan juices. Cook and stir till gravy is thickened and bubbly. Pass with roast. Makes 6 servings.

SNOWCAP POT ROAST

In Dutch oven, brown one 4-pound beef arm or blade pot roast on both sides over low heat with 1 clove garlic, minced, in 1 tablespoon hot shortening. Add ½ teaspoon dried marjoram, crushed, ¼ teaspoon ground nutmeg, and dash *each* salt and pepper. Pour 1 cup red Burgundy over meat. Cook, covered, in slow oven (325°) for 2½ to 3 hours.

To serve, remove bone and excess fat. Top meat with ½ cup dairy sour cream; sprinkle with 2 tablespoons chopped green onion and dash paprika. Pour meat juices and fat into large measuring cup; skim off fat. Add water to measure 1½ cups; return juices to pan. Blend 1½ tablespoons cornstarch with 2 tablespoons cold water; stir into juices. Cook and stir till thick and bubbly. Serves 6 to 8.

TO BROWN MEAT

Use trimmed fat from meat for browning instead of shortening, if desired. Trim excess fat from meat. Heat trimmings over low heat in Dutch oven until about 2 tablespoons melted fat accumulates; be certain fat does not smoke. **Discard trimmings.** This is enough fat to brown a 3- or 4-pound pot roast.

To give roast rich brown appearance, coat meat with all-purpose flour seasoned with salt and pepper; brown roast, uncovered, over low heat, on all sides in hot shortening.

SIMMERED BEEF SHANKS

 2 tablespoons all-purpose flour
 1 tablespoon salt
 ¼ teaspoon pepper
 3 to 4 pounds crosscut beef
   shanks
 1 tablespoon shortening
 1 cup tomato juice
 2 tablespoons snipped parsley
 ½ teaspoon dried basil, crushed
 4 medium potatoes, pared and
   quartered
 2 tablespoons all-purpose flour

Combine 2 tablespoons flour, salt, and pepper in a paper or plastic bag; add beef shanks, one at a time, and shake to coat. Brown meat in hot shortening in Dutch oven. Add tomato juice, parsley, and basil. Cover and simmer 1½ hours. Add potatoes; cover and simmer 30 to 45 minutes more or till potatoes are tender. Remove meat and potatoes; skim off excess fat from pan juices.

Add enough water to juices to make 1 cup liquid; return to pan. Mix together ½ cup cold water and 2 tablespoons flour; stir into juices. Cook and stir till thickened and bubbly. Serve with potatoes. Serves 4 to 6.

To please robust appetites, serve Beef Stew Bake. It's an easier version of the old-time favorite and cooks in the oven.

Discover good old-fashioned flavor in Simmered Beef Shanks. Here's real eating enjoyment that won't strain the budget.

CORNED BEEF DINNER

Place one 3- to 4-pound corned beef brisket in Dutch oven. Barely cover with water. Add ½ cup chopped onion. If seasonings not in package, add 2 bay leaves and 6 whole black peppercorns. Cover; simmer till almost tender, about 2½ to 3 hours. Add 8 sweet potatoes, pared, and cook 30 minutes more. Add two 10-ounce packages frozen Brussels sprouts and cook 15 minutes longer. Remove bay leaves; serve vegetables with meat. Serves 8.

BEEF STEW BAKE

In heavy skillet, brown 1½ pounds beef stew meat, cut in 1½-inch cubes, in 2 tablespoons hot shortening; drain off excess fat. Add one 10½-ounce can mushroom gravy, 1 cup tomato juice, ½ envelope (¼ cup) *dry* onion soup mix, and 1 teaspoon prepared horseradish. Simmer, covered, for 5 minutes. Place 4 medium potatoes, pared and quartered, in bottom of 2-quart casserole. Top with meat mixture. Bake, covered, at 350° for 1½ hours or till meat and potatoes are tender, stirring once or twice during baking. Serves 6.

CORNED BEEF AND APPLES

Cook ¼ cup chopped onion in 1 tablespoon butter till tender but not brown. Add to 4 pared tart apples sliced into large bowl. Combine ⅓ cup brown sugar, 2 tablespoons all-purpose flour, and dash ground cloves. Toss with apples and onion in bowl.

Turn into a 9-inch pie plate. Combine 2 tablespoons water and 1 tablespoon lemon juice. Drizzle over apples. Slice 8 ounces cooked corned beef into 12 slices. Place atop apples; cover with foil. Bake in a moderate oven (350°) for 45 minutes, or till apples are tender. Makes 4 servings.

CHINESE STEW

Season 2 pounds beef stew meat, cut in 1½-inch cubes, with ⅛ teaspoon pepper. Brown in 1 tablespoon hot shortening in large, heavy skillet. Pour off excess fat.

Add one 10½-ounce can condensed golden mushroom soup, ¼ cup water, 2 tablespoons soy sauce, and 1 small onion, thinly sliced, to meat in skillet. Cover and simmer 1¼ to 1½ hours or until meat is tender.

Add six 1-inch crosswise slices Chinese cabbage and one 5-ounce can bamboo shoots, drained and rinsed, to meat in skillet. Cover and simmer for 20 minutes longer, or till cabbage slices are tender. Serve stew over hot cooked rice. Makes 6 servings.

The best way to use the good meat left on the bones after serving a standing rib roast is to prepare Deviled Beef Bones.

BEEF AND SPROUTS

 2 pounds beef stew meat, cut in 1½-inch cubes
 2 tablespoons shortening
 1 clove garlic, minced
 2 medium onions, sliced
 2 tablespoons vinegar
 1 teaspoon paprika
 1 teaspoon salt
 ¼ teaspoon dried marjoram, crushed
 1 cup water

• • •

 ½ teaspoon grated lemon peel
 ½ teaspoon caraway seed
 1 10-ounce package frozen Brussels sprouts

• • •

 2 tablespoons all-purpose flour
 ¼ cup water
   Hot cooked noodles

In large saucepan, brown meat in hot shortening; remove meat. Add garlic and onions; cook till tender. Stir in vinegar, paprika, salt, and marjoram. Add meat and 1 cup water; cover and simmer 1 hour and 20 minutes. Add lemon peel, caraway seed, and frozen Brussels sprouts. Cover; bring to boiling over high heat. Reduce heat and simmer 10 minutes longer, or till sprouts are tender. Blend together flour and ¼ cup cold water; stir into stew. Cook and stir till thickened and bubbly. Serve over cooked noodles. Makes 6 servings.

DEVILED BEEF BONES

 ¾ cup extra-hot catsup
 2 tablespoons Worcestershire sauce
 1 tablespoon vinegar
 1½ teaspoons celery seed
 1 teaspoon Dijon-style mustard
   Dash bottled hot pepper sauce
   Beef bones (with meat on) from cooked standing rib roast*

In skillet, combine first 6 ingredients. Heat to boiling. Add bones; simmer, covered, about 20 minutes, spooning sauce over beef bones 2 or 3 times. Pass any extra sauce. Makes about 1 cup sauce (enough for 4 to 6 bones).

*Or buy beef ribs your meatman has removed when preparing rolled roasts—roast them, then simmer in the zippy sauce.

Young, tender veal is flavorful

SPINACH-STUFFED VEAL

Cook one 10-ounce package frozen chopped spinach, thawed, ½ cup chopped carrot, ½ cup chopped celery, ¼ cup chopped onion, and 1 clove garlic, minced, in ¼ cup hot salad oil till tender but not brown. Stir in ¼ cup water, 2 teaspoons chicken-flavored gravy base, 2 tablespoons catsup, 1 teaspoon salt, and ¼ teaspoon dried oregano, crushed; mix.

Remove from heat; add 1 cup soft bread crumbs and 1 beaten egg. Spoon stuffing onto half of one 3½-pound boneless breast of veal; fold over other half. Skewer closed. Place on rack in shallow roasting pan. Lay 6 to 8 slices bacon atop veal. Roast, uncovered, in slow oven (325°) for about 4 hours or till meat is tender. Makes 6 to 8 servings.

VEAL ROAST

Season a bone-in veal roast from leg or loin (rib roast, loin roast, or sirloin roast), or a boneless rolled shoulder roast. Place, fat side up, on rack in shallow roasting pan. Lay 5 bacon slices over top of veal. Insert meat thermometer making sure it does not rest on bone or in fat. Roast in slow oven (325°) according to directions in Veal Roasting Chart or till meat thermometer registers 170°. Let roast stand 15 minutes before carving to allow meat to firm so slicing will be easier.

VEAL AND PORK ROAST

1½ to 2 pounds boneless pork loin*
3½ to 4 pounds boneless leg of
      veal, shank half*
¼ cup salad oil
¼ cup dry sherry
1 tablespoon lemon juice
½ teaspoon salt
¼ teaspoon pepper
¼ teaspoon dried oregano, crushed
½ clove garlic, crushed

*Have meatman roll boneless pork loin inside boneless leg of veal and tie securely.

Center roast on rotisserie spit. Adjust holding forks and tighten screws. Test balance. Insert meat thermometer. Attach spit to rotisserie and turn on motor.

Roast at 325° for about 4½ to 5 hours, or till meat thermometer registers 170°. (To roast in oven instead of on rotisserie, lay strips of bacon over meat. Place veal on rack in shallow roasting pan.)

Combine salad oil and next 6 ingredients; use to baste roast occasionally during cooking. Makes 10 to 12 servings.

Veal and pork combo

Veal and Pork Roast is an interesting→ blend of flavors roasted on the rotisserie. A hot fruit compote tops off the meal.

	VEAL ROASTING CHART		
Cut	Approximate Weight (Pounds)	Internal Temp. on Removal from Oven	Approximate Cooking Time (Total Time)
Roast meat at constant oven temperature of 325°.			
Leg	5 to 8	170°	2¾ to 3¾ hours
Loin	4 to 6	170°	2½ to 3 hours
Rolled Shoulder	4 to 6	170°	3½ to 3¾ hours

Veal cuts

For Basic Bone Identification Chart and How Much Meat to Serve, see Index.

1. *Arm Roast*—is cut from the arm section of the shoulder. It can be identified by the round arm bone and may have a cross section of the rib bone exposed. Roast or braise this cut. *Rolled Shoulder Roast*—is a boneless cut which is rolled and tied with twine. It's cut from the shoulder and may have a thin layer of fat covering the outside. Roast or braise. *Arm Steak*—sliced from the Arm Roast, can be identified by the round arm bone. A cross section of the rib bone may be present depending upon the thickness of the cut. Panfry or braise this steak.

2. *Mock Chicken Legs*—are made from ground veal formed around a wooden skewer to look like the shape of chicken legs. They are coated with fine crumbs. Panfry or braise Mock Chicken Legs. *Blade Roast*—is cut from the shoulder next to the rib section of the loin. It can be identified by the blade bone and a cross section of the rib bone. Braise this cut. *Blade Steak*—is a thin slice cut off the Blade Roast. Identify this cut by the blade bone, sometimes called the 7-bone. Panfry or braise this blade steak.

3. *Standing Rump Roast*—can be identified by its triangular shape and by the round leg bone. The larger face area connects with the sirloin section while the smaller face area connects with the leg. Roast or braise this cut. *Rolled Rump Roast*—is the Standing Rump Roast which has been boned, rolled, and tied with twine. A thin fat layer will cover one side. Roast or braise. *Cutlet (round steak)* —is sliced from the center of the leg. It contains the top of the round, bottom of the round, and the eye muscles. (Top and bottom muscles may be sold separately.) The round steak can be identified by the round leg bone; the cutlet is a round steak with the bone removed. Panfry or braise cutlets and round steaks.

1. *Arm Roast*, left; *Rolled Shoulder Roast*, upper right; *Arm Steak*, lower right.

2. *Mock Chicken Legs*, left; *Blade Roast*, upper right; *Blade Steak*, lower right.

3. *Rump Roast: Standing*, top, *Rolled*, left; *Cutlet (round steak)*, bottom.

4. *Loin Roast*, top; *Loin Chop*, lower left; *Loin Kidney Chop*, lower right.

5. *Sirloin Roast*, upper left; *Sirloin Steak*, lower right.

6. *Rib Roast*, upper left; *Frenched Rib Roast*, upper right; *Rib Chops*, bottom.

4. *Loin Roast*—can be identified by the T-bone. The finger of the T-bone separates the loin eye, the larger muscle, from the tenderloin, the smaller muscle. It is cut from the center of the loin section. Roast this tender cut. *Loin Chop*—is a slice cut off the Loin Roast. It also can be identified by the T-bone. The loin eye and the tenderloin are the two muscles. Braise or panfry this tender chop. *Loin Kidney Chop*—is a Loin Chop with a slice of kidney included. It can easily be identified by the T-bone. It will have the kidney slice attached on the tenderloin side of the chop. The tenderloin will be small in size. Braise this chop with the kidney attached. If this chop is cut thinner, ½ inch or less, it can be panfried.

5. *Sirloin Roast*—is cut from the sirloin section of the loin which is between the leg and the center loin section. This roast can be identified by the wedge bone (hip bone). Some fat is interspersed between the muscles, and a thin layer of fat covers the outside. Roast this cut. *Sirloin Steak* —sliced from the Sirloin Roast can also be identified by the wedge bone. The size and shape of this steak and of the wedge bone will vary according to each slice. Braise or panfry this sirloin steak.

6. *Rib Roast*—can be identified by the rib bones. It is cut from the rib section of the loin which is between the shoulder and the center loin. The large and predominant muscle is the rib eye. A thin layer of fat covers the outer surface. Roast this tender cut. *Frenched Rib Roast*—is an identical cut to the Rib Roast except that it has been "frenched." To "french," meat is removed from about a 1-inch section of the ribs and paper frills are placed on the exposed bones. Roast this fancy cut. Two Frenched Rib Roasts can be tied together with the rib bones around the inside and the rib eye muscle toward the outside to form a crown. This is called a Crown Roast. Fill the center with stuffing and roast. *Rib Chops*—are cut from the rib section of the loin and can be identified by the rib bone. The predominant muscle is the rib eye. This chop can also be "frenched" and a paper frill put on the end for a fancy serving. Braise or panfry.

BREADED VEAL CUTLETS

2 pounds veal cutlets *or* round
    steak, cut ½ inch thick
Salt
Pepper
1 cup fine dry bread crumbs
2 slightly beaten eggs
2 tablespoons water

   . . .

⅓ cup shortening
½ cup dairy sour cream
1 10½-ounce can condensed cream
   of mushroom soup

Cut veal into 6 serving-size pieces. Season
with salt and pepper. Dip veal into bread
crumbs, then into eggs mixed with water, and
back again into bread crumbs.

In skillet, brown meat on both sides in hot
shortening. Transfer cutlets to 13x9x2-inch
baking pan. Pour 2 tablespoons water in
bottom of pan. Cover pan lightly with foil;
bake in moderate oven (350°) for 30 minutes.
Uncover and bake 15 minutes longer. For
gravy, combine sour cream and mushroom
soup; cook and stir over low heat just till
heated through. Serve with meat. Serves 6.

Veal Roll-ups are a combination of tender
veal stuffed with cream cheese and deviled ham. Accompany with green beans.

WIENER SCHNITZEL

1½ pounds veal cutlets *or* round
    steak, cut ½ inch thick
¼ cup all-purpose flour
1 beaten egg
1 tablespoon milk
1 cup fine dry bread crumbs
¼ cup shortening
Lemon wedges

Cut meat into 4 pieces; pound ¼ to ⅛ inch
thick. Cut small slits around edges to prevent
curling. Coat meat with flour seasoned with 1
teaspoon salt and ¼ teaspoon pepper. Combine egg and milk. Dip floured cutlets in egg
mixture, then in bread crumbs. In skillet,
cook meat in hot shortening 2 to 3 minutes on
each side or till tender and golden brown.
Serve with lemon wedges. Makes 4 servings.

Wiener Schnitzel a la Holstein: Prepare Wiener Schnitzel. In skillet, fry 4 eggs in
butter till whites are set. Add 1 tablespoon
water. Cover; cook till eggs are done. Place 1
cooked egg on each veal cutlet. Sprinkle each
cooked egg with snipped parsley.

VEAL ROLL-UPS

4 boneless veal cutlets (about 1
   pound)
1 4½-ounce can deviled ham
1 tablespoon chopped onion
1 3-ounce package cream cheese
1 beaten egg
½ cup fine dry bread crumbs
2 tablespoons butter or margarine
¾ cup water
1 envelope dry mushroom gravy mix
¼ cup dry sherry

With meat mallet, pound cutlets very thin.
Mix deviled ham with onion; spread on cutlets just to edge. Slice cream cheese into 12
narrow strips; place 3 strips on each cutlet.
Roll cutlets jelly-roll style; fasten with wooden
picks. Dip rolls in beaten egg, then in crumbs.
Melt butter or margarine in skillet; add veal
rolls and brown on all sides. Arrange browned
rolls in 10x6x1½-inch baking dish; remove
picks. Pour water into skillet; add gravy mix
and sherry. Cook and stir till mixture is
bubbly; pour over veal rolls. Bake, covered,
at 350° for 45 minutes or till tender. Serves 4.

VEAL BIRDS

- 2 pounds boneless veal round steak, ½ inch thick, cut in serving pieces
- 3 cups dry bread cubes
- 3 tablespoons butter, melted
- 2 tablespoons chopped onion
- ½ teaspoon salt
- ½ teaspoon poultry seasoning
- 3 tablespoons shortening
- 1 10½-ounce can condensed cream of mushroom soup

With meat mallet, pound steak till very thin. Sprinkle liberally with salt and pepper. For stuffing, combine bread cubes, next 4 ingredients, and dash pepper; add enough water to moisten, about 2 teaspoons. Top veal with bread mixture. Roll jelly-roll style; fasten with wooden picks. Brown in hot shortening. Mix together soup and ¼ cup water; pour over meat. Cover tightly and cook slowly 1 hour or till tender, turning veal birds occasionally. Makes 6 servings.

ITALIAN VEAL CHOPS

- ½ cup salad oil
- 1 clove garlic, minced
- 1 teaspoon dried oregano, crushed
- 6 veal loin chops, ½ to ¾ inch thick (about 1¾ pounds)
- 4 ounces medium noodles, cooked and drained
- 2 tablespoons butter, melted
- 2 tablespoons grated Parmesan cheese
- ½ cup cold chicken broth
- 1 teaspoon cornstarch

Combine oil, garlic, and oregano. Place chops in shallow dish; pour oil mixture over. Refrigerate for 2 to 3 hours, turning once. Drain chops reserving marinade. In skillet, brown chops on both sides in small amount of reserved marinade. Reduce heat; cover and simmer for 25 to 30 minutes or till tender. Toss hot noodles with mixture of butter and cheese; spoon onto warm platter. Arrange veal chops atop. Blend chicken broth into cornstarch; stir into pan drippings. Cook and stir over low heat till thickened and bubbly. Spoon over chops. Makes 6 servings.

VEAL CHOPS

Coat 4 veal chops, ½ to ¾ inch thick, with flour*. In skillet, brown chops on both sides in hot shortening; season with salt and pepper. Add ½ cup water. Cover; cook slowly about 45 minutes or till meat is tender. Add more water to veal chops if necessary during cooking. Makes 4 servings.

*Or, dip chops into mixture of 1 slightly beaten egg and 1 tablespoon water, then into ¼ cup finely crushed saltine cracker crumbs.

VEAL STEW

- 1 pound veal, cut in 1-inch cubes
  All-purpose flour
- 3 tablespoons shortening
- 2¼ cups hot water
- ½ cup diced potatoes
- ½ cup diced carrots
- ¼ cup chopped celery
- ¼ cup chopped onion
- 1 bay leaf
- 1 teaspoon Worcestershire sauce
- ¾ teaspoon salt
  Dash pepper
  Fluffy Dumplings
- 1 8-ounce can tomato sauce
- ½ cup canned peas
- 2 tablespoons all-purpose flour
- ¼ cup cold water

Coat meat with flour; brown slowly in hot shortening. Add 2¼ cups water; cover and simmer (don't boil) for 1 hour. Add potatoes, carrots, celery, onion, bay leaf, Worcestershire sauce, salt, and pepper. Continue cooking 15 to 20 minutes or till meat is tender.

Meanwhile, prepare *Fluffy Dumplings:* Sift together 1 cup sifted all-purpose flour, 2 teaspoons baking powder, and ½ teaspoon salt. Combine ½ cup milk and 2 tablespoons salad oil; add to dry ingredients, stirring with fork just till flour is moistened.

Add tomato sauce and peas to stew; bring to boiling. Drop dumpling mixture from tablespoon atop bubbling stew. Cover tightly. Reduce heat (don't lift cover) and simmer 12 to 15 minutes longer; remove dumplings and bay leaf. In shaker, mix flour with ¼ cup cold water. Stir into stew; cook and stir till mixture thickens and bubbles. Serve with Fluffy Dumplings. Makes 4 or 5 servings.

CITY CHICKEN

      2 pounds veal, cut in 1½-inch
        cubes
      ⅔ cup finely crushed saltine
        cracker crumbs
    1½ teaspoons salt
      1 teaspoon paprika
      ¾ teaspoon poultry seasoning
      ½ teaspoon monosodium glutamate
      1 slightly beaten egg
      2 tablespoons milk
      3 tablespoons shortening
      1 chicken bouillon cube

Thread veal cubes onto six 9-inch skewers. Combine crumbs and next 4 ingredients. Combine egg and milk. Dip meat in egg mixture, then in crumbs. In skillet, brown meat slowly on all sides in hot shortening. Dissolve bouillon cube in ½ cup boiling water; add to meat. Cover and bake at 350° for 45 minutes. Uncover; bake 30 minutes. Serves 6.

VEAL WITH DUMPLINGS

    1½ pounds veal, cut in 1-inch cubes
      3 tablespoons all-purpose flour
      2 tablespoons shortening
      4 cups tomato juice
      2 teaspoons salt
    1½ teaspoons monosodium glutamate
      4 to 6 drops bottled hot pepper
        sauce
      1 cup diced pared potatoes
      ½ cup sliced celery
      ½ cup chopped onion
      2 tablespoons snipped parsley
      1 10-ounce package corn-bread mix

Coat meat with flour. In Dutch oven, brown meat slowly on all sides in hot shortening; add tomato juice, salt, monosodium glutamate, and hot pepper sauce. Cover; simmer (don't boil) for 45 minutes. Add potatoes, celery, and onion; cover and continue cooking about 30 minutes or till vegetables are almost done.

For corn-bread dumplings, add parsley to corn-bread mix. Using only ⅓ *cup milk*, prepare batter according to package directions. Drop rounded tablespoon of corn-bread batter onto hot bubbling stew. Cover tightly and cook (don't lift cover) about 10 minutes or till dumplings are done. Makes 6 servings.

BARBECUED VEAL

      3 pounds veal, cut in 1-inch cubes
      2 tablespoons shortening
      1 8-ounce can tomato sauce
      ½ cup catsup
      ½ cup water
      1 medium onion, sliced
      ½ cup chopped celery
      2 tablespoons brown sugar
      2 tablespoons prepared mustard
      1 tablespoon Worcestershire sauce
        Hot cooked rice

In skillet, brown meat slowly on all sides in hot shortening; season with salt and pepper. Combine remaining ingredients except rice and pour over meat. Pour into 2-quart casserole. Cover and bake at 350° for 1¾ hours; uncover and bake 15 minutes longer. Serve over rice. Makes 6 to 8 servings.

SWEET-SOUR VEAL

      1 20½-ounce can pineapple tidbits
    1½ pounds veal, cut in 1½-inch
        cubes
      2 tablespoons shortening or salad
        oil
      ½ cup chopped onion
      ½ teaspoon salt
        Dash pepper
      1 beef bouillon cube
    1¼ cups boiling water
      1 cup sliced celery
      3 tablespoons cornstarch
      3 tablespoons soy sauce
      2 tablespoons vinegar
      1 teaspoon monosodium glutamate
      1 3-ounce can sliced mushrooms,
        drained (½ cup)
        Hot cooked rice

Drain pineapple, reserving syrup. In skillet, brown veal on all sides in hot shortening. Add onion, salt, pepper, and reserved syrup. Dissolve bouillon cube in boiling water; pour over meat. Cover; simmer 50 minutes. Add celery; cook 10 minutes more or till meat is tender. Mix cornstarch with soy sauce, vinegar, and monosodium glutamate; stir into hot mixture. Cook and stir till thickened and bubbly. Add pineapple and mushrooms; heat through. Serve over rice. Serves 6.

VEAL PARMIGIANO

Melt 3 tablespoons butter or margarine in 10x6x1½-inch baking dish. Combine ½ cup cornflake crumbs, ¼ cup grated Parmesan cheese, ½ teaspoon salt, and dash pepper. Cut 1 pound veal cutlets *or* round steak, about ¼ inch thick, into 4 serving-size pieces; dip in 1 slightly beaten egg, then in cornflake crumb mixture. Place in baking dish. Bake in hot oven (400°) for 20 minutes. Turn meat; bake 15 to 20 minutes more or till meat is tender.

Meanwhile, combine one 8-ounce can (1 cup) tomato sauce, ½ teaspoon dried oregano, crushed, ½ teaspoon sugar, and dash onion salt; heat to boiling, stirring frequently. Pour tomato sauce over meat. Top with 4 ounces sliced mozzarella cheese. Return casserole to oven to melt cheese. Makes 4 servings.

VEAL SCALLOPINI

      1 tablespoon all-purpose flour
      ½ teaspoon salt
        Dash pepper
      4 veal cutlets (about 1 pound)
      ¼ cup salad oil
      ½ medium onion, thinly sliced
      1 16-ounce can tomatoes, cut up
      1 3-ounce can (⅔ cup) sliced
        mushrooms, undrained
      1 tablespoon snipped parsley
      1 tablespoon capers, drained
      ¼ teaspoon garlic salt
      ¼ teaspoon dried oregano, crushed
        Hot buttered noodles

Combine flour, salt, and pepper; coat veal lightly with flour mixture. In medium skillet, brown meat slowly in hot oil. Remove meat from skillet. Add onion to skillet; cook till tender but not brown.

Add cooked meat, tomatoes, mushrooms with liquid, snipped parsley, capers, garlic salt, and oregano. Cover and simmer for 20 to 25 minutes or till veal is tender, stirring occasionally. Arrange veal on hot buttered noodles; top with sauce. Makes 4 servings.

An Italian dish

A tomato sauce flavored with oregano is →
poured over tender veal cutlets in Veal Scallopini. Top with snipped parsley.

Palate tempting pork

GINGERED PORK SIRLOIN

1 3-pound pork sirloin roast *or* blade loin roast
1 tablespoon finely chopped candied ginger
2 to 3 tablespoons soy sauce

Make deep slits at 1½-inch intervals over meat surface; insert ginger into slits. Place on a rack in shallow roasting pan; brush with some of the soy sauce. Roast, uncovered, at 325° for 2½ hours or till meat thermometer registers 170°. Brush with the soy sauce about every 30 minutes. Makes 6 servings.

GLAZED BOSTON SHOULDER

1 4- to 6-pound fresh Boston shoulder
½ cup apricot preserves
2 teaspoons vinegar
1 teaspoon prepared mustard
¼ teaspoon ground ginger

Place meat on rack in shallow roasting pan. Roast at 325° for about 4 hours or till meat thermometer registers 185°. Combine remaining ingredients. Remove meat; spoon on sauce. Roast 15 minutes. Serves 12 to 16.

CHERRY-SAUCED PORK LOIN

1 4- to 5-pound pork loin roast, boned, rolled, and tied
½ teaspoon salt
½ teaspoon pepper
Dash dried thyme, crushed
• • •
1 cup cherry preserves
¼ cup red wine vinegar
2 tablespoons light corn syrup
¼ teaspoon ground cinnamon
¼ teaspoon ground nutmeg
¼ teaspoon ground cloves
¼ cup toasted slivered almonds

Rub roast with mixture of salt, pepper, and thyme. Place on rack in 13x9x2-inch baking pan. Roast, uncovered, in slow oven (325°) for about 2½ hours.

Meanwhile, make cherry sauce in small saucepan by combining cherry preserves, vinegar, corn syrup, cinnamon, nutmeg, cloves, and ¼ teaspoon salt. Heat to boiling, stirring occasionally; reduce heat and simmer 2 minutes. Add toasted almonds.

Spoon sauce over roast and continue roasting for about 30 minutes longer, or till meat thermometer registers 170°. Baste roast with sauce several times. Pass sauce with roast. Makes 10 to 12 servings.

Cut	Approximate Weight (Pounds)	Internal Temp. on Removal from Oven	Approximate Cooking Time (Total Time)
FRESH AND SMOKED PORK ROASTING CHART			
Roast meat at constant oven temperature of 325°.			
Loin, center	3 to 5	170°	2½ to 3 hours
Loin, half	5 to 7	170°	3½ to 4¼ hours
Loin, blade or sirloin	3 to 4	170°	2¼ to 2¾ hours
Loin, center; rolled	3 to 4	170°	2½ to 3 hours
Boston Shoulder	4 to 6	185°	3½ to 4½ hours
Boston Shoulder Roll	3 to 5	185°	3 to 3½ hours
Leg (fresh ham)	10 to 14	185°	5½ to 6½ hours
Leg, half (fresh ham)	5 to 7	170°	3½ to 4½ hours
Picnic (smoked, cook-before-eating)	5 to 8	170°	3 to 4 hours

MARINATED PORK ROAST

    ½ cup soy sauce
    ½ cup sherry
    2 cloves garlic, minced
    1 tablespoon dry mustard
    1 teaspoon ground ginger
    1 teaspoon dried thyme, crushed
    1 4- to 5-pound pork loin roast,
        boned, rolled, and tied
       Currant Sauce

Blend first 6 ingredients. Place roast in clear plastic bag; set in deep bowl. Pour marinade in bag and close. Marinate 2 to 3 hours at room temperature or overnight in refrigerator. Occasionally press bag against meat to distribute marinade. Remove meat from marinade; place on rack in shallow roasting pan. Roast, uncovered, at 325° for 2½ to 3 hours or till meat thermometer registers 170°. Baste with marinade during last hour. Serve with Currant Sauce. Serves 10 to 12.

Currant Sauce: In a small saucepan, heat one 10-ounce jar currant jelly until melted; add 2 tablespoons sherry and 1 tablespoon soy sauce. Stir and simmer 2 minutes.

PORK ROAST WITH STUFFING

    ¾ cup chopped celery
    ½ cup chopped onion
    6 tablespoons butter or margarine
            • • •
    3 cups corn bread stuffing mix
    1½ cups chopped pared apple
    ¾ cup water
    ½ teaspoon salt
    ½ teaspoon dried rosemary, crushed
    1 4- to 4½-pound pork rib roast*

Cook celery and onion in butter till tender. Combine stuffing mix, apple, water, salt, and rosemary; add celery mixture. Toss together lightly. Loosely stuff about ⅓ cup mixture in each pocket of roast.

Place meat, fat side up, in shallow roasting pan. Roast, uncovered, at 325° for 2½ to 3 hours or till meat thermometer registers 170°. Bake extra stuffing in small casserole for the last 30 minutes of roasting time. Remove backbone of roast and serve. Makes 8 servings.

*Have meatman loosen backbone of roast and cut pockets between ribs for stuffing.

ROAST PORK TENDERLOIN

Arrange 2 slices bacon over top of one 1-pound pork tenderloin. Place roast on rack in shallow roasting pan, tucking thin end of meat under. Roast, uncovered, in moderate oven (350°) for 35 to 45 minutes or till meat thermometer registers 170°.

Cook ⅓ cup chopped onion in 1 tablespoon butter or margarine till tender but not brown. Add one 8-ounce can tomato sauce, 3 tablespoons chopped sweet pickle, 2 tablespoons vinegar, 1 tablespoon snipped parsley, and 1 teaspoon sugar; simmer sauce, uncovered, for 10 minutes. Serve sauce with roast tenderloin. Makes 4 or 5 servings.

Stuffing made with apple and corn bread puffs between pork ribs of Pork Roast with Stuffing. Trim with spiced apples.

Pork cuts

For Basic Bone Identification Chart and How Much Meat to Serve, see Index.

1. *Tenderloin*—is the small muscle which lies on one side of the T-bone and is centered in the loin. Roast or braise this boneless cut or panfry the tenderloin slices. *Sirloin Roast*—cut from the loin section, can be identified by the wedge bone (hip bone). The largest muscle is the loin eye; the smaller muscle, tenderloin, tapers away as it approaches the hip. Roast this cut. *Loin Chop*—is cut from the center of the loin and can be identified by the T-bone. The larger muscle is the loin eye separated from the smaller muscle, the tenderloin, by the T-bone. Braise, panfry, or broil this chop.

2. *Fresh Boston Shoulder*—often called the Boston Butt, contains the blade bone exposed on two sides. Roast this cut. *Smoked Shoulder Roll (butt)*—comes from the largest muscle of the Fresh Boston Shoulder. This boneless cut is cured and smoked. Roast or cook in liquid. *Blade Steak*—is cut from the Fresh Boston Shoulder. It is identified by the blade bone. Broil, braise, or panfry this cut.

3. *Crown Roast*—consists of two pork loins with 6 to 10 center ribs from each. The ends of the ribs are "frenched" (meat removed from about a 1-inch section) and the backbone removed. Then the two pieces are tied together to form a crown. Roast and fill the center with stuffing. *Center Loin Roast*—is cut from the middle of the loin. The larger muscle is the loin eye, the smaller the tenderloin. To identify this roast look for the T-bone separating the two muscles. Roast for juicy and tender servings. *Rib Chops*—are usually identified by the rib bone. Cut from the rib section of the loin, the only muscle is the loin eye. For stuffed pork chops, either extra thick chops or two rib chops are ordered. The pockets (horizontal slits made to hold stuffing) are cut on the rib or fat side. Roast or braise.

1. *Tenderloin*, left; *Sirloin Roast*, upper right; *Loin Chop*, lower right.

2. *Fresh Boston Shoulder*, top; *Smoked Shoulder Roll*, left; *Blade Steak*, right.

3. *Crown Roast*, upper left; *Center Loin Roast*, upper right; *Rib Chops*, bottom.

4. *Canadian-style Bacon*, left; *Boneless Center Loin Roast, Butterfly Chop*, right.

5. *Back Ribs*, left; *Blade Loin Roast*, upper right; *Rib Center Chop*, lower right.

6. *Spareribs*, left; *Salt Side*, top right; *Bacon, Slab and Sliced*, bottom right.

4. *Canadian-style Bacon*—is made by curing and smoking the boneless loin. This formed cut is available fully-cooked and cook-before-eating. It can be identified by its long, round shape and the characteristic pinkish color of cured and smoked pork. When purchased in one piece, roast. Broil, panbroil, or panfry the sliced Canadian-style Bacon. *Boneless Center Loin Roast*—is the loin eye, the largest muscle in the loin section. It is cut from the Center Loin Roast. Roast for a delicious entree. *Butterfly Chop*—is made from a boned chop or a thick slice of a boneless cut of meat such as a Boneless Center Loin Roast. A lengthwise slit is made almost all the way through, then spread flat. This forms a butterfly-shaped cut which looks bigger and cooks faster. Braise or broil this boneless cut.

5. *Back Ribs*—are also called Country-style Back Ribs. These ribs contain the rib bones cut from the rib area of the loin. The thicker layer of meat covering the ribs comes from the loin eye. Roast or braise these "meaty" ribs. *Blade Loin Roast*—is cut from the rib section of the loin (next to the shoulder). It is identified on one side by the rib bone, on the other by the blade bone, from which it is named. The loin eye is the larger and predominant muscle. Roast this cut. *Rib Chop (center cut)*—can be identified by the rib bone and its general shape. It is cut from the center loin on the rib side, and as a result no tenderloin muscle will be present. The only muscle is the loin eye. Braise, panfry, or broil rib chops.

6. *Spareribs*—come from the "rib cage" and contain the breastbone, rib bones, and rib cartilage. A thin covering of meat surrounds the ribs. Roast, braise, or cook the spareribs in liquid. *Salt Side*—used mainly for seasoning, comes from the side of pork. It is cured by dry salt. Look for the layers of fat and lean and the deposit of salt on the outer surface. Cook the Salt Side in liquid, panbroil, or panfry. *Bacon*—can be purchased in a slab or sliced thick or thin. It is the fresh side of pork which has been cured and smoked. Bacon is sliced after removing the skin or rind. Broil, panbroil, or panfry.

Smoked pork cuts

7. *Smoked Picnic Shoulder*—is often incorrectly called Picnic Ham because of its smoky ham flavor. It is cut from the lower shoulder and arm section (front leg) while a Ham is cut from the hind legs. The Picnic Shoulder contains the shank, arm, and blade bones. The shoulder muscles are interspersed with fat and skin covers the shank end. It is cured and smoked and available both fully cooked and cook before eating. A whole Picnic Shoulder or a half can be purchased. Roast or cook it in liquid. *Canned Smoked Picnic Shoulder*—weighs 3 to 5 pounds. This boneless cut is fully cooked and should be refrigerated. Heat or serve it cold, sliced. A Fresh Picnic Shoulder is the same cut except that it has not been cured and smoked. Roast this cut.

8. *Smoked Center Loin Roast*—is cut from the middle section of the loin. It can be identified by the T-bone. The larger muscle is the loin eye, the smaller the tenderloin. It is usually fully cooked and just needs heating. *Smoked Loin Chops*—are cut from the Smoked Center Loin Roast. They are identified by the T-bone with the finger bone separating the loin eye from the tenderloin. Broil or panfry these smoked pork chops.

9. *Smoked Spareribs*—are cut from the "rib cage" and are identical to the fresh Spareribs except for the smoking and sometimes curing. They contain the breastbone, rib bones, and rib cartilage. A thin covering of meat surrounds the ribs. Roast, braise, or cook the spareribs in liquid. The smoky flavor adds an interesting variation to barbecued ribs. *Smoked Hocks*—are cut just above the pig's feet. They are then cured and smoked. This bony shank cut can be identified by the round bone. Braise or cook hocks in liquid. Fresh Hocks are also available and are identical to the Smoked Hocks except for curing and smoking. Braise or cook in liquid.

7. *Canned Smoked Picnic Shoulder*, top; *Smoked Picnic Shoulder*, halves, bottom.

8. *Smoked Center Loin Roast*, center; *Smoked Loin Chops*, lower left.

9. *Smoked Spareribs*, lower left and center; *Smoked Hocks*, upper right.

GLAZED SHOULDER BUTT

Place one 2- to 3-pound smoked pork shoulder butt in large Dutch oven; cover with water. Add 1 medium onion, sliced, 3 whole cloves, 1 bay leaf, one 3-inch stick cinnamon, and ½ teaspoon celery seed. Cover tightly; simmer 2 hours. Remove meat from liquid.

Place meat on rack in shallow roasting pan. Combine ½ cup brown sugar, 1 tablespoon all-purpose flour, ½ teaspoon dry mustard, ⅛ teaspoon ground cloves, and 2 tablespoons water. Brush on meat and bake in moderate oven (350°) for 20 to 30 minutes. Serves 6 to 8.

GINGERY PORK CROWN

1   4- to 5-pound crown roast of pork*
½   cup pineapple juice
1   tablespoon minced preserved or candied ginger
2   tablespoons light molasses

Place roast in shallow roasting pan, bone ends down. Insert meat thermometer in loin part of roast, making sure thermometer does not rest on bone or in fat. Roast at 325° about 2¼ to 2¾ hours, or till meat thermometer registers 170°. Combine remaining ingredients; baste roast with glaze 4 times during last hour of roasting. Serves 8 to 10.

*Have meatman tie roast securely around loin area as well as near bones.

BACON-MACARONI BAKE

1   7-ounce package elbow macaroni
½   pound sliced bacon
½   cup chopped onion
4   ounces sharp process American cheese, grated (1 cup)
1   10¾-ounce can condensed tomato soup
1   cup milk

Cook macaroni using package directions; drain. Cook bacon till crisp; drain, reserving 2 tablespoons drippings. Crumble bacon. Cook onion in reserved bacon drippings till tender. Combine macaroni, bacon, onion, and next 3 ingredients. Turn into 2-quart casserole. Bake at 375° for 45 minutes or till hot. Serves 6.

BACON

Fried: Put bacon slices in unheated skillet. Cook over moderately low heat for 6 to 8 minutes, turning often. Drain. For crisp bacon, spoon off fat while cooking.

Broiled: Separate slices and place on cold rack of broiler pan. Broil 3 to 5 inches from heat; turn only once; watch closely.

Oven-baked: Place separated bacon slices on a rack in shallow baking pan. Bake at 400° for 10 minutes. Needs no turning or draining.

CANADIAN-STYLE BACON

Panbroiled: Slash edges of ¼-inch thick Canadian-style bacon slices. Brush preheated skillet lightly with oil. Brown bacon quickly, about 2 to 3 minutes per side.

Baked: Place one 2-pound piece Canadian-style bacon in shallow baking pan. Bake, uncovered, at 325° for 1¼ hours. Spoon currant jelly over last 10 minutes to glaze.

If pork crown roast is not to be filled, turn roast bone ends down and use bones as a rack. Insert thermometer in loin part.

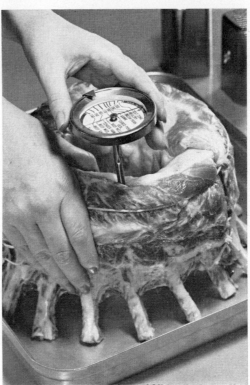

For stuffing, choose thick or double rib pork chops. Have meatman cut pockets along fat side. Fill lightly with stuffing.

STUFFED PORK CHOPS

    6 pork chops, 1¼ to 1½ inches thick (3½ to 4 pounds)
1½ cups toasted bread cubes
    ½ cup chopped unpared apple
    2 ounces sharp natural Cheddar cheese, shredded (½ cup)
    2 tablespoons light raisins
    2 tablespoons butter or margarine, melted
    2 tablespoons orange juice
    ¼ teaspoon salt
    ⅛ teaspoon ground cinnamon

Have a pocket cut in each chop along the fat side. Salt and pepper inside of pockets. Toss together bread cubes, apple, cheese, and raisins. Combine melted butter, orange juice, salt, and cinnamon; pour over bread-fruit mixture and mix gently. Stuff pork chops lightly. Place in a shallow baking pan. Bake at 350° for 1¼ hours. Cover lightly with foil; bake 15 minutes more. Makes 6 servings.

ORANGE-GLAZED CHOPS

In skillet, brown 4 pork chops, ¾ inch thick, on both sides in 1 tablespoon hot shortening; season with salt and pepper. Drain off excess fat. Combine ½ cup orange juice, 2 tablespoons brown sugar, 2 tablespoons orange marmalade, and 1 tablespoon vinegar; pour over chops. Cover and simmer 45 minutes or till chops are tender. Remove chops to a warm platter. Spoon sauce over chops. Makes 4 servings.

GOURMET PORK CHOPS

    6 loin pork chops, ½ inch thick
    2 tablespoons all-purpose flour
    1 teaspoon salt
       Dash pepper
    2 tablespoons shortening
    1 10½-ounce can condensed cream of mushroom soup
    ½ teaspoon ground ginger
    ¼ teaspoon dried rosemary, crushed
    1 3½-ounce can French-fried onions
    ½ cup dairy sour cream

Coat chops with a mixture of flour, salt, and pepper. In skillet, brown on both sides in hot shortening. Place in 11x7x1½-inch baking dish. Combine soup, ¾ cup water, ginger, and rosemary; pour over chops. Sprinkle with *half* the onions. Cover and bake at 350° for 50 minutes, or till meat is tender.

Uncover; sprinkle with remaining onions and continue baking 10 minutes. Remove meat to platter. Blend sour cream into soup mixture; heat. Pass with meat. Serves 6.

BRAISED PORK CHOPS

Brown ¾- to 1-inch thick pork chops slowly on both sides in small amount hot shortening; pour off excess fat. Season; add a little hot water, if desired. Cover tightly; cook over low heat for 45 to 60 minutes or till tender. Make gravy from pan juices, if desired.

Men will love these

The enticing aroma of fruit-cheese Stuffed →
Pork Chops will whet any appetite. Accompany meat with creamy cabbage slaw.

PORK CHOPS IN SOUR CREAM

6 loin pork chops, ½ inch thick
¾ teaspoon dried sage, crushed
½ teaspoon salt
2 tablespoons shortening
2 medium onions, sliced
1 beef bouillon cube
¼ cup boiling water
½ cup dairy sour cream
1 tablespoon all-purpose flour
2 tablespoons snipped parsley

Rub pork chops with a mixture of sage, salt, and dash pepper. Brown lightly on both sides in hot shortening. Drain off excess fat; add onions. Dissolve bouillon cube in ¼ cup boiling water. Pour over chops. Cover and simmer 30 minutes or till meat is done. Place meat on serving platter. Prepare gravy by combining sour cream and flour in small bowl. Slowly stir in meat drippings. Return mixture to skillet; cook and stir just till boiling. Add water till gravy is desired consistency. Serve over pork chops; garnish with snipped parsley. Makes 6 servings.

PORK CHOPS SUPREME

6 pork chops, ¾ inch thick
  Paprika
2 tablespoons shortening
½ cup finely chopped celery
½ envelope (¼ cup) *dry* onion
  soup mix
2 tablespoons all-purpose flour
1 tablespoon dry parsley flakes
1 6-ounce can (⅔ cup) evaporated
  milk
1 3-ounce can chopped mushrooms,
  drained (½ cup)

Season pork chops with paprika, salt, and pepper. In skillet, brown chops slowly on both sides in hot shortening. Drain off excess fat. Add 1 cup water, celery, and soup mix. Cover and cook over low heat 40 to 45 minutes, or till chops are tender. Remove chops from skillet. Combine flour, parsley flakes, and ¼ cup cold water. Blend into pan juices. Add evaporated milk and mushrooms. Cook and stir over low heat till thickened and bubbly. Spoon a little gravy over chops; pass extra gravy. Makes 6 servings.

AMBER SKILLET DINNER

Combine ¼ cup all-purpose flour, 1 teaspoon salt, and ½ teaspoon pepper; coat 4 pork chops, cut ¾ inch thick. Brown chops on both sides in 1 tablespoon hot shortening. Add 1 medium onion, sliced, 1 cup prune juice, 1 tablespoon lemon juice, and ¼ teaspoon *each* salt, pepper, ground cinnamon, and ground ginger; stir. Add one 16-ounce can whole potatoes; cover and simmer 1 hour. Serves 4.

PORK CHOP RISOTTO BAKE

¾ cup brown rice
1 10½-ounce can
  condensed beef broth
4 smoked pork chops
1 tablespoon shortening
2 medium carrots, cut in julienne
  strips
½ cup coarsely chopped onion
½ cup sauterne
¼ teaspoon dried marjoram, crushed
⅛ teaspoon dried oregano, crushed

Combine rice, broth, and ¼ cup water; bring to boiling. Simmer, covered, 50 minutes. Brown chops lightly on both sides in hot shortening. Combine remaining ingredients, ½ teaspoon salt, and dash pepper; stir into rice. Turn into 10x6x1½-inch baking dish; arrange chops on top. Bake, covered, at 350° for 1 hour, stirring rice once or twice. Serves 4.

BARBECUE PORK CHOPS

1 10¾-ounce can condensed
  tomato soup
2 tablespoons brown sugar
2 tablespoons vinegar
2 teaspoons Worcestershire sauce
1 teaspoon instant minced onion
½ teaspoon *dry* Italian salad
  dressing mix
½ teaspoon dry mustard
6 pork chops, 1 inch thick
2 tablespoons shortening

Combine first 7 ingredients. Brown chops on both sides in hot shortening. Pour off excess fat. Pour sauce over chops. Cover; simmer about 1 hour, basting occasionally. Serves 6.

SWEET-SOUR PORK

Brown 1½ pounds lean pork, cut in 2x½-inch strips, in 2 tablespoons hot shortening. Stir in 1 cup water, 1 chicken bouillon cube, and ¼ teaspoon salt. Cover; simmer about 1 hour. Drain one 20½-ounce can pineapple chunks, reserving syrup. Combine ¼ cup brown sugar and 2 tablespoons cornstarch in saucepan; add reserved pineapple syrup, ¼ cup vinegar, 1 tablespoon soy sauce, and ½ teaspoon salt. Cook and stir till bubbly.

Add sauce to pork; mix well. Stir in pineapple, 1 medium green pepper, cut in strips, and ¼ cup thinly sliced onion. Cook 2 to 3 minutes. Serve over hot cooked rice. Serves 6.

HOCKS AND KRAUT

With scissors, snip two 16-ounce cans sauerkraut to cut up long strips. In greased 2-quart casserole, combine kraut, 2 tablespoons brown sugar, and ½ teaspoon caraway seed. Fold in 1 unpared large tart apple, sliced. Place 1 medium onion, sliced, over kraut mixture; top with 4 large smoked ham hocks (3 pounds). Cover and bake in a slow oven (325°) for 3½ to 4 hours. Makes 4 servings.

To set an Oriental mood, cook Chinese Pork Saute in a wok pan—a basin-shaped saucepan available in some Oriental shops.

CHEESE NOODLE CASSEROLE

- 1 pound diced uncooked pork
- 1 tablespoon shortening
- 1 10½-ounce can condensed chicken rice soup
- ½ cup chopped green pepper
- ¼ cup chopped canned pimiento
- 1 17-ounce can (2 cups) cream-style corn
- 8 ounces sharp process American cheese, shredded (2 cups)
- 4 ounces medium egg noodles

In skillet, brown pork in hot shortening. Stir in soup; cover and simmer for 45 to 60 minutes, or till tender. Stir in remaining ingredients *except* noodles. Cook noodles according to package directions; drain. Stir into pork mixture; turn into a 2-quart casserole. Bake, covered, at 350° for 45 minutes. Serves 6.

CHINESE PORK SAUTE

- ⅓ cup finely chopped uncooked pork
- 1 tablespoon peanut or salad oil
- 1 5-ounce can water chestnuts, drained and sliced
- 1 7-ounce package frozen Chinese pea pods, thawed
- 1 teaspoon monosodium glutamate
- 1 cup chicken broth
- 1 tablespoon cornstarch

In skillet, brown pork in hot oil. Add next 3 ingredients; then add broth. Steam, covered, over high heat about 3 minutes. Combine cornstarch and 2 tablespoons cold water; push vegetables aside and add cornstarch mixture to broth; cook and stir till slightly thickened. Add salt to taste. Makes 3 or 4 servings.

BREADED PORK TENDERLOIN

Mix 1 beaten egg and 1 tablespoon milk. Dip 6 pork tenderloin patties *or* pork cutlets (1 pound) in egg mixture, then in ½ cup fine dry bread crumbs. Brown in 2 tablespoons hot shortening. Season with salt. Add ¼ cup water; cover. Cook over low heat for 40 minutes. Lift meat occasionally to prevent sticking. For crisp coating, uncover the last 15 minutes. Makes 6 servings.

RIBS WITH ONION SAUCE

- 4 pounds pork spareribs, cut in serving pieces
- 2 cups sliced onion
- 2 cloves garlic, minced
- 1 tablespoon salad oil
- ¼ cup vinegar
- ¼ cup chili sauce
- 3 tablespoons brown sugar
- 2 tablespoons lemon juice
- 2 tablespoons Worcestershire sauce
- 1 teaspoon dry mustard

Roast ribs, meaty side down, in shallow roasting pan at 450° for 30 minutes. Drain off excess fat. Turn ribs meaty side up. Meanwhile, cook onion and garlic in hot oil till tender; add remaining ingredients, ½ cup water, and 1½ teaspoons salt. Simmer 10 minutes. Pour sauce over ribs. Reduce oven temperature to 350°; bake ribs about 1½ hours or till tender, basting occasionally with sauce. If sauce gets too thick, add more water. Serves 4 to 6.

SWEET-SOUR SPARERIBS

- 4 pounds pork spareribs, cut in serving pieces
- 1 20½-ounce can pineapple tidbits
- ⅓ cup chopped celery
- ⅓ cup chopped green pepper
- 2 tablespoons butter or margarine
- 2 tablespoons cornstarch
- 1 clove garlic, minced
- ⅓ cup vinegar
- 2 tablespoons soy sauce
- 1 tablespoon sugar
- ½ teaspoon ground ginger

Place ribs, meaty side down, in shallow roasting pan. Season with salt and pepper. Roast at 450° for 30 minutes. Drain off excess fat. Turn ribs meaty side up. Reduce oven temperature to 350° and continue roasting for 1 hour. Meanwhile, drain pineapple reserving syrup. In saucepan, cook celery and green pepper in butter till tender. Combine cornstarch and reserved pineapple syrup; add to saucepan; cook and stir till mixture thickens and bubbles. Stir in pineapple, garlic, vinegar, soy sauce, sugar, ginger, and ½ teaspoon salt; pour over ribs. Roast 30 minutes or till tender, basting occasionally. Serves 4 to 6.

PLUM-GLAZED RIBS

- 4 pounds pork back ribs, cut in serving pieces
- 2 teaspoons salt
- 1 10-ounce jar plum preserves
- ¼ cup frozen orange juice concentrate, thawed
- 1 tablespoon vinegar
- ½ teaspoon Worcestershire sauce

Place ribs, meaty side down, in shallow roasting pan. Roast at 450° for 30 minutes. Remove meat from oven; drain off excess fat. Turn ribs meaty side up; season with the salt. Reduce oven temperature to 350° and continue roasting for 1 hour; drain.

Meanwhile, prepare plum glaze by combining preserves, orange juice concentrate, vinegar, and Worcestershire sauce; blend. Pour glaze over ribs; roast 30 minutes or till tender, basting occasionally. Serves 4 to 6.

BARBECUED SPARERIBS

- 4 pounds pork spareribs, cut in serving pieces
- 1 lemon, thinly sliced
- 1 large onion, thinly sliced
- 1½ cups water
- 1 cup catsup
- ⅓ cup Worcestershire sauce
- 1 teaspoon chili powder
- 1 teaspoon salt
  Dash bottled hot pepper sauce

Place ribs, meaty side down, in shallow roasting pan. Season with salt. Roast in very hot oven (450°) for 30 minutes. Drain off excess fat. Turn ribs meaty side up. Top ribs with slices of unpeeled lemon and onion.

Reduce oven temperature to 350°. Continue roasting ribs for 30 minutes. Combine water, catsup, Worcestershire sauce, chili powder, salt, and hot pepper sauce. Bring to boiling and pour over ribs. Continue roasting for 1 hour, basting ribs occasionally. If sauce gets too thick, add more water. Serves 4 to 6.

A Hawaiian special

You'll almost feel the tropical breezes →
when you eat these mouth-watering
Sweet-sour Spareribs with pineapple.

Ham for all occasions

HAM WITH NECTARINES

1 fully-cooked center-cut ham slice, cut 2 inches thick (about 3 pounds)
1 cup sugar
2 tablespoons cornstarch
2 teaspoons seasoned salt
2 teaspoons dry mustard
½ teaspoon paprika
⅓ cup orange juice
¼ cup vinegar
2 slightly beaten egg yolks
2 or 3 fresh nectarines, sliced (about 1½ cups) *or* 1 12-ounce package frozen sliced peaches, thawed and drained

Slash edge of ham. Place on rack in shallow baking pan; bake at 350° for 40 minutes.

Meanwhile, in a saucepan mix sugar, cornstarch, seasoned salt, mustard, and paprika. Blend in 1 cup cold water, orange juice, and vinegar. Cook over low heat, stirring constantly, until thickened and smooth. Stir a small amount of hot mixture into egg yolks; return quickly to hot mixture. Cook and stir 1 minute or till bubbly. Add nectarines.

Place ham slice on serving plate; spoon on some of the nectarine sauce. Pass remaining sauce with ham. Makes 8 to 10 servings.

HAM AND CHEDDAR RICE

6 fully-cooked ham slices, cut ½ inch thick (about 2 pounds)
4 cups hot cooked rice
4 ounces natural Cheddar cheese, shredded (1 cup)
¼ cup sliced green onion (with tops)
2 tablespoons snipped parsley
¼ teaspoon salt

Slash edges of ham slices. Broil 2 inches from heat for 4 minutes on each side. Toss together rice, cheese, onion, parsley, and salt. Arrange rice mixture on platter; top with ham slices. Makes 6 servings.

CRANBERRY TOPPED HAM

1 fully-cooked ham slice, cut 1 inch thick (about 2 pounds)
1 8-ounce can (1 cup) whole cranberry sauce
½ teaspoon prepared mustard
Dash ground cloves

Slash edge of ham slice. Place in a shallow baking pan. Combine the cranberry sauce, prepared mustard, and cloves; spread over ham. Bake in a moderate oven (350°) for 40 to 45 minutes. Makes 6 servings.

OLD-FASHIONED PEA SOUP

1 pound (2¼ cups) dry green split peas
2 quarts water
• • •
1 meaty ham bone
1 cup chopped onion
¼ teaspoon garlic salt
¼ teaspoon dried marjoram, crushed
Dash pepper
• • •
1 cup chopped celery
1 cup chopped carrot
½ to 1 teaspoon salt

In a large saucepan, cover peas with 2 quarts water; soak overnight. (Or, combine peas and water. Bring to boiling; boil gently 2 minutes; soak 1 hour.)

Add ham bone, onion, garlic salt, marjoram, and pepper. Bring to boiling; cover, reduce heat, and simmer 2 hours. Stir occasionally. Remove bone and cut off meat. Dice meat and return to soup with celery and carrot. Cook slowly 45 minutes, stirring occasionally. Add salt to taste. Serves 8 to 10.

Three ways to use ham

Ham with Nectarines, Ham and Cheddar → Rice, or Old-fashioned Pea Soup all provide the mainstay for any meal.

Ham cuts

1. *Rolled Hams*—present no carving problems since they are boneless, thus producing uniform slices. Whole rolls, in a casing, average 7 to 10 pounds, but halves or 1½- to 2-pound pieces are also available. Since they are fully cooked, they need no further cooking, but slices can be baked, broiled, or panfried.

2. *Semi-boneless Hams*—usually have only the round leg bone left in this compact 8- to 12-pound piece of meat. The shank portion is rounded off. Some retailers have pieces available that weigh as little as 4 pounds. These hams are skinless and are carefully trimmed except for a thin layer of fat that protects the lean portion from drying out if the ham is heated before serving. They are usually purchased in a casing, stockinette, or paper wrapped. The majority of these hams are fully-cooked.

3. *Ham Shank Portion*—has a tapering shape and a collar of skin covering the hock and part of the meaty area. It contains the hind shank bones and part of the leg bone, and costs less per pound than the butt half, which has a greater proportion of meat. Bake or simmer the shank in liquid—great for split pea soup.
Ham Butt Portion—is full and oval for easy slicing. The pelvic bone and part of the leg bone are found in this cut. Both butt and shank portions can be either cook-before-eating or fully-cooked.
Center Ham Slices—are identified by the round leg bone and are thin, oval-shaped pieces cut from the center of the ham. When cut about 1 inch thick, as shown, the slices weigh 1- to 1¾-pounds and are ideal for serving a small family. They can be purchased as either cook-before-eating or fully-cooked slices. Broil, pan-broil, panfry, or bake slices.
Whole Hams—are also available which have the shank and butt in one piece. They weigh from 10 to 18 pounds. Some whole hams have the shanks removed and are called skinless and shankless hams.

1. *Rolled Hams:* whole roll, left; half, upper right; piece, lower right.

2. *Semi-boneless Hams:* whole ham, top; two halves, bottom. Usually fully-cooked.

3. *Shank Portion*, upper left; *Butt Portion*, upper right; *Center Slices*, lower.

4. *Canned Hams: Unsmoked*, upper left; *Smoked*, lower left and right.

5. *Sliced "Boiled" or Cooked Ham* makes perfect sandwiches with Swiss cheese.

6. *Formed Hams:* whole ham, top; two quarters, lower left; half, lower right.

4. *Canned Hams*—come in a range of sizes from 1½ to 10 pounds. All are cured and while the majority of canned hams are not smoked, some are available that have been smoked. Canned hams are solid, boneless pieces of meat that are fully-cooked and easy to serve right from the can. Some hams come with a glaze and special flavor built in. Remember, unless the label says otherwise, canned hams should be kept refrigerated. And even though they are fully-cooked, they may be heated before serving with a glaze or heated as is and served with a sauce.

5. *Sliced "Boiled" or Cooked Hams*—are not really boiled. Instead, they are gently simmered, steamed, or slowly baked to enhance the delicate ham flavor. This boneless meat can be purchased sliced by the pound or already vacuum sealed in clear plastic wrap.

6. *Formed Hams*—are boneless and usually fully-cooked so that they need no further cooking. This type of ham has a thin cover of surface fat which bastes the ham when it is baked to serve it hot. All other fat has been removed, so it's perfect to slice cold for sandwiches. The whole ham weighs 7 to 10 pounds and halves or quarters are also available.

Meat curing and smoking was once used primarily as a means of preserving meat, especially during the hot summer months, but the distinctive flavor that it produces still makes cured meats popular today. The curing solution is a brine mixture. Because the meat shrinks during processing, the brine is pumped into the meat up to its original weight. It is then allowed to cure for several days, depending on the flavor desired. The curing causes a change in flavor and color of the meat. The next step is a smoking process, giving ham a distinctive flavor. Chips of special woods, such as hickory or maple, are used during the smoking of hams.

When selecting and preparing hams, keep in mind that they fall into two categories: fully-cooked hams—need no further cooking, and cook-before-eating hams—are partially cooked in processing but need further cooking.

HOW TO COOK HAM

Roasting or Baking: Place whole hams or ham pieces fat side up on rack in shallow pan. Do not cover or add water. Score ham if glaze is to be added later. Insert meat thermometer. Bake at 325° according to Ham Roasting Chart. If desired, glaze ham during last 30 minutes of baking time.

Broiling Ham Slices: Slash fat edge of ham at 1-inch intervals to prevent meat from curling during cooking. Place meat on cold rack of broiler pan. Broil 3 inches from heat using chart below, turning once.

Panfrying Ham Slices: In heavy skillet, cook ham in small amount of hot shortening over medium heat according to chart below. Turn meat occasionally until heated through.

GLAZES FOR HAM

Apricot-honey Glaze: In saucepan, combine ½ cup *each* apricot jam and honey, 1 tablespoon cornstarch, 3 tablespoons lemon juice, and ¼ teaspoon ground cloves. Heat, stirring constantly, till thickened and bubbly. Last 30 minutes of baking time, spoon glaze over ham; baste occasionally. Makes 1 cup.

Jewel Glaze: In saucepan, combine one 10-ounce jar currant jelly, ½ cup light corn syrup, ½ teaspoon grated lemon peel, ¼ cup lemon juice, ¼ teaspoon *each* ground cloves, ground cinnamon, and ground allspice. Bring to boil over low heat; remove. Stir in 8 ounces chopped mixed candied fruits and peels. Last 30 minutes of baking time, spoon glaze over ham; baste occasionally. Makes 2 cups.

HAM ROASTING CHART

Cut	Approximate Weight (Pounds)	Internal Temp. on Removal from Oven	Approximate Cooking Time (Total Time)
Roast meat at constant oven temperature of 325°.			
Ham (fully-cooked)			
half, boneless	4 to 5	130°	1½ to 2 hrs.
whole, boneless	8 to 10	130°	2 to 2¼ hrs.
half	5 to 7	130°	1¾ to 2¼ hrs.
whole	10 to 14	130°	2½ to 3 hrs.
Ham (cook-before-eating)			
shank or butt	3 to 4	160°	2 to 2¼ hrs.
half	5 to 7	160°	2½ to 3 hrs.
whole	10 to 14	160°	3½ to 4 hrs.

To broil* or panfry fully-cooked ham slices		
Ham Slices, Bone-in ¾ inch thick	1 to 1¼ pounds	Broil 10 to 12 minutes Panfry 12 to 15 minutes
Ham Slices, Bone-in 1 inch thick	1¼ to 1¾ pounds	Broil 14 to 16 minutes Panfry 16 to 18 minutes
Ham Slices, Boneless ⅜ inch thick	3 ounces	Broil 4 to 5 minutes Panfry 4 to 5 minutes
Ham Slices, Boneless ¼ inch thick	2 ounces	Broil 3 to 4 minutes Panfry 3 to 4 minutes
To broil* or panfry cook-before-eating ham slices		
Ham Slices, Bone-in ¾ inch thick	1 to 1¼ pounds	Broil 13 to 14 minutes Panfry 15 to 20 minutes
Ham Slices, Bone-in 1 inch thick	1¼ to 1¾ pounds	Broil 18 to 20 minutes Panfry 20 to 22 minutes
*Broil 3 inches from heat.		

HAM TROPICALE*

1 fully-cooked boneless whole ham
1 15-ounce can sliced peaches
1 8¾-ounce can crushed
   pineapple
2 tablespoons cornstarch
½ teaspoon ground cinnamon
   Dash ground cloves
⅓ cup frozen orange juice
   concentrate, thawed
½ cup whole maraschino cherries
¼ cup light raisins
½ cup broken pecan halves

Place ham on rack in shallow roasting pan. Score ham in diamonds, cutting only ¼ inch deep. Insert meat thermometer. Roast according to Ham Roasting Chart.

Drain peaches and pineapple, reserving syrups. In saucepan, combine cornstarch and spices. Stir in reserved syrups, orange juice concentrate, and 1 cup water; cook and stir till mixture thickens and bubbles. Spoon some sauce over ham last 30 minutes of baking time. Continue baking; baste occasionally.

Reserve a few peach slices and whole cherries for garnish. Cut up remaining peaches and slice remaining cherries. To same sauce, add peaches, pineapple, cherries, raisins, and pecans. Simmer 10 minutes. Garnish with reserved peaches and cherries; spoon on a little fruit sauce. Pass remaining sauce.

As shown across from the Contents page.

Score ham fat in diamond pattern—cuts should be only ¼ inch deep. A 12x2-inch paper strip is a handy cutting guide.

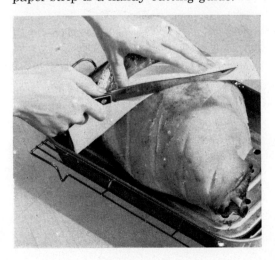

MUSTARD SAUCE

2 beaten egg yolks
1 tablespoon sugar
3 tablespoons prepared mustard
2 tablespoons vinegar
1 tablespoon water
1 tablespoon prepared horseradish
1 tablespoon butter or margarine
½ teaspoon salt
½ cup whipping cream, whipped

In top of double boiler, combine all ingredients except whipped cream; mix well. Place over boiling water; cook and stir till thickened, about 2 minutes. Remove from heat. Stir till sauce is smooth; cool. Fold in whipped cream; refrigerate. Makes 1 cup.

RAISIN SAUCE

½ cup brown sugar
2 tablespoons cornstarch
1 teaspoon dry mustard
1 tablespoon vinegar
1 cup raisins
¼ teaspoon grated lemon peel
2 tablespoons lemon juice

In saucepan, mix together first 3 ingredients. Slowly add vinegar, next 3 ingredients, and 1½ cups water. Stir over medium heat till thick and bubbly. Serve hot. Makes 2½ cups.

Spoon glaze evenly over ham during last 30 minutes of baking. For heavier coating, spoon glaze over several times.

HAM AND VEGETABLE STEW

In Dutch oven, brown 1 pound fully-cooked ham, cut in 1-inch pieces, in 2 tablespoons shortening. Remove ham. Cook ¾ cup chopped green pepper, ½ cup chopped onion, and 1 clove garlic, minced, in Dutch oven till tender but not brown.

Add ham, one 10-ounce package frozen green beans, 3 medium potatoes, cut in 1-inch cubes, one 28-ounce can tomatoes, cut up, 1 cup water, and 1 teaspoon salt to Dutch oven. Bring to boiling; cover and simmer 35 minutes or till tender. Combine 3 tablespoons all-purpose flour and ¼ cup cold water; stir into stew. Cook and stir till mixture thickens and bubbles; cook 1 minute longer. Serves 6.

HAM AND POTATO SCALLOP

 1 fully-cooked ham slice, cut ½ inch thick (about 1 pound)
 5 cups thinly sliced pared potatoes
 1 10½-ounce can condensed cream of mushroom soup
 ¼ cup milk
 ½ cup chopped onion
 ¼ cup chopped green pepper
   Dash pepper
 2 tablespoons butter or margarine

Cut ham in serving or bite-size pieces. Place *half* the potatoes in greased 2-quart casserole. Cover with ham pieces. Place remaining potatoes atop. Combine soup, milk, onion, green pepper, and pepper; pour over potatoes. Dot with butter. Cover and bake in moderate oven (350°) 1 hour. Remove cover; bake 45 minutes longer or till potatoes are done. Trim with snipped parsley. Makes 6 servings.

CREAMED HAM

In saucepan, melt ¼ cup butter or margarine; blend in ¼ cup all-purpose flour and ¼ teaspoon salt. Add 2 cups milk all at once. Cook and stir till thick and bubbly. Add 2 cups diced fully-cooked ham, one 3-ounce can sliced mushrooms, drained, 2 tablespoons chopped green pepper, and ½ teaspoon prepared mustard; heat through. Serve over hot toast points; trim with diced canned pimiento. Makes 4 or 5 servings.

SWEET-SOUR HAM OVER RICE

 2½ cups packaged precooked rice
 1 16-ounce can (2 cups) apricot halves
 1½ pounds fully-cooked ham, cut in strips (about 3 cups)
 2 green peppers, cut in 1-inch pieces
 1 cup chicken broth
 ⅓ cup sugar
 ¼ cup vinegar
 3 tablespoons butter or margarine
 3 tablespoons soy sauce
 1 teaspoon monosodium glutamate
 4 tablespoons cornstarch

Cook rice according to package directions. Meanwhile, drain apricots, reserving syrup. In large saucepan combine apricot syrup, ham, green pepper, ¾ *cup* of the chicken broth, sugar, vinegar, butter, soy sauce, and monosodium glutamate. Bring to boiling; cover and simmer for 10 minutes.

Blend cornstarch and the remaining ¼ cup *cold* chicken broth; add to ham mixture. Cook and stir till boiling; boil 2 minutes more. Add apricots and remove from heat. Spoon over servings of hot cooked rice. Makes 6 servings.

Make colorful Sweet-sour Ham Over Rice to give your meal an Oriental touch. Serve sherbet and fortune cookies for dessert.

1. *Virginia-style* or *Smithfield* hams are great served thinly sliced with turkey.

2. *Country-style* hams are similar to the Smithfield hams and need slow cooking.

3. *Prosciutto* is delicious eaten the Italian way—with chilled honeydew melon.

Specialty hams

1. *Virginia-style* and true *Smithfield* hams have several specific requirements. The hams must be processed in a particular locality. (For Smithfield hams, it must be within the limits of Smithfield, Virginia.) They are dry salt cured, smoked over hickory logs, and then hung to age for 6 months to develop flavor and texture.

Sometimes the hogs are peanut fed and because of the special diet, the meat is rich and lean and after curing the fat is clear and amber colored. A coarse black pepper is used on the surface. After cooking, the meat is a deep red color and has a very distinctive flavor.

To prepare Smithfield hams, soak in cold water from 24 to 48 hours, then wash and scrape. Put ham in a large kettle and cover completely with water. Bring water to boiling and simmer till a skewer can easily be inserted and removed from ham, about 25 minutes per pound. Additional hot water should be added as needed to keep ham covered while cooking.

After cooking, the skin is then carefully removed and the meat can be glazed in the oven if desired. Slice meat paper-thin to serve. Some prefer to slice the ham lengthwise, others slice across the grain.

2. *Country-style* hams are another Southern tradition and are processed in much the same way as the Smithfield ham. These hams were developed by the early settlers to keep through the hot summer without refrigeration. They are also scrubbed or trimmed, soaked, and simmered before browning and glazing.

3. *Prosciutto* is the Italian version of a Virginia-style ham and is highly esteemed by gourmets. The special method of processing concentrates the flavor in these hams so that very thin slices are the rule. The lean, whole ham is pressed and aged in a spice mixture till it has a concentrated, rich flavor. This ham can also be sliced lengthwise or across the grain and is delicious on a cold meat tray or as an appetizer with fruit.

Lamb puts
spring into mealtime

<table>
<tr><td colspan="3">LAMB CHOP BROILING CHART</td></tr>
<tr><td colspan="3">Broil chops so surface is 3 inches from heat.</td></tr>
<tr><td>Thickness of
Lamb Chop</td><td>Medium</td><td>Well-done</td></tr>
<tr><td></td><td colspan="2">(total time in minutes)</td></tr>
<tr><td>¾ inch</td><td>10 to 12</td><td>13 to 15</td></tr>
<tr><td>1 inch</td><td>11 to 13</td><td>16 to 18</td></tr>
<tr><td>1½ inches</td><td>15 to 18</td><td>20 to 22</td></tr>
</table>

LAMB CHOPS ORIENTAL

6 shoulder lamb chops,
   ¾ inch thick
½ cup soy sauce
1 clove garlic, minced

Slash fat edges of chops. Place in shallow baking dish. Combine soy sauce, ½ cup water, and garlic; pour over chops. Cover; refrigerate several hours; turn once. Place chops on rack of broiler pan; broil 3 inches from heat about 10 minutes. Turn chops and broil 5 to 8 minutes longer. Makes 6 servings.

ORANGE LAMB CHOPS

6 shoulder lamb chops, ¾
   inch thick
½ teaspoon shredded orange peel
¼ cup orange juice
½ teaspoon dried thyme, crushed
1 tablespoon shortening
1 3-ounce can sliced mushrooms,
   drained (½ cup)

Trim excess fat from chops. Combine orange peel, juice, and thyme; spoon over chops. Let stand 1 hour at room temperature or several hours in refrigerator, turning chops once or twice. Drain, reserving orange mixture. Brown chops on both sides in hot shortening; season with salt and pepper. Add orange mixture and mushrooms. Cover; simmer 40 minutes. Uncover; simmer about 5 minutes more. Makes 6 servings.

CURRIED LAMB CHOPS

6 Saratoga lamb chops
2 tablespoons shortening
1 17-ounce can apricot halves
1 tablespoon lemon juice
¼ cup sliced green onions (with tops)
½ teaspoon curry powder
1 tablespoon cornstarch
   Hot cooked rice

Brown chops in hot shortening; season with salt and pepper. Drain off excess fat. Drain apricots, reserving syrup. Combine syrup, lemon juice, onion, and curry. Pour over chops. Cover; simmer about 40 to 45 minutes. Remove chops from skillet. Mix cornstarch with 1 tablespoon cold water; stir into sauce. Cook and stir till thick and bubbly. Add drained apricots; heat through. Serve sauce with chops and rice. Makes 6 servings.

TANGY LAMB CHOPS

8 loin lamb chops, 1 inch thick
2 tablespoons chopped onion
2 tablespoons butter, melted
1 3-ounce can sliced mushrooms,
   drained (½ cup)
½ cup dairy sour cream
2 tablespoons milk
   Dash dried marjoram, crushed

Broil chops according to Lamb Chop Broiling Chart. Meanwhile, cook onion in butter till tender. Blend in remaining ingredients, dash salt, and dash pepper. Cook and stir over low heat till sauce is heated through. Serve sauce with chops. Makes 4 servings.

Lamb chops with elegance

Serve mouth-watering Orange Lamb →
Chops. Complete the meal with a tossed salad and sesame-topped biscuits.

Lamb cuts

For Basic Bone Identification Chart and How Much Meat to Serve, see Index.

1. *Square Cut Shoulder Roast*—can be identified by its shape, square. This shoulder cut contains the arm bone, blade bone, ribs, and part of the neck bone. The arm bone is exposed on one side, the blade bone on another side. The outside is covered with a layer of fat and fell (a thin skin or membrane covering the fat). Roast this cut. *Rolled Shoulder Roast*—is a boneless cut made from the Square Cut Shoulder Roast. Thin layers of fat are distributed throughout the roast with a thin layer covering the outside. After boning, the meat is rolled and secured with twine or netting. Roast or braise this Rolled Shoulder Roast for best results.

2. *Cushion Shoulder Roast*—is the Square Cut Shoulder Roast with the bones removed. The pocket openings made when the bones are removed are closed with twine. The appearance of a cushion has influenced the naming of this cut. Roast. *Saratoga Chops*—are made from a shoulder muscle which is rolled and fastened with skewers, then cut into chops. Broil, panbroil, panfry, or braise this lean cut.

3. *Blade Chop*—can be identified by the blade bone. It is cut from the blade side of the Square Cut Shoulder Roast. The outer surface is covered with a thin layer of fat and fell. Broil, panbroil, panfry, or braise this chop. *Arm Chop*—identified by the round bone, is cut from the arm side of the Square Cut Shoulder Roast. This chop is lean and the bone waste is slight. A thin layer of fat and fell cover the outside of this chop. Broil, panbroil, panfry, or braise this chop. *Shanks*—cut from the arm (front legs) of the lamb can be identified by the round arm bone. A very thin layer of fat and fell covers the outer surface. Because of the elongated shape and position of the shanks, they are sometimes called "lamb drumsticks." Braise or cook the shanks in liquid.

1. *Square Cut Shoulder Roast*, top; *Rolled Shoulder Roast* (netted), bottom.

2. *Cushion Shoulder Roast*, upper left; *Saratoga Chops* (shoulder), lower right.

3. *Blade Chop*, upper left; *Arm Chop*, lower left; *Shanks*, right.

4. *Frenched Rib Roast*, top; *Rib Chops*, left; *Frenched Rib Chops*, lower right.

5. *Riblets*, upper left; *Ribs*, middle right; *Stuffed Breast Chop*, lower left.

6. *Loin Roast*, upper left; *Loin Chop*, upper right; *English Chop*, lower left.

4. *Frenched Rib Roast*—contains 7 to 8 ribs with the meat removed from about a 1-inch section (Frenched). The predominant muscle is the rib eye covered with a layer of fat and fell. When this cut is not "Frenched," it's called Rib Roast or Lamb Rack. Have meatman loosen or remove the backbone when purchased. Roast this cut. *Rib Chops*—are cut from the Rib Roast and can usually be identified by the rib bone. The large muscle is the rib eye. The outside layer of fat has the fell removed. Broil, panbroil, or panfry these chops. *Frenched Rib Chops*—are Rib Chops which have been "Frenched." Broil, panbroil, or panfry these chops.

5. *Riblets*—are cut between the rib bones from the breast section and contain rib cartilage and rib bones. Layers of muscle are alternated with layers of fat. Grill, braise, or cook the riblets in liquid. *Ribs*—come from the breast section and contain rib bones and rib cartilage. A thin covering of meat surrounds the ribs. Roast or braise lamb ribs. *Stuffed Breast Chops*—are cut from the whole breast of lamb which contains layers of muscle and fat. A slit is cut through the breast forming a pocket which is then stuffed with ground lamb or a ground lamb mixture. The chops, also called Scotch Chops, are then cut by slicing between the ribs of the breast. Braise, broil, or panbroil chops.

6. *Loin Roast*—can be identified by the T-bone. Cut from the loin section, the larger muscle is the loin eye. The smaller muscle is the tenderloin separated from the loin eye by the finger of the T-bone. Roast this tender cut. *Loin Chop*—is cut from the Loin Roast and can be identified by the T-bone. The larger muscle is the loin eye, the smaller the tenderloin. Broil, panbroil, or panfry this chop. *English Chop*—is also called a Double Loin Chop. Usually the entire loin section is split lengthwise through the center of the backbone forming two sections. For this chop it is not. The loin section is kept whole and a cross-sectional slice is made. Each side of the slice contains the loin eye, the larger muscle, separated from the tenderloin by the finger of the T-bone. For a large serving, broil or panfry this cut.

Lamb cuts

7. *Boneless English Roast*—is also called a Rolled Double Loin. The whole loin section, which has not been split through the center of the backbone to form two sections, is used for this roast. It is boned, rolled, and tied. The muscles are two loin eyes and two tenderloins. Roast this tender cut. *Cubes for Kabobs*—are cut from either the shoulder or leg of lamb and are boneless. They can be purchased in bulk or threaded on wooden skewers. Marinate, if desired, and broil. *Boneless English Chop*—sliced from the Boneless English Roast, is also called a Boneless Double Loin Chop. The loin eye and tenderloin are the muscles present. Broil or panfry this tender Double Loin Chop.

7. *Boneless English: Roast*, upper left, *Chop*, lower; *Cubes for Kabobs*, right.

8. *Center Leg Roast*—is cut between the shank half and the sirloin half of the leg. Roast this tender cut. *Leg Steak*—can be identified by the round leg bone. It is cut from the center of the American or Frenched Leg. Broil, panbroil, panfry, or braise this steak. *Sirloin Chop*—comes from the sirloin section of the lamb which is between the loin section and the leg. The wedge bone (hip bone) will vary in shape depending upon where the chop is cut in the sirloin. The muscles found in this chop are the top sirloin, flank, and sometimes the tenderloin. Broil, panbroil, or panfry this tender Sirloin Chop.

8. *Center Leg Roast*, upper left; *Leg Steak*, right; *Sirloin Chop*, lower left.

9. *American Leg*—has the sirloin half of the leg removed. (The sirloin half is the portion of the leg which is connected to the sirloin section on one side and the leg on the other side.) The shank bone is also removed and the meat is folded back into the pocket left by boning. Roast this cut. *Frenched Leg*—has the sirloin section of the leg removed. The shank bone is "Frenched" and a paper frill is placed over the bone. Roast this cut. *Boneless Leg of Lamb*—is formed from a full leg (both shank half and sirloin half of leg). The leg is boned, rolled, and either netted or tied with twine. Roast this boneless cut.

9. *Leg: American*, left, *Frenched*, right; *Boneless Leg of Lamb*, bottom.

LAMB WITH PLUM SAUCE

Place one 4- to 5-pound leg of lamb, fat side up, on rack in shallow roasting pan. Season. Roast at 325° for 2½ to 3 hours or till meat thermometer registers 175° to 180°.

Meanwhile, drain one 16-ounce can purple plums, reserving ¼ cup syrup. Pit and sieve plums. Combine reserved syrup, plums, 2 tablespoons lemon juice, 1 tablespoon soy sauce, 1 teaspoon Worcestershire sauce, ½ teaspoon dried basil, crushed, and ½ clove garlic, crushed. Baste lamb 4 times during last hour of roasting. Simmer remaining sauce 5 minutes. Pass with meat. Makes 8 to 10 servings.

SAVORY LAMB ROLL

  1 tablespoon all-purpose flour
  2 teaspoons salt
  1 clove garlic, minced
  1 tablespoon lemon juice
  1 3- to 4-pound boned and rolled
      lamb shoulder roast
  3 tablespoons all-purpose flour

Combine 1 tablespoon flour, salt, dash pepper, garlic, and lemon juice. Spread over meat. Place lamb on large sheet of heavy foil; wrap securely. Place in shallow roasting pan. Roast in hot oven (425°) about 3 hours or till meat thermometer registers 175° to 180°; open foil last 30 minutes of roasting. Remove meat to warm serving platter.

Pour juices into large measuring cup; add water to make 1¾ cups liquid and transfer to saucepan. Combine 3 tablespoons flour and ½ cup cold water; stir into juices. Cook and stir till thick and bubbly. Add dash of kitchen bouquet, if desired; season. Serves 6 to 8.

FRUITED LEG OF LAMB

Cut 2 or 3 slits in one 5- to 6-pound leg of lamb; insert 1 clove garlic, sliced. Rub mixture of 1 teaspoon *each* ground ginger and dry mustard over lamb. Place meat, fat side up, on rack in shallow roasting pan. Roast in slow oven (325°) for 3 to 3½ hours or till meat thermometer registers 175° to 180°.

Meanwhile, dissolve ½ cup cherry jam in 1 cup hot strong coffee; stir in 2 tablespoons port wine. After meat has roasted 1 hour, pour sauce over lamb. Baste occasionally during remainder of roasting period. Place meat on warm serving platter.

Pour meat juices into large measuring cup. Skim off fat, returning 2 tablespoons fat to pan. Blend in 2 tablespoons all-purpose flour; cook and stir till bubbly. Remove pan from heat. Add water to meat juices to make 1½ cups liquid. Add liquid to flour mixture all at once; cook and stir till thickened and bubbly. Season to taste. Pass sauce with lamb. Makes 10 servings.

STUFFED LAMB SHOULDER

Rub outside of one 3- to 3½-pound boneless cushion lamb shoulder roast with salt and pepper. Stuff pocket of meat with Savory Stuffing. Fasten edges with skewers. Place on rack in shallow roasting pan. Roast at 325° about 2 hours. During last 30 minutes of roasting, lay 5 bacon slices over meat. Remove skewers before carving. Serves 6.

Savory Stuffing: Combine 4 cups ½-inch dry bread cubes, 3 tablespoons chopped onion, ½ teaspoon poultry seasoning, ¼ teaspoon salt, and dash pepper. Add ¼ cup melted butter and ¼ cup hot water; toss gently.

LAMB ROASTING CHART			
Cut	Approximate Weight (Pounds)	Internal Temp. on Removal from Oven	Approximate Cooking Time (Total Time)
Roast meat at constant oven temperature of 325°.			
Leg, whole	5 to 8	175° to 180°	3½ to 3¾ hours
Leg, half	3 to 4	175° to 180°	3 to 3½ hours
Square Cut Shoulder	4 to 6	175° to 180°	2½ to 3 hours
Rolled Shoulder	3 to 5	175° to 180°	2¾ to 3 hours

HONEY-LIME LAMB ROAST

2 lamb rib roasts with backbones loosened (3 to 4 pounds total)
¾ cup honey
2 teaspoons grated lime peel
⅓ cup lime juice

Season lamb roasts with salt. Place meat, rib side down, in roasting pan. Roast at 325° for 1 hour or till meat thermometer registers 180°. Meanwhile, heat honey, lime peel, and juice in saucepan. Baste meat with glaze during last 30 minutes of roasting time. Serves 6 to 8.

MINT SAUCES

Fresh Mint Sauce: Combine ¼ cup snipped fresh mint leaves, ¼ cup light corn syrup, and 1 tablespoon lemon juice. Blend together ¼ cup water and 1½ teaspoons cornstarch; add to mint mixture. Cook and stir over medium heat till mixture thickens and bubbles; strain. Stir in 1 drop green food coloring. Makes ½ cup.

In-a-hurry Mint Sauce: Combine ½ cup mint jelly and 2 teaspoons lemon juice. Heat slowly, stirring occasionally, till jelly is melted. Serve with lamb. Makes ½ cup.

Tangy Mint Sauce: In small saucepan, combine ½ cup mint-flavored apple jelly, 2 tablespoon butter or margarine, 2 tablespoons cider vinegar, 1 tablespoon lemon juice, and ½ teaspoon dry mustard. Cook and stir over medium heat till jelly melts and mixture comes to a boil. Makes ¾ cup.

BARBECUED LAMB RIBLETS

Brown 3- to 4-pounds lamb riblets slowly in skillet. Drain off excess fat. Season with salt and pepper; top with 1 lemon, sliced. Combine ¾ cup catsup, ¾ cup water, ½ cup chopped onion, 2 tablespoons brown sugar, 3 tablespoons Worcestershire sauce, 1 tablespoon vinegar, 1½ teaspoons monosodium glutamate, ¾ teaspoon salt, and dash bottled hot pepper sauce; pour over meat. Cover; simmer about 1½ hours or till done. Remove meat to serving dish. Skim off excess fat from sauce. Pass sauce with meat. Serves 6 to 8.

LAMB WITH VEGETABLES

4 lamb steaks, ½ inch thick
½ teaspoon dried rosemary, crushed
¼ teaspoon salt
Dash pepper
1 tablespoon shortening

. . .

¼ cup chopped onion
2 tablespoons chopped green pepper
1 clove garlic, crushed
1 3-ounce can sliced mushrooms, drained (½ cup)
2 medium tomatoes, sliced
¼ cup dry white wine
2 tablespoons cold water
1 tablespoon all-purpose flour

Season steaks with mixture of rosemary, salt, and pepper. In skillet, brown steaks on both sides in hot shortening. Add onion, green pepper, and garlic; cook till tender. Add mushrooms, tomatoes, and wine. Cook, covered, over low heat for 30 minutes; uncover and simmer 15 minutes more or till meat is tender. Remove meat and vegetables to serving dish.

Pour remaining meat juices into measuring cup. Add enough water to make 1 cup liquid; return to skillet. Blend together water and flour; stir into meat juices. Cook and stir till mixture thickens and bubbles. Serve sauce with lamb steaks. Makes 4 servings.

GARLIC LAMB KABOBS

1½ pounds boneless lamb, cut in 1-inch cubes
1 cup garlic salad dressing *or* 1 envelope *dry* garlic salad dressing mix*
2 medium green peppers, cut in squares
1 16-ounce can small onions

Place meat in shallow dish. Pour dressing over meat. Let stand 2 hours at room temperature or overnight in refrigerator, turning occasionally. Drain meat, reserving liquid. Thread meat and vegetables on skewers in the following order: lamb, green pepper, lamb, onion. Broil 4 inches from heat about 15 minutes, turning once. Baste meat and vegetables occasionally with dressing. Makes 6 servings.

*Prepare mix, following package directions.

CURRIED LAMB

2 pounds boneless lamb, cut in
¾-inch cubes
2 tablespoons shortening
1 medium onion, sliced
1½ teaspoons salt
Dash freshly ground pepper
1 bay leaf

. . .

¼ cup all-purpose flour
1½ to 2 teaspoons curry powder
1 tablespoon snipped parsley
Hot cooked rice
Curry condiments

In skillet, brown cubed meat in hot shortening. Add 1½ cups water, onion, salt, pepper, and bay leaf. Cover and cook slowly for 1½ hours or till meat is tender.

Remove meat from pan. Pour meat juices into large measuring cup; skim off excess fat. Add enough water to make 1½ cups liquid. Mix flour and curry powder; blend with ½ cup cold water. Pour meat juices back into pan; stir in flour mixture. Cook, stirring constantly, until mixture thickens and bubbles. Add meat and parsley to sauce; heat through. Serve lamb with hot cooked rice. Offer bowls of curry condiments—raisins, peanuts, flaked coconut, or chutney. Makes 6 servings.

DILLED LAMB STEW

2 pounds boneless lamb, cut in
¾-inch cubes
2 tablespoons shortening
1 teaspoon salt
½ teaspoon dillweed
2 cups water
2 cups sliced carrot
1 cup sliced celery
2 tablespoons all-purpose flour
¾ cup cold water
1 cup dairy sour cream

Brown lamb in hot shortening. Season with mixture of salt and dillweed; add 2 cups water. Cover and simmer about 35 minutes, or till meat is almost tender. Add carrot and celery; cook 15 minutes. Blend flour and ¾ cup water; stir into stew. Cook till mixture thickens and bubbles. Stir in sour cream; heat through; do not boil. Makes 6 servings.

SHEPHERD'S LAMB STEW

1 pound boneless lamb, cut in
1-inch cubes
3 tablespoons all-purpose flour
2 tablespoons shortening
1 envelope *dry* onion gravy mix
¾ teaspoon salt
¼ teaspoon monosodium glutamate
⅛ teaspoon garlic powder
Dash paprika
Dash pepper
2 cups cold water
2 potatoes, pared, halved, and
cut in ½-inch slices
1 10-ounce package frozen green
beans

Coat meat with flour; brown in hot shortening. Drain off excess fat. Combine gravy mix, salt, monosodium glutamate, garlic powder, paprika, pepper, and any remaining flour; stir in water and add to meat. Cook, stirring occasionally, till mixture thickens and bubbles. Cover and simmer 30 minutes. Add potatoes and beans. Return to boiling, then reduce heat. Cover and simmer 30 minutes more or till vegetables are tender. Serves 4.

Shepherd's Lamb Stew offers a hearty mixture of lamb, potatoes, and green beans. It's served in a rich brown sauce prepared with ease from a gravy mix.

Lamb shanks cooked slowly

Here's eating enjoyment for the budget-conscious. The slow, moist cooking makes Herbed Lamb Shanks an easy success.

HERBED LAMB SHANKS

    4 lamb shanks, about 2½ pounds
    1 tablespoon butter or margarine
 1½ cups water
    1 teaspoon salt
    ¼ cup all-purpose flour
    2 tablespoons butter or margarine, melted
    ½ cup water
    1 clove garlic, minced
    1 tablespoon snipped parsley
    ⅛ teaspoon dried marjoram, crushed
       Dash ground mace
       Hot cooked noodles

In large skillet, brown lamb shanks in 1 tablespoon butter. Add 1½ cups water and salt. Cook, covered, over low heat for 1 hour. In small skillet, add flour to 2 tablespoons melted butter; cook and stir over low heat till mixture is browned. Add to meat. Cook and stir till gravy thickens and bubbles. Stir in ½ cup water, garlic, parsley, marjoram, and mace. Cook, covered, about 1 hour more or till meat is tender. Arrange lamb shanks on a bed of hot cooked noodles; spoon on a little gravy. Pass remaining gravy. Makes 4 servings.

ZIPPY LAMB SHANKS

    4 lamb shanks, about 2½ pounds
       Salt
       Pepper
    2 tablespoons shortening
    1 medium onion, sliced
    ½ cup sliced celery
    1 small clove garlic, minced
    ½ cup catsup
 1½ teaspoons Worcestershire sauce
       Hot cooked rice

Season lamb shanks with salt and pepper. In skillet, brown meat in hot shortening. Combine onion, celery, garlic, catsup, ½ cup water, and Worcestershire sauce; add to meat. Simmer, covered, for 1½ hours or till meat is tender. Skim off excess fat. Serve with hot cooked rice. Makes 4 servings.

Ever-popular ground meat served plain or fancy

STUFFED HAMBURGER ROLL

¼ cup chopped onion
2½ cups ¼-inch bread cubes, toasted (about 4 slices)
1½ pounds ground beef
1 egg
½ teaspoon salt
¼ teaspoon dried sage, crushed
4 ounces sharp process American cheese, shredded (1 cup)

Combine onion and ⅓ cup water; simmer, covered, 5 minutes. Add bread cubes; toss. Combine meat, egg, seasonings, and dash pepper. On waxed paper, pat meat into 14x8-inch rectangle. Spread bread mixture over; sprinkle ¾ *cup* cheese atop. Starting at narrow end, roll meat mixture. Place seam side down in 8½x4½x2½-inch loaf dish. Bake, uncovered, at 350° 70 minutes. Top with remaining cheese; bake till melted. Serves 6.

MEAT LOAF SUPREME

1 pound ground pork
1 pound ground beef
1 cup shredded carrot
1 cup coarsely crushed saltine cracker crumbs (22 crackers)
1 cup dairy sour cream
¼ cup chopped onion
1 teaspoon salt
Dash pepper
Mushroom Sauce

Combine all ingredients except Mushroom Sauce; mix. Press into 9x5x3-inch loaf pan. Bake at 350° about 1½ hours. Let stand 10 minutes; remove from pan. Serve with *Mushroom Sauce:* Dissolve 1 beef bouillon cube, crushed, in drippings from meat loaf. Combine with ½ cup dairy sour cream, 1 tablespoon all-purpose flour, and one 3-ounce can broiled sliced mushrooms, undrained. Heat just till boiling. Serves 8 to 10.

TARGET MEAT LOAVES

Combine 1 pound ground beef, 1 egg, ½ cup coarsely crushed saltine cracker crumbs, ¼ cup finely chopped celery, ¼ cup milk, 2 tablespoons finely chopped onion, ½ teaspoon salt, ¼ teaspoon garlic salt, ¼ teaspoon ground sage, and dash dried oregano, crushed. Mix well. Hard cook 6 eggs; shell. Shape about ⅓ cup meat mixture around each egg. Arrange in 10x6x1½-inch baking dish. Cook ¼ cup chopped onion in 1 tablespoon butter or margarine till tender but not brown. Stir in one 8-ounce can tomato sauce, ¼ cup water, and 2 tablespoons snipped parsley. Pour over meat. Bake, uncovered, at 350° for 45 minutes. Cut 1½ slices sharp process American cheese into 6 triangles. Spoon sauce over loaves; top each with cheese triangle. Bake till cheese melts. Serves 6.

GLAZED HAM RING

1½ pounds ground ham
1¼ pounds ground pork
2 beaten eggs
1½ cups soft bread crumbs
½ cup chopped onion
½ cup milk
Sweet-sour Glaze

Thoroughly combine first 6 ingredients. Press mixture into lightly oiled 6-cup ring mold. Invert on shallow baking pan; remove mold. Bake at 350° for 1¼ hours. Prepare *Sweet-sour Glaze:* Blend ½ cup brown sugar and 1 tablespoon prepared mustard. Stir in 2 tablespoons vinegar and 1 tablespoon water. The last 30 minutes of baking time, spoon glaze over ham ring. Baste 3 or 4 times. Serves 8 to 10.

Perfect for company

Who can resist this mouth-watering display. Fill the center of Glazed Ham Ring with creamed peas and new potatoes.

KRAUT-PORK PINWHEEL

Combine 1 pound ground fresh pork, ½ cup fine dry bread crumbs, 1 slightly beaten egg, 1 teaspoon salt, ½ teaspoon Worcestershire sauce, and dash pepper; mix thoroughly. On waxed paper, pat ground meat mixture to a 10x7-inch rectangle.

Combine one 16-ounce can (2 cups) sauerkraut, drained and snipped, and ¼ cup chopped onion; spread evenly over meat. Starting at narrow end, roll up jelly-roll fashion; place seam side down in a shallow baking dish. Arrange 5 bacon slices across top. Bake in moderate oven (350°) for 40 to 45 minutes. Makes 5 or 6 servings.

PORK-APRICOT LOAF

Combine 1½ cups soft bread crumbs (about 2 slices) and ¾ cup milk; let stand for 5 minutes. Add 1 pound ground ham, 1 pound ground fresh pork, 1 cup snipped dried apricots, 2 eggs, 2 tablespoons snipped parsley, and 2 tablespoons chopped onion; mix bread crumbs and meat mixture together thoroughly.

Combine ½ cup brown sugar and 1 teaspoon all-purpose flour; sprinkle in bottom of a 9x5x3-inch loaf pan. Pat ground meat mixture into pan. Bake in a moderate oven (350°) for 1 hour and 15 minutes. Makes 8 servings.

For even-sized meatballs, pat meat mixture into a rectangle, then cut into squares. Roll each square in a ball.

QUICK SWEDISH MEATBALLS

    2   pounds ground beef
    2   cups soft bread crumbs
    2   3-ounce packages cream cheese
    ¼   cup *dry* onion soup mix
    ½   teaspoon salt
    ½   teaspoon ground nutmeg
    2½ cups milk
    2   tablespoons all-purpose flour

Thoroughly combine the meat, bread crumbs, cheese, soup mix, salt, nutmeg, and ½ *cup* of the milk. Shape into about 40 small balls. Brown lightly in large skillet, shaking skillet to keep balls round. Cover and cook 20 to 25 minutes or till done. Remove meat; drain off excess fat, leaving ¼ cup fat in skillet. Blend flour into fat; stir in remaining milk all at once. Cook and stir till thick and bubbly. Return meatballs to skillet; cover and cook till heated through. Makes 10 to 12 servings.

SAUCY ITALIAN MEATBALLS

        Spaghetti Sauce
    4   slices bread
    2   eggs
    1   pound ground beef
    ¼   cup grated Parmesan cheese
    2   tablespoons snipped parsley
    1   teaspoon salt
    ¼   teaspoon dried oregano, crushed
    2   tablespoons salad oil
        Hot cooked spaghetti

Spaghetti Sauce: Cook ¾ cup chopped onion and 1 clove garlic, minced, in 3 tablespoons hot salad oil till tender but not brown. Stir in two 16-ounce cans tomatoes, cut up, two 6-ounce cans (1⅓ cups) tomato paste, 2 cups water, 1½ teaspoons dried oregano, crushed, 1½ teaspoons salt, 1 teaspoon sugar, ½ teaspoon pepper, and 1 bay leaf. Simmer, uncovered, for 30 minutes; remove bay leaf.

Meanwhile, soak bread in ½ cup water 2 to 3 minutes. Add eggs, mixing well. Combine with ground beef, Parmesan cheese, parsley, salt, oregano, and dash pepper. With wet hands, form into small balls (about 24). Brown slowly in hot salad oil. Add meatballs to Spaghetti Sauce; simmer, loosely covered, for 30 minutes. Serve over hot spaghetti. Pass extra Parmesan cheese. Serves 6.

Try a new way with meatballs. Serve Glazed Ham-raisin Balls—you can't miss with this pork and ham combination.

DILLED VEAL SPECIAL

  1 pound ground veal
  4 slices bacon, crisp-cooked, drained, and crumbled
  ¼ cup fine dry bread crumbs
  ¼ cup milk
  1 beaten egg
  ¼ teaspoon dillweed
  1 chicken bouillon cube
  ½ teaspoon kitchen bouquet
  1 tablespoon cornstarch
    Hot cooked rice with parsley

Combine first 6 ingredients and ½ teaspoon salt; mix thoroughly. Shape into 24 balls. Dissolve bouillon cube in 1½ cups boiling water; add kitchen bouquet. Pour into large skillet. Add meatballs and bring to boiling. Cook, covered, for 15 minutes; turn balls once during cooking. Transfer balls to serving dish. Blend 1 tablespoon cold water into cornstarch; stir into broth in skillet. Cook and stir over low heat till thickened and bubbly. Pour sauce over veal balls; serve with hot cooked rice with parsley. Makes 6 servings.

GLAZED HAM-RAISIN BALLS

  ½ pound ground ham
  ½ pound ground fresh pork
  1 cup raisin bran flakes
  1 6-ounce can (⅔ cup) evaporated milk
  1 egg
  1 tablespoon finely chopped onion
    Dash salt
    Dash pepper
    Dash dried thyme, crushed
  ¼ cup brown sugar
  ¼ cup corn syrup
  1 tablespoon vinegar
  ½ teaspoon dry mustard

Thoroughly mix ground ham, ground pork, raisin bran flakes, evaporated milk, egg, onion, salt, pepper, and thyme. Shape into 8 to 10 meatballs, using about ¼ cup ground meat mixture for each ball. Place in an 11x7x1½-inch baking pan. Bake, uncovered, in a moderate oven (350°) for 30 minutes.

In a small saucepan combine brown sugar, corn syrup, vinegar, and dry mustard; bring to boiling. Pour over ham balls and bake 20 minutes more, basting with the sauce once or twice during baking. Makes 4 or 5 servings.

For a tasty change of pace, Dilled Veal Special fits the bill. Spoon these tiny meatballs over fluffy hot cooked rice.

Tips for better burgers

Buying: You'll find your meatman offers a choice of ground beef. *Hamburger* usually has a fairly high proportion of suet. It's good for full-flavored burgers and has a lower price per pound in the meat counter. *Ground chuck* (meat from the shoulder) contains less fat than hamburger and shrinks less in cooking. This type is well-suited for most ground beef dishes. *Ground round steak* is the leanest of all ground beef and perfect for calorie watchers. For juicier burgers, have the meatman grind 2 or 3 ounces of suet with each pound of round steak. Remember, a medium or coarse grind gives burgers a lighter texture.

Making Patties: Handle meat gently when shaping into patties. Too much handling gives burgers a compact texture. To enhance flavors, mix in ½ teaspoon monosodium glutamate for each pound of ground beef. Or, try your hand with herbs for accent.

Want patties to be the same size? Use a ⅓- or ½-cup measure as a quantity guide. Another way to form patties that are the same size is to pat meat till ½ inch thick between two big sheets of waxed paper. Cut burgers with a jumbo cookie cutter. Remember, though, a light touch is important.

Prepare patties ahead for a crowd. Stack patties, putting waxed paper between each layer; wrap. Refrigerate till ready to use.

Cooking: Avoid overcooking for a juicy, tender product. When broiling or panfrying, gently turn meat once during cooking.

To shape patties, place meat on waxed paper. Gently form into a roll 3 inches thick. Cut into ½- to ¾-inch slices.

HAMBURGERS

Panbroiled: Shape 1 pound ground beef into 4 patties, ¾ inch thick. Sprinkle sizzling hot skillet with salt. Cook burgers over high heat 4 to 5 minutes on *each* side. Partially cover if meat spatters.

Broiled: Combine 1 pound ground beef, ½ teaspoon salt, and dash pepper. Shape into 4 patties, ¾ inch thick. Broil 3 inches from heat 6 minutes; turn; broil 4 minutes longer.

APPLE-BEEF PATTIES

    1 pound ground beef
    1 cup cooked long-grain rice
    1 slightly beaten egg
    1 teaspoon monosodium glutamate
    1 teaspoon Worcestershire sauce
    ½ of a 5-ounce jar spiced apple
      rings (5 rings)
    ¼ cup corn syrup
    1 tablespoon lemon juice
    2 teaspoons cornstarch

Combine first 5 ingredients, ½ cup water, and 1 teaspoon salt. Shape into 5 thick patties; place in shallow baking pan. Drain 5 apple rings, reserving ½ cup syrup. Press 1 ring onto each patty. Bake, uncovered, at 350° for 35 minutes. Combine apple and corn syrups and lemon juice in saucepan. Stir 2 teaspoons cold water into cornstarch; add to syrup mixture. Cook and stir till bubbly; spoon onto meat. Bake 5 minutes. Serves 5.

SKILLETBURGERS

Brown 1 pound ground beef. Add 1 cup *each* chopped onion and celery; cook till tender but not brown. Add one 8-ounce can tomato sauce, one 10¾-ounce can condensed tomato soup, dash bottled hot pepper sauce, ¾ teaspoon salt, ½ teaspoon monosodium glutamate, and ¼ teaspoon chili powder. Simmer, uncovered, about 30 minutes. Spoon into split toasted buns. Makes 8 to 10 skilletburgers.

Perk up beef patties

Colorful spiced apple rings bake atop →
Apple-beef Patties. The spicy glaze adds gloss and zest to a ground beef special.

SOUR CREAM BURGERS

1½ pounds ground beef
1 cup dairy sour cream
2 tablespoons Worcestershire sauce
1 tablespoon instant minced onion
1 teaspoon salt
1 cup cornflakes

Thoroughly combine ground beef, sour cream, Worcestershire sauce, onion, and salt. Crush cornflakes slightly. Gently stir into meat mixture. Let stand ½ hour. Shape into 6 patties about ½ inch thick. Broil 4 inches from heat for 6 minutes; turn and broil 6 minutes longer or till done. Makes 6 burgers.

TERIYAKI BURGERS

Combine 1½ pounds ground beef, 1½ cups soft bread crumbs (2 slices), ¼ cup chopped onion, 2 slightly beaten eggs, 2 tablespoons sugar, ¼ cup water, 3 tablespoons soy sauce, 1 small clove garlic, crushed, ¼ teaspoon monosodium glutamate, and dash ground ginger; mix well. Shape into 6 patties. Broil 4 to 5 inches from heat for 10 minutes, turning once. Makes 6 burgers.

STUFFINGBURGERS

1 cup packaged herb-seasoned stuffing mix
¾ cup milk
1 teaspoon instant minced onion
• • •
1 pound ground beef
1 teaspoon salt
½ teaspoon monosodium glutamate
¼ teaspoon pepper
Hamburger buns, split and toasted
Onion rings
Sliced tomatoes

Combine stuffing mix (dry), milk, and onion; let stand till all stuffing mix is moistened. Add beef, salt, monosodium glutamate, and pepper; mix well. Shape into 4 or 5 patties; broil about 4 inches from heat for 7 to 8 minutes; turn. Broil 4 to 5 minutes more; place on bun halves. Top with onions and tomatoes; cover with top of bun. Makes 4 or 5 servings.

VEAL PATTIES

1½ pounds ground veal
¼ cup butter or margarine, melted
1 teaspoon lemon juice
½ teaspoon paprika
½ teaspoon salt
⅛ teaspoon ground nutmeg
Dash pepper
1 beaten egg
2 tablespoons water
½ cup fine dry bread crumbs
2 tablespoons shortening

Combine meat, butter, lemon juice, paprika, salt, nutmeg, and pepper; form into 6 patties. Mix egg with water. Dip patties into egg mixture, then into bread crumbs. Brown on both sides in hot shortening; reduce heat and cook 15 minutes. Makes 6 servings.

LAMB BROILER DINNER

1 pound ground lamb
1 teaspoon salt
Dash monosodium glutamate
Dash dried thyme *or* marjoram, crushed
¼ cup milk
• • •
1 16-ounce can potatoes, drained
2 tablespoons butter or margarine, melted
2 bacon slices, halved
Salt and pepper
Paprika
1 16-ounce can peach halves, drained
Mint jelly

Mix ground lamb with 1 teaspoon salt, monosodium glutamate, thyme *or* marjoram, and milk. Shape lightly into 4 oval patties. Score with handle of wooden spoon or spatula.

Place drained potatoes in foilware pan (or make your own) and drizzle with butter. Arrange meat patties and foilware pan on broiler pan. Broil 4 to 5 inches from heat for 12 minutes. Turn patties; broil 2 minutes more. Top each patty with bacon. Turn potatoes; sprinkle with salt, pepper, and paprika. Place peach halves on broiler pan; broil 5 minutes. Fill peach centers with mint jelly; broil 5 to 7 minutes more. Makes 4 servings.

SAUSAGE-ZUCCHINI BOATS

  4 medium zucchini (2 pounds)
¼ pound bulk pork sausage
¼ cup chopped onion
½ cup grated Parmesan cheese
½ cup finely crushed saltine cracker crumbs
  1 slightly beaten egg
½ teaspoon monosodium glutamate
¼ teaspoon salt
¼ teaspoon dried thyme, crushed
    Dash garlic salt
    Dash pepper
    Paprika

Cook whole zucchini in boiling salted water till barely tender, 7 to 10 minutes. Cut each in half lengthwise; scoop squash from shells and mash. Cook sausage and onion; drain off excess fat. Stir in mashed zucchini. Reserving 2 tablespoons Parmesan cheese, add remaining ingredients except paprika; mix well. Spoon into zucchini shells. Place shells in a shallow baking dish. Sprinkle with reserved Parmesan cheese and dash with paprika. Bake at 350° for 25 to 30 minutes. Makes 4 servings.

SAUSAGE AND MOSTACCIOLI

1½ pounds bulk pork sausage
½ cup chopped onion
¼ cup chopped green pepper
  1 clove garlic, crushed
  1 16-ounce can tomatoes, cut up
  1 6-ounce can tomato paste
½ teaspoon salt
⅛ teaspoon pepper
¼ teaspoon dried oregano, crushed
  8 ounces (3½ cups) mostaccioli, cooked and drained
  6 ounces sharp process American cheese, shredded (1½ cups)

Cook sausage, onion, green pepper, and garlic till meat is brown and vegetables are tender. Drain off excess fat. Add tomatoes, tomato paste, ½ cup water, salt, pepper, and oregano. Stir in cooked mostaccioli. Turn *half* the mostaccioli mixture into a 2-quart baking dish. Top with *half* the cheese. Add remaining mostaccioli mixture. Bake at 350° for 25 minutes. Top with remaining cheese. Heat 5 minutes more. Makes 6 to 8 servings.

SAUSAGE AND MUFFIN BAKE

  3 English muffins, split and toasted
½ pound bulk pork sausage
½ pound ground beef
½ teaspoon salt
  4 ounces sharp process American cheese, shredded (1 cup)
    • • •
  1 envelope onion sauce mix
1½ cups milk
  2 beaten eggs
  1 large tomato, cut in 6 slices

Place an English muffin half in each of 6 buttered 1-cup casseroles. In medium skillet, combine meats and salt. Brown meat; drain off excess fat. Divide meat mixture between casseroles; sprinkle with the cheese.

Combine onion sauce mix and milk; stir in eggs. Pour about ⅓ cup egg mixture into each casserole. Top each casserole with a tomato slice. Bake in moderate oven (350°) for 15 to 20 minutes. Makes 6 servings.

English muffins topped with a blend of sausage, beef, and cheese are crowned with tomato slices. Individual casseroles are perfect for Sausage and Muffin Bake.

CHOPPED MEAT SUEY

In skillet, brown 1 pound ground pork; spoon off excess fat. Dissolve 1 chicken bouillon cube in 1 cup boiling water; add to meat. Stir in 2 cups celery cut in 1-inch pieces and 1/3 cup green onions (with tops) cut in 1/2-inch pieces. Cook, covered, over medium-low heat till celery and green onions are almost crisp tender, about 10 minutes.

Mix 2 tablespoons cornstarch with 1/3 cup cold water; add 1 tablespoon molasses and 1 tablespoon soy sauce. Stir into meat mixture. Cook and stir till thickened and bubbly. Add one 16-ounce can chop suey vegetables, drained; cook till heated through. Serve over mounds of fluffy hot cooked rice. Pass additional soy sauce. Makes 4 servings.

SPANISH RICE SKILLET

In 12-inch skillet, cook 4 slices bacon till crisp; drain. Leaving 1 tablespoon bacon drippings in skillet, cook 1 pound ground beef, 1/2 cup finely chopped onion, and 1/4 cup chopped green pepper till meat is brown and vegetables are tender. Add one 16-ounce can tomatoes, cut up, 1 cup water, 3/4 cup uncooked long-grain rice, 1/2 cup chili sauce, 1 teaspoon salt, 1 teaspoon brown sugar, 1/2 teaspoon Worcestershire sauce, and dash pepper. Simmer, covered, 35 minutes. Crumble bacon atop. Makes 6 to 8 servings.

HAMBURGER SKILLET

 1 pound ground beef
 1 16-ounce can (2 cups) cut green
     beans, undrained
 1 10½-ounce can pizza sauce
 2 teaspoons instant minced onion
· · ·
 1 cup packaged biscuit mix
 1/3 cup milk

In skillet, brown beef; spoon off excess fat. Season with pepper. Stir in beans, pizza sauce, and onion; heat till boiling. Combine biscuit mix and milk; beat vigorously till stiff but sticky, about 20 strokes. Drop by rounded tablespoon atop boiling meat mixture. Cover and simmer about 12 minutes (do not lift cover during cooking). Makes 4 or 5 servings.

SAVORY CABBAGE ROLLS

 1 pound ground beef
 ½ pound ground pork
 1 cup cooked long-grain rice
 1 16-ounce can (2 cups) tomatoes,
     cut up
 ¼ cup chopped onion
 1½ teaspoons salt
 ½ teaspoon monosodium glutamate
     Dash pepper
· · ·
 10 cabbage leaves
 1 tablespoon cornstarch
 1 tablespoon cold water

Combine beef, pork, rice, 3/4 *cup* of the tomatoes, onion, salt, monosodium glutamate, and pepper; mix well. Immerse cabbage leaves in boiling water for 3 minutes or just till limp; drain. Spoon meat mixture onto leaves; roll each leaf around meat, turning ends under. Place in large saucepan or Dutch oven; pour remaining tomatoes over rolls. Cover; simmer 30 minutes. Remove rolls to warm platter. Mix cornstarch with cold water; stir into liquid in saucepan. Cook and stir over medium heat till mixture thickens and bubbles. Serve with cabbage rolls. Makes 5 servings.

Prepare Hamburger Skillet when time is short. This meal-in-a-dish supper is great with crisp relishes and mugs of milk.

CHILI-BURGER STACK-UPS

In medium skillet, cook 1 pound ground beef, ½ cup chopped onion, and 1 clove garlic, minced, till meat is brown and vegetables are tender. Stir in one 16-ounce can tomatoes, cut up, one 6-ounce can tomato paste, ¼ cup chopped green pepper, 1½ teaspoons seasoned salt, 1 teaspoon chili powder, and ¼ teaspoon dried oregano, crushed. Simmer, covered, for 15 minutes, stirring once.

For pancakes, combine one 10-ounce package corn bread mix, 1¼ cups milk, and 1 slightly beaten egg; beat with rotary beater till smooth. Using 2 tablespoons batter for each pancake, bake on hot, lightly greased griddle. Keep baked pancakes warm in oven till all batter is used.

On serving platter, place 6 pancakes. Top with ⅓ of the meat mixture; sprinkle with about 4 teaspoons grated Parmesan cheese. Top each with second pancake, then with half the remaining meat mixture and 4 teaspoons grated Parmesan cheese. Repeat with remaining pancakes, meat mixture, and 4 teaspoons Parmesan cheese. Makes 6 servings.

For an intriguing yet tempting display, it's Chili-burger Stack-ups with layers of pancakes, saucy ground beef, and cheese.

VEAL SKILLET

Cook 1 pound ground veal and ½ cup chopped onion in 3 tablespoons hot shortening till meat is lightly browned. Add one 28-ounce can tomatoes, cut up, 1 cup uncooked elbow macaroni, 2 tablespoons snipped parsley, 1 teaspoon salt, dash pepper, and 1 teaspoon lemon juice. Simmer, covered, for 25 minutes or till macaroni is tender. Serves 6.

LAMB PINWHEELS

½ pound ground lamb
1 2-ounce can chopped mushrooms, drained
2 tablespoons finely chopped onion
1 tablespoon sweet pickle relish
1 tablespoon snipped parsley

• • •

1½ cups sifted all-purpose flour
1½ teaspoons baking powder
½ teaspoon salt
¼ teaspoon ground sage
¼ cup shortening
½ cup milk
Gravy

In skillet, combine lamb, mushrooms, onion, pickle relish, parsley, ¼ teaspoon salt, and dash pepper. Cover and cook for 10 minutes over medium-low heat, stirring occasionally. Spoon off excess pan juices.

Sift together flour, baking powder, salt, and sage. Cut in shortening with pastry blender or blending fork till mixture looks like coarse cornmeal. Add milk all at once and stir just till blended. On a lightly floured surface, roll pastry from center to edge till dough forms a 10x7-inch rectangle.

Spread meat mixture over dough in an even layer. Starting at narrow end, roll jelly-roll style. Place seam side down on lightly greased baking sheet. Bake in hot oven (425°) for 30 minutes or till pastry is lightly browned.

For *Gravy:* Cook 2 tablespoons chopped onion in 2 tablespoons butter or margarine till tender but not brown. Blend in 2 tablespoons all-purpose flour. Add one 10½-ounce can condensed beef broth all at once; cook and stir till mixture thickens and bubbles. Season with salt and pepper. Serve over slices of meat roll. Serves 4 to 6.

Variety meats to select

LIVER AND TOMATO SKILLET

  1 pound beef liver, ½ inch thick,
     cut in serving pieces
  ¼ cup all-purpose flour
  2 tablespoons shortening
  ½ cup chopped onion
  ¼ cup chopped green pepper
  1 16-ounce can tomatoes, cut up
  1 teaspoon sugar
  ½ teaspoon salt
  ¼ teaspoon dried basil, crushed
     Dash garlic powder
  ½ teaspoon Worcestershire sauce
     Hot cooked rice

Coat liver with flour. In skillet, brown quickly in hot shortening; season with salt and pepper. Remove liver. In same skillet, cook onion till tender but not brown. Stir in remaining ingredients except rice. Add liver to sauce. Simmer, uncovered, for 15 minutes. Serve over rice. Makes 4 or 5 servings.

BACON AND LIVER BAKE

  6 slices bacon, chopped
  1 cup chopped onion
  ¼ cup all-purpose flour
  1 pound beef liver, cut in
     serving pieces
1½ cups milk
  ¼ cup fine dry bread crumbs
  1 tablespoon butter, melted

Combine bacon and onion in skillet. Cook till bacon is crisp and onion is tender. Remove, reserving drippings in skillet. Combine flour, 1 teaspoon salt, and dash pepper. Coat liver with flour mixture. Reserve remaining flour mixture. Brown liver in bacon drippings. Remove liver to 10x6x1½-inch baking dish.

Blend reserved flour mixture with drippings in skillet till smooth. Add milk. Cook and stir till thickened and bubbly. Pour sauce over liver. Sprinkle bacon and onion over all. Combine crumbs and melted butter; sprinkle atop liver mixture. Bake, uncovered, at 350° about 25 minutes. Makes 4 servings.

LIVER

Remove membrane and veins from 1 pound calves liver, ⅜ to ½ inch thick. Cook in one of the ways below. Makes 4 servings.

Panfried: Dip slices of liver in seasoned all-purpose flour. Brown quickly on one side in ¼ cup hot shortening, about 1 minute; turn, cook 2 to 3 minutes. Don't overcook.

Broiled: Dip slices of liver in 2 tablespoons butter, melted, *or* French salad dressing. Broil 3 inches from heat for 3 minutes. Turn, top with bacon slices, and broil 3 minutes longer; turn bacon once.

Braised: Dip slices of liver in ¼ cup all-purpose flour seasoned with salt and pepper. Brown quickly on both sides in 3 to 4 tablespoons hot shortening. Reduce heat. Dissolve 1 beef bouillon cube in ½ cup boiling water; add to skillet with 1 medium onion, thinly sliced. Cook over low heat 15 to 20 minutes.

French Fried: Cut liver in strips, ½ inch wide. Let stand in ½ cup French salad dressing 30 minutes; drain. Dip in 1 beaten egg; roll in 1 cup saltine cracker crumbs. Fry in deep hot fat (360°) about 2 minutes. Drain.

CREAMY LIVER OVER RICE

  1 pound beef liver, cubed
  ¼ cup all-purpose flour
  2 tablespoons shortening
  ¼ teaspoon salt
     Dash pepper
  ⅓ cup milk
  1 10½-ounce can condensed cream
     of chicken soup
  2 hard-cooked eggs, chopped
  2 tablespoons snipped parsley
     Hot cooked rice

Coat liver with flour. In 10-inch skillet, brown liver in hot shortening, stirring often. Season with salt and pepper. Blend milk into soup; pour over liver. Cover and cook 10 minutes over low heat, stirring occasionally. Add chopped hard-cooked eggs; cover and simmer 5 minutes longer. Stir in snipped parsley. Serve over hot cooked rice. Makes 4 servings.

Liver Kabobs make a tasty main dish. Cubes of liver, marinated in a tangy mustard mixture, are coated with bread crumbs, then threaded on long skewers.

LIVER KABOBS

Combine 2 tablespoons salad oil, 2 tablespoons Dijon-style mustard, 1 tablespoon lemon juice, 1 tablespoon catsup, 2 teaspoons Worcestershire sauce, $\frac{1}{2}$ teaspoon onion powder, and dash cayenne. Add 1 pound beef liver, 1 inch thick, cut in 2-inch cubes; stir to coat. Refrigerate 3 to 4 hours, turning meat occasionally. Remove liver from mixture.

Drain one 8-ounce can tiny whole onions and cut 1 green pepper in large pieces. Roll liver in $\frac{2}{3}$ cup fine dry bread crumbs. Thread long skewers with liver, green pepper pieces, and whole onions. Place on greased rack of broiler pan. Broil 6 inches from heat for about 5 minutes on each of two sides, or till liver is tender. Add 2 tomatoes, cut in eighths, to ends of skewers the last few minutes of cooking time just to heat. Serve kabobs on hot cooked rice. Makes 4 servings.

LIVER LOAF

1 pound calves liver
1 medium onion, quartered
1 pound ground pork
1 cup soft bread crumbs
1 teaspoon salt
  Dash pepper
1 teaspoon Worcestershire sauce
$\frac{1}{2}$ teaspoon celery salt
2 beaten eggs
3 slices bacon, halved

In saucepan, cover liver with hot water; simmer 5 minutes. Drain; reserve 1 cup stock.

Put liver and onion through medium blade of food chopper. Add pork, next 6 ingredients, and reserved stock. Form mixture into loaf in $8\frac{1}{2}$x$4\frac{1}{2}$x$2\frac{1}{2}$-inch baking dish. Top with bacon. Bake at 350° for 1 hour. Drain off excess fat. Let stand 10 minutes. Serves 8.

KIDNEY IN WINE SAUCE

   2 pounds beef kidneys
   1 10½-ounce can condensed beef
      broth
   ½ cup chopped onion
   1 clove garlic, minced
   ½ teaspoon salt
   1 cup coarsely chopped carrot
   1 cup coarsely chopped celery
     • • •
   2 tablespoons dry red wine
   2 tablespoons cold water
   2 tablespoons all-purpose flour
      Hot cooked rice

Remove membranes and hard parts from kidneys and cut meat into 1-inch pieces. In saucepan, combine kidney, beef broth, onion, garlic, and salt. Cover tightly; cook slowly 1½ hours. Add carrots and celery; continue cooking till tender, about 25 minutes longer. Blend wine, water, and flour together till smooth. Stir into kidney mixture; cook and stir till thickened and bubbly. Serve over hot cooked rice. Makes 4 to 6 servings.

Before cooking kidney, remove any membrane and white hard parts in center with a sharp knife. Then cook as desired.

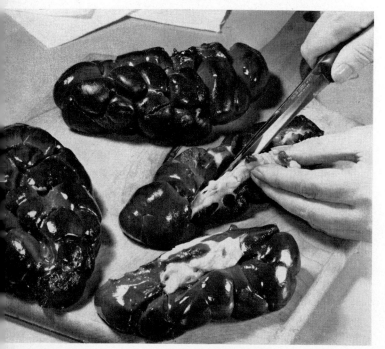

KIDNEY KABOBS

Remove membranes from 4 lamb kidneys. Cut kidneys in quarters, removing any veins and fat. Thread pieces on four 9-inch metal skewers, alternating with 4 slices bacon cut in 2-inch pieces, threaded on accordion fashion. Add 4 mushroom caps to each skewer and brush meat and mushrooms generously with 2 tablespoons butter, melted. Broil 3 inches from heat 7 minutes. Turn and broil 9 to 10 minutes longer or till browned. On separate skewers, broil 8 cherry tomatoes just long enough to heat. Serve with kabobs. Makes 4 servings.

BEEF AND KIDNEY PIE

   1 beef kidney
   1 quart water
   1 tablespoon salt
     • • •
   1 pound beef round steak, cut in
      ½-inch cubes
   ¼ cup all-purpose flour
   2 tablespoons shortening
   1 medium onion, sliced
     • • •
   ½ cup cold water
   ¼ cup all-purpose flour
   1 teaspoon salt
      Dash pepper
      Plain Pastry (see Index)
      Milk

Remove membrane and hard parts, if any, from kidney. In saucepan, combine kidney, 1 quart water, and 1 tablespoon salt. Soak 1 hour; drain. Cover with cold water. Bring to boil; simmer, covered, 20 minutes. Drain meat; cut in ½-inch cubes; set aside.

Coat cubed round steak with ¼ cup all-purpose flour. In Dutch oven, brown steak in hot shortening. Add sliced onion and 2 cups water. Cover; simmer 30 minutes or till tender. In shaker, mix ½ cup cold water, ¼ cup all-purpose flour, 1 teaspoon salt, and pepper. Stir into hot mixture. Cook and stir till slightly thickened and bubbly. Add kidney; heat.

Prepare pastry; roll into circle ½ to 1 inch larger than casserole. Pour meat into 2-quart casserole. Place pastry atop *hot* meat mixture; cut slits in top. Turn under edge and flute. Brush top with milk. Bake at 450° for 20 to 25 minutes. Makes 6 servings.

STUFFED BEEF HEART

　　1　beef heart
　　2　tablespoons chopped onion
　　2　tablespoons shortening
　1½　cups coarsely crushed saltine
　　　　cracker crumbs
　　¼　teaspoon celery salt
　　1　10½-ounce can condensed beef
　　　　broth
　　3　whole black peppercorns
　　2　whole cloves
　　1　bay leaf

Prepare heart for stuffing (see pictures below). Cook onion in shortening till tender. Add crumbs, celery salt, ⅛ teaspoon pepper, and ⅓ cup water; mix. Stuff into heart. Cover opening with foil; tie securely. Place in Dutch oven. Add ½ cup water and remaining ingredients. Cover; simmer 2½ hours. Remove skewers and string. Makes 6 servings.

CHICKEN-FRIED HEART

Slice one 2-pound beef heart in ½-inch thick slices. Coat with seasoned flour. Brown on all sides in small amount hot shortening. Add small amount hot water; cover tightly. Cook slowly about 2 hours or till tender. Add more water, if needed. Makes 6 servings.

To stuff a heart, remove the hard parts. Close the slit with metal skewers, then lace and tie with string forming pocket.

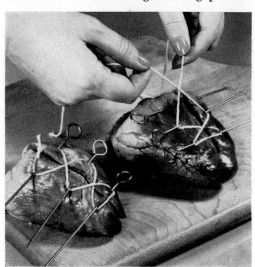

OLD-TIME OXTAIL STEW

　　2　pounds oxtail, cut in 1½-inch
　　　　lengths
　　　　All-purpose flour
　　2　tablespoons shortening
　　1　medium onion, sliced
　　1　16-ounce can (2 cups) tomatoes
　　1　10½-ounce can condensed beef
　　　　broth
　1½　teaspoons salt
　　¼　teaspoon pepper
　　8　small onions, halved
　　4　potatoes, pared and quartered
　　4　carrots, pared and quartered

Coat meat with flour. In Dutch oven, brown meat in hot shortening. Add sliced onion, tomatoes, broth, salt, and pepper. Cover; simmer 2 hours or till meat is just tender. Add halved onions, potatoes, and carrots; cover and simmer 1 hour. Skim off fat. Remove meat and vegetables. Thicken broth.

For pressure pan: Coat meat with flour; brown in hot shortening. Add sliced onion, tomatoes, broth, salt, and pepper. Cook at 15 pounds pressure for 35 minutes. Reduce pressure under cold running water. Add vegetables; return to 15 pounds pressure; cook 10 minutes. Reduce pressure under cold running water. Skim off fat. Remove meat and vegetables. Thicken broth. Makes 6 servings.

For ease of stuffing, place tied heart in small bowl. Fill lightly with stuffing and cover opening with foil; tie in place.

SPICED TONGUE

Place one 3- to 4-pound beef tongue in Dutch oven. Cover with 3 quarts water. Add 16 whole cloves, 12 whole black peppercorns, 2 teaspoons salt, 6 bay leaves, and ¼ cup vinegar. Cover and simmer till tender, allowing 1 hour *per pound*. Chill in liquid. Remove meat. Cut off gristle from large end. Peel off skin. Slice in thin crosswise slices. Makes 4 servings per pound.

CHEESY TONGUE ON RICE

In heavy saucepan, toss 8 ounces sharp process American cheese, shredded, with ½ teaspoon dry mustard. Add ¾ cup milk. Stir over low heat till cheese melts and is smooth. Stir in ½ teaspoon Worcestershire sauce and dash cayenne. Stir small amount of hot mixture into 1 well-beaten egg. Return to hot mixture. Stir in 1½ cups cooked tongue cut in thin strips 3 inches long. Cook and stir over low heat till mixture is thick and creamy. Serve over cooked rice. Serves 4.

To peel tongue, plunge into cold water after cooking to help loosen skin. Slit skin on underside from large end to tip.

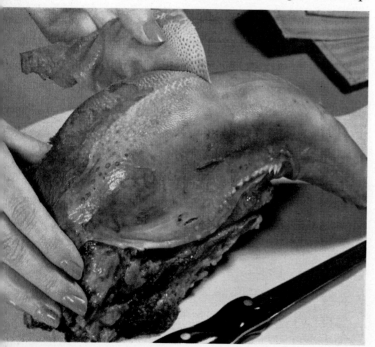

TONGUE 'N BEAN SKILLET

    2 tablespoons chopped onion
    1 tablespoon butter or margarine
    1 beef bouillon cube
    2 teaspoons cornstarch
    ⅓ cup catsup
    ⅛ teaspoon dried thyme, crushed
    2 cups thinly sliced cooked
        beef tongue
    1 10-ounce package frozen baby
        lima beans, cooked and drained

In skillet, cook onion in butter till tender but not brown. Dissolve bouillon cube in ¾ cup boiling water. Blend cornstarch and catsup. Stir into bouillon. Add thyme. Combine with cooked onion, tongue, and beans. Simmer about 5 minutes. Makes 4 or 5 servings.

TONGUE STUFFED PEPPERS

    4 large green peppers
    ¼ cup chopped onion
    2 tablespoons butter or margarine
    1 12-ounce can whole kernel corn,
        drained
    1 cup soft bread crumbs
    1 cup diced cooked tongue
    ½ cup chili sauce

Cut off tops of green peppers; remove seeds and membrane. Precook pepper cups in boiling salted water about 5 minutes; drain. Season pepper shells with salt and pepper. Cook onion in butter till tender. Combine with remaining ingredients. Stuff peppers. Stand upright in small baking dish. Bake, uncovered, at 350° for 20 to 25 minutes. Serves 4.

SWEETBREAD BAKE

    1 pound sweetbreads
    1 slightly beaten egg
    ½ cup fine dry bread crumbs
    6 slices bacon

Cook sweetbreads in simmering water 20 minutes. Cut into 6 serving-size pieces. Dip into mixture of egg and 1 tablespoon water, then into crumbs. Wrap each in bacon and fasten with wooden pick. Bake in shallow pan at 400° for 35 minutes. Serves 4 to 6.

CREAMED SWEETBREADS

Cover 1 pound sweetbreads with 1 quart water, ½ teaspoon salt, and 1 tablespoon vinegar. Simmer 20 minutes or till tender. Drain; cube, removing white membrane.

In saucepan, melt ¼ cup butter over low heat. Blend in 3 tablespoons all-purpose flour, ½ teaspoon salt, and dash pepper. Add 2 cups milk all at once. Cook quickly, stirring constantly, till mixture thickens and bubbles. Add sweetbreads and one 10-ounce package frozen peas with mushrooms, cooked and drained. Heat, stirring gently. Serve over toast points or in pastry shells. Serves 6.

DEEP-FRIED BRAINS

    2 brains (about 1 pound)
      Vinegar *or* lemon juice
    1 slightly beaten egg
    1 tablespoon milk
    1 cup finely crushed saltine
      cracker crumbs

Simmer brains 20 minutes in water to which 1 tablespoon vinegar *or* lemon juice and 1 teaspoon salt have been added for each quart water. Drain. Remove membrane, if any, and cut brains in half lengthwise.

Dip brains into mixture of egg and milk, then in crumbs. Fry in deep hot fat (360°) about 2 minutes or till crisp and brown. Serve with tartar sauce. Makes 4 servings.

SCRAMBLED BRAINS

Cover ¼ pound brains with cold water; add 1½ teaspoons vinegar. Soak 30 minutes; drain. Remove loose fatty membrane. Cover brains with water; add ½ teaspoon salt. Simmer 20 to 30 minutes. Drain; chill in cold water. Finely chop brains. Brown in 2 tablespoons butter. Combine 4 beaten eggs, 1 tablespoon milk, and ¼ teaspoon salt; add to brains. Turn heat low. Don't disturb mixture till it starts to set on bottom and sides, then lift and fold over with wide spatula so uncooked part goes to bottom. Avoid breaking up eggs any more than necessary. Continue cooking 5 to 8 minutes till eggs are cooked throughout, but still glossy and moist. Remove from heat immediately. Serves 4.

PEPPERPOT SOUP

    ½ pound honeycomb tripe
    ½ cup chopped green pepper
    ½ cup chopped onion
    ¼ cup chopped celery
    2 tablespoons butter or margarine
    2 tablespoons all-purpose flour
    3 cups chicken broth
    1 teaspoon celery salt
    ⅛ teaspoon pepper
    ½ cup light cream
    2 tablespoons butter or margarine

In covered saucepan, simmer tripe 3 hours in water to which 1 teaspoon salt has been added for each quart of water. Drain and dice finely, making about 1 cup.

Cook green pepper, onion, and celery in 2 tablespoons butter till onion is tender but not brown. Blend in flour; add chicken broth all at once. Cook and stir till thickened and bubbly. Add diced tripe, celery salt, and pepper. Cover and simmer 1 hour. To serve, add cream and 2 tablespoons butter or margarine; heat through. Makes 4 servings.

Three different kinds of variety meats—upper left, sweetbreads; right, honeycomb tripe; center and front, brains.

Add quick-cooking fish and seafood to the menu

FRESH COOKED SHRIMP

2 tablespoons vinegar
2 bay leaves
1 teaspoon mixed pickling spices
2 branches celery, cut up
2 pounds fresh or frozen shrimp in shells

Combine 6 cups water, 2 tablespoons salt, vinegar, bay leaves, pickling spices, and celery; bring to boiling. Add shrimp either in shells *or* peeled and cleaned. Heat to boiling, then lower heat and simmer gently till shrimp turn pink, about 1 to 3 minutes; drain. If cooked in shell, peel and clean.

Note: When cooking shrimp for highly seasoned dishes, omit vinegar and spices.

SHRIMP QUICHE

4 ounces process Swiss cheese, shredded (1 cup)
4 ounces Gruyere cheese, shredded
1 tablespoon all-purpose flour
3 eggs
1 cup light cream
½ teaspoon prepared mustard
¼ teaspoon Worcestershire sauce
Dash bottled hot pepper sauce
Plain Pastry (see Index)
1 10-ounce package frozen, peeled, and cleaned shrimp, thawed and diced (about 1 cup)

Toss together Swiss cheese, Gruyere cheese, and flour. Beat together next 5 ingredients, ¼ teaspoon salt, and dash pepper. Prepare pastry; line 6 individual bakers. Divide about ¾ of the cheese mixture between the pastry-lined bakers; add diced shrimp and remaining cheese. Pour in egg mixture. Bake in hot oven (400°) for about 30 minutes, or till knife inserted just off center comes out clean. If desired, garnish with whole cooked shrimp and parsley. Makes 6 servings.

SHRIMP FOO YONG

¾ cup chopped, cooked, and cleaned shrimp
1 cup bean sprouts, rinsed and drained
2 tablespoons finely chopped water chestnuts
1 tablespoon chopped green onion
3 fresh mushrooms, chopped
1 teaspoon monosodium glutamate
4 eggs
2 tablespoons salad oil
Foo Yong Sauce

Combine first 7 ingredients, adding eggs last. Mix well. Grease griddle or skillet with salad oil. Drop about ⅓ cup egg mixture onto hot griddle; cook over medium heat till lightly browned, turning once. Stack 3 cakes together for a serving.

Serve with *Foo Yong Sauce:* In small saucepan, blend 1 tablespoon cornstarch, 1 teaspoon monosodium glutamate, and ¼ teaspoon sugar. Gradually stir in 2 tablespoons soy sauce. Add 1 cup chicken broth. Cook and stir till mixture thickens and bubbles. Serves 3.

FRENCH FRIED SHRIMP

Combine 1 cup sifted all-purpose flour, ½ teaspoon sugar, ½ teaspoon salt, 1 slightly beaten egg, 1 cup ice water, and 2 tablespoons salad oil; beat smooth. Shell 2 pounds fresh or frozen shrimp, leaving last section and tail intact. Butterfly shrimp by cutting almost through at center back without severing tail end. Remove black vein; flatten.

Dry shrimp well. Dip into batter; fry in deep hot fat (375°) till golden. Drain.

A luncheon on the patio

A crisp green salad with hearts of palm →
and cooling iced tea accents this elegant meal featuring individual Shrimp Quiche.

DETERMINE HOW MUCH SHRIMP YOU NEED BY HOW YOU WANT TO USE IT

SHRIMP IN 1 POUND

Size	Number of raw shrimp in shell from 1 pound
Jumbo size	*15 to 18*
Average size	*26 to 30*
Tiny	*60 or more*

BUY IN SHELL OR SHELLED

Amount needed	Amount to buy
For each 1 cup cleaned, cooked shrimp	*12 ounces raw shrimp in shell* **or** *7 or 8 ounces frozen shelled shrimp* **or** *1 4½- or 5-ounce can shrimp*

SHRIMP IN CASSEROLE OR SAUCE

Servings	Amount needed
For 4 servings of casserole or creamy sauce (approximate)	*1 pound shrimp in shell* **or** *1⅓ cups cleaned, cooked shrimp* **or** *1 or 2 4½- or 5-ounce cans (1 or 2 cups) shrimp*

JIFFY SHRIMP SKILLET

In skillet, place one 10-ounce can frozen condensed cream of shrimp soup, thawed; add ¾ cup water and stir to blend. Cover; bring just to boiling. Stir in ⅔ cup uncooked packaged precooked rice, one 7- or 8-ounce package frozen, cleaned, and peeled shrimp, ⅓ cup chopped celery, ⅓ cup chopped green pepper, ¼ teaspoon salt, and ½ to 1 teaspoon curry powder. Cover; return to boiling. Reduce heat; simmer 10 minutes or till rice and shrimp are done, stirring occasionally. Just before serving, add ⅓ cup sliced pitted ripe olives. Sprinkle with 2 tablespoons toasted slivered almonds. Serves 3 or 4.

SHRIMP BUFFET CASSEROLE

In skillet, cook ½ cup chopped onion and ½ cup chopped green pepper in 2 tablespoons butter or margarine till tender but not brown. Stir in 3 cups cooked, cleaned shrimp, 2 cups cooked rice, one 10½-ounce can condensed tomato soup, ¾ cup milk, ¼ cup sherry, 1 tablespoon lemon juice, ¼ teaspoon salt, and ¼ teaspoon ground nutmeg.

Pour into a 2-quart casserole. Bake at 350° for 35 minutes, stirring once. Garnish with parsley. Makes 6 to 8 servings.

OYSTER STEW

- 2 tablespoons all-purpose flour
- 1 teaspoon Worcestershire sauce
  Dash bottled hot pepper sauce
- 1 pint shucked oysters, undrained
- ¼ cup butter or margarine
- 1 quart milk, scalded

Blend together first 3 ingredients, 1½ teaspoons salt, and 2 tablespoons water in 3-quart soup kettle. Add oysters and butter. Simmer over very low heat 3 to 4 minutes, stirring gently till edges of oysters curl. Add hot milk; remove from heat. Cover; let stand 15 minutes. Reheat briefly. Top servings with pats of butter. Makes 4 or 5 servings.

SCALLOPED OYSTERS

- 1 pint shucked oysters
- 2 cups coarsely crushed saltine cracker crumbs (44 crackers)
- ½ cup butter or margarine, melted
- ¾ cup light cream
- ¼ teaspoon Worcestershire sauce

Drain oysters, reserving ¼ cup liquor. Combine crumbs and butter. Spread a *third* of crumbs in 8x1½-inch round pan. Cover with *half* the oysters. Sprinkle with pepper. Using another *third* of the crumbs, spread a second layer; cover with remaining oysters. Sprinkle oyster mixture with pepper.

Combine cream, Worcestershire sauce, reserved oyster liquor, and ½ teaspoon salt. Pour over oysters. Top with remaining crumbs. Bake in moderate oven (350°) about 40 minutes or till done. Makes 4 servings.

FRIED OYSTERS, SCALLOPS

Drain oysters or scallops; dry between paper towels. Roll in all-purpose flour seasoned with salt and pepper. Dip into mixture of 1 beaten egg and 1 tablespoon water, then into fine dry bread crumbs. Fry till golden brown in deep hot fat (375°) about 2 minutes. Drain. Serve hot with Tartar Sauce (see Index).

STEAMED CLAMS

Thoroughly wash 2 dozen soft-shelled clams in shells (oval shape). Cover with salt water (⅓ cup salt to 1 gallon cold water). Let stand 15 minutes; rinse. Repeat twice. Place on rack in kettle with 1 cup hot water; steam, tightly covered, till shells open, about 5 minutes. Cut out edible portion; serve on half shell with melted butter. Serves 4.

CLAM-MUSHROOM BAKE

  1 dozen (½ cup clam meat) large hard-shelled clams *or* 1 7½-ounce can minced clams, drained
  1 3-ounce can chopped mushrooms, drained
  ¼ cup chopped onion
  3 tablespoons butter or margarine

     • • •

  2 tablespoons all-purpose flour
    Dash salt
    Dash pepper
  ½ cup milk

     • • •

  ½ cup soft bread crumbs
  2 tablespoons butter or margarine, melted

For fresh clams, prepare following directions for Steamed Clams (see directions above) *or* open unsteamed clams following pictures on this page. Remove edible portion and chop.

Cook mushrooms and onion in 3 tablespoons butter till tender but not brown. Blend in flour, salt, and pepper. Add milk all at once. Cook quickly, stirring constantly, till mixture is thickened and bubbly. Stir in clams. Pour into 4 baking shells. Combine bread crumbs and melted butter; sprinkle atop each shell. Bake at 400° for 10 to 15 minutes or till lightly browned. Makes 4 servings.

To open hard-shelled clam or oyster: Hold shell in palm of hand, with hinge against palm. Insert knife between halves.

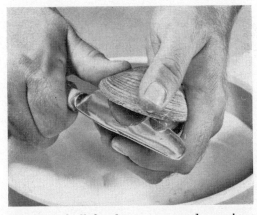

Holding shell firmly, cut around opening. Twist knife up slightly to pry open shell. Pull top shelf half up with thumb.

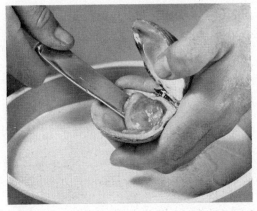

Cut both muscles free from two halves of shell. To serve oysters or clams on the half shell, remove one half of the shell.

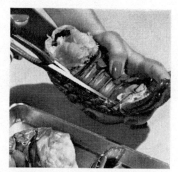  

To remove meat from lobster tails: Drain boiled tails. With scissors, remove thin membrane by cutting along sides of shell. Insert index finger between shell and meat; push against meat.

To butterfly lobster tails: Partially thaw frozen tails. Cut through center of hard top shell and meat but not through the thin undershell membrane. Spread open to expose meat on upper side.

To loosen meat from broiled lobster tails: Insert fork between shell and cooked meat; lift to give lobster a built-up look. Brush with melted butter and sprinkle with a dash of paprika.

LOBSTER

Boiled: Select active live lobster. Plunge lobster into enough boiling salted water to cover. Return to boil then reduce heat and simmer for 20 minutes. Remove lobster from boiling salted water at once.

Place with back side down on cutting board; using a sharp knife, cut body in half lengthwise. Remove the black vein that runs to tip of tail. Discard all organs in body section near head except red coral roe (in females only) and brownish-green liver. Crack claws. Serve with cups of melted butter. Or, chill and use meat in casseroles or salads.

Broiled: Select active live lobster. Plunge lobster into enough boiling salted water to cover. Return to boil; cook 2 minutes. Remove lobster from water; place with back side down on cutting board.

Using a sharp knife, split body lengthwise from head to tail. Cut off head, if desired. Using scissors, snip out under shell membrane of tail section. Remove black vein that runs down to tail. Discard all organs in body section except brownish-green liver and red coral roe (in females only). Crack claws.

Place on broiler rack, shell side up; broil 5 inches from heat for 7 minutes. Turn; flatten open to expose meat. Brush with melted butter. Season with salt and pepper. Broil 7 to 8 minutes more. Serve with additional melted butter and lemon wedges. Allow 1 to 1½ pound lobster per serving.

ROCK LOBSTER TAILS

Boiled: Drop frozen rock lobster tails into enough boiling salted water to cover. Return to boil; reduce heat and simmer 3 ounce tails for 3 to 4 minutes, 6 ounce tails 8 minutes, and 8 ounce tails 11 minutes. Drain.

Prepare for serving by removing meat from tails. With scissors, remove the undershell (thin membrane) by cutting along sides of shell. Insert index finger between hard top shell and meat; push firmly, separating the shell from the meat. Serve with melted butter. Or, chill the lobster meat and use meat for salads, casseroles, or sandwich fillings.

Broiled: With sharp knife, cut down through the center of hard top shell of frozen tail. Cut through meat, but not through undershell (thin membrane). Spread open, butterfly-style, to expose meat on top. Protect tail "fans" by covering with foil. Place tails on broiler rack with shell side down. Mix a few drops bottled hot pepper sauce into melted butter; brush liberally over meat.

Broil 4 to 5 inches from heat 10 minutes for 3 ounce tails; 17 minutes for 6 to 8 ounce tails. Do not turn. Brush often with melted butter. Avoid overcooking. Tails are done when meat loses its translucency and can be flaked easily with a fork.

To prepare for serving, loosen meat by inserting fork between shell and meat. Brush with melted butter; garnish with paprika. Serve with melted butter and lemon wedges.

LOBSTER-SHRIMP CHOWDER

Cook ¼ cup chopped celery and 2 tablespoons finely chopped onion in 2 tablespoons butter or margarine till tender. Add one 10-ounce can frozen condensed cream of shrimp soup, one 10½-ounce can condensed cream of mushroom soup, 1 soup can milk, and 1 cup light cream to celery mixture.

Heat till frozen shrimp soup thaws, stirring occasionally. Stir in one 5-ounce can lobster *or* one 7½-ounce can crab meat, drained, flaked, and cartilage removed, ¼ cup dry sherry, and 1 tablespoon snipped parsley. Cook till heated through. Serves 4 to 6.

LOBSTER NEWBURG

    6 tablespoons butter or margarine
    2 tablespoons all-purpose flour
    1½ cups light cream
    3 beaten egg yolks
    1 5-ounce can (1 cup) lobster,
      broken in large pieces
    3 tablespoons dry white wine
    2 teaspoons lemon juice
    ¼ teaspoon salt
      Paprika
      Pastry Petal Cups

Melt butter or margarine in a 10-inch skillet; blend in flour. Add light cream all at once. Cook, stirring constantly, till mixture thickens and bubbles.

Stir small amount of hot sauce mixture into egg yolks; return to hot mixture; cook, stirring constantly, till thickened. Add lobster; heat through. Add white wine, lemon juice, and salt. Sprinkle with paprika. Serve lobster sauce in Pastry Petal Cups or over toast points. Makes 4 or 5 servings.

Pastry Petal Cups: Make one recipe Plain Pastry (see next column). Roll to ⅛ inch thickness; cut into 2¼-inch rounds. In each of five muffin cups, place one pastry round in bottom and overlap four pastry rounds on sides; press together to seal. Prick. Bake at 450° for 10 to 12 minutes. Cool.

Crab Meat Newburg: Substitute 1 cup flaked, cooked crab meat for lobster.

Shrimp Newburg: Substitute 2 cups cleaned cooked shrimp for the lobster.

CRAB JAMBALAYA

Cook 6 slices bacon till crisp; drain, reserving 2 tablespoons drippings. Crumble bacon; set aside. Cook ½ cup *each* chopped onion and chopped celery and ¼ cup chopped green pepper in reserved drippings till tender.

Add one 28-ounce can tomatoes, cut up, ¼ cup uncooked long-grain rice, 1 teaspoon Worcestershire sauce, ½ teaspoon salt, and dash pepper to vegetables. Simmer, covered, for 20 to 25 minutes or till rice is tender, stirring occasionally. Add one 7½-ounce can crab meat, drained, flaked, and cartilage removed; heat through. Spoon into serving bowl; top with reserved bacon. Serves 4 to 6.

CRAB-ARTICHOKE BAKE

Toss two 7½-ounce cans crab meat, drained, flaked, and cartilage removed, with 1 cup cubed process Swiss cheese, ⅓ cup chopped green pepper, ¼ cup finely chopped onion, and 1 teaspoon salt. Blend ½ cup mayonnaise or salad dressing and 2 teaspoons lemon juice together; toss with crab mixture.

Place 5 artichokes in boiling salted water with 1 tablespoon *each* salad oil and lemon juice, and 2 cloves garlic. Simmer, covered, 20 to 30 minutes or till leaf pulls out easily; drain. Remove small center leaves, leaving a cup. Discard chokes. Fill with salad.

Place in a 12x7½x2-inch baking dish. Pour hot water around them ¼ inch deep. Cover; bake at 375° for 35 minutes. Serves 5.

PLAIN PASTRY

    1½ cups sifted all-purpose flour
    ½ teaspoon salt
    ½ cup shortening
    4 to 5 tablespoons cold water

Sift flour and salt together; cut in shortening till pieces are size of small peas. Sprinkle 1 tablespoon water over part of mixture. Gently toss with fork; push to side of bowl. Repeat till all is moistened. Form into ball.

Flatten on lightly floured surface. Roll ⅛ inch thick. Fit into pie plate; trim and flute edge. Prick. (If filling and crust are baked together, do not prick.) Bake at 450° for 10 to 12 minutes. Makes 1 single-crust pie.

Green pepper strips and sauteed onion trim a platter of delicately flavored Halibut Royale. Choose lemon wedges and tartar sauce as accompaniments.

HALIBUT ROYALE

    3 tablespoons lemon juice
    1 teaspoon salt
    ½ teaspoon paprika
    6 halibut steaks
            • • •
    ½ cup chopped onion
    2 tablespoons butter or margarine
    6 green pepper strips

In shallow dish, combine lemon juice, salt, and paprika. Add halibut and marinate for one hour, turning steaks after first half hour. Cook chopped onion in butter or margarine till tender but not brown.

Place steaks in greased 10x6x1½-inch baking dish. Top with green pepper strips and sprinkle with cooked onion. Bake in very hot oven (450°) about 10 minutes or till fish flakes easily with fork. Makes 6 servings.

STUFFED FILLET ROLL-UPS

Cook 2 tablespoons chopped onion in 2 tablespoons butter till tender. Stir in 2 cups soft bread crumbs, ¼ teaspoon poultry seasoning, ⅛ teaspoon salt, dash pepper, and 2 tablespoons mayonnaise. Cut one 1-pound package frozen haddock fillets in 4 strips, about 8x1½-inches. Spread each with bread stuffing; roll up, jelly-roll fashion. Place in 3-cup casserole. Bake, covered, at 375° for 25 minutes. Uncover; bake 10 minutes. Serve with Egg Sauce. Makes 4 servings.

Egg Sauce: Cook 2 tablespoons chopped green onion in 3 tablespoons butter till tender but not brown. Blend in 2 tablespoons all-purpose flour, ½ teaspoon salt, and dash pepper. Add 1¼ cups milk, ½ teaspoon prepared mustard, and 1 teaspoon Worcestershire sauce. Cook and stir till bubbly. Add 1 finely chopped hard-cooked egg. Heat.

UNCOOKED FISH CUTS

Dressed or pan-dressed for small fish: Scales, head, tail, and fins are removed.

Steaks: Cross-sectional slices are cut ⅝ to 1 inch thick from dressed fish.

Fillets: Sides of the fish are cut lengthwise away from the backbone.

MARKET FORMS OF FISH

Fresh and frozen fish can be purchased in many different forms with the three basic forms shown above. A *Whole Fish* is just as it comes from the water. Before cooking, the fish is scaled and dressed. *Butterfly Fillets* are the two side fillets cut lengthwise away from the backbone and held together by the uncut meat and skin from the underside of fish. *Chunks* are cross sections of large dressed fish and contain a cross section of the backbone. Frozen *Fish Portions and Sticks* are cut from frozen fish blocks and are breaded.

FISH BUYING GUIDE

Buy the following amounts of fish for one serving: whole, ¾ pound; dressed, ½ pound; fillets, steaks, or portions, ⅓ pound; and fish sticks, ¼ pound. This allows about 3 ounces cooked, boneless fish per serving.

FRIED FISH

Wash cleaned fresh- or salt-water fish; dry thoroughly. Dip in 1 beaten egg mixed with 1 tablespoon water, then in bread crumbs, seasoned all-purpose flour, or cornmeal. Brown fish in ¼ inch hot shortening on both sides.

Small fish may be fried whole. Bone and cut large fish in steaks or fillets before frying.

BAKED FISH FILLETS

  1 pound fish fillets
  1 tablespoon lemon juice
  ⅛ teaspoon paprika
  3 tablespoons butter or margarine, melted
  1 tablespoon all-purpose flour
  ½ cup milk
  ¼ cup fine dry bread crumbs
  1 tablespoon snipped parsley

Cut fillets in serving pieces. Place in greased shallow baking dish. Sprinkle with lemon juice, paprika, and dash *each* salt and pepper. In saucepan, blend *1 tablespoon* of the melted butter with flour and dash *each* salt and pepper; add milk all at once.

Cook and stir till thick and bubbly; pour over fish. Blend crumbs with remaining butter; sprinkle over fish. Bake at 350° for 35 minutes. Trim with parsley. Serves 3 or 4.

LEMON-STUFFED FISH

Cook ½ cup finely chopped celery and ¼ cup chopped onion in 3 tablespoons butter or margarine till crisp-tender; pour over 4 cups ½-inch dry bread cubes. Add 1 tablespoon snipped parsley, ½ teaspoon grated lemon peel, ½ teaspoon salt, dash pepper, and 4 teaspoons lemon juice. Toss together.

Partially thaw two 1-pound packages frozen fish fillets. Slice each block of fish in half lengthwise through center making 4 thinner pieces. Place 2 pieces in greased 13x9x2-inch baking pan. Spoon half of stuffing on each piece; top with remaining 2 pieces of fish.

Brush fish with 1 tablespoon butter or margarine, melted; sprinkle with salt. Cover pan with foil; bake at 350° for 20 to 25 minutes or till fish flakes easily with a fork. Sprinkle with paprika. Makes 6 servings.

COMPANY TUNA BAKE

1 3-ounce package cream cheese, softened
1 10½-ounce can condensed cream of mushroom soup
1 6½-, 7-, or 9¼-ounce can tuna, drained and flaked
1 tablespoon chopped canned pimiento
1 tablespoon chopped onion
1 teaspoon prepared mustard
⅓ cup milk
½ 7-ounce package (1 cup) elbow macaroni, cooked and drained
½ cup fine dry bread crumbs
2 tablespoons butter or margarine, melted

Blend cheese into soup using electric or rotary beater. Stir in next 6 ingredients. Pour into 1½-quart casserole. Mix crumbs and butter; sprinkle over top.

Bake at 375° for 35 to 40 minutes or till heated through. Garnish with additional pimiento and parsley, if desired. Serves 4 or 5.

TUNA TETRAZZINI

½ cup chopped onion
1 tablespoon butter or margarine
1 10½-ounce can condensed cream of mushroom soup
⅔ cup milk
⅓ cup grated Parmesan cheese
1 9¼-ounce can tuna, drained
6 ounces medium noodles, cooked and drained
1 3-ounce can sliced mushrooms, drained (½ cup)
½ cup chopped ripe olives
2 tablespoons snipped parsley
2 teaspoons lemon juice
2 tablespoons grated Parmesan cheese
Paprika

Cook onion in butter till tender but not brown. Add soup, milk, and ⅓ cup cheese; heat and stir. Break tuna in chunks; add tuna and next 5 ingredients to soup mixture. Pour into 2-quart casserole. Sprinkle with cheese and paprika. Bake in moderate oven (375°) for 30 to 35 minutes. Makes 6 servings.

PASTRY-TOPPED FISH BAKE

2 beaten eggs
½ cup milk
1 tablespoon butter or margarine, melted
2 tablespoons finely chopped onion
2 tablespoons snipped parsley
2 6½- or 7-ounce cans tuna *or* 1 16-ounce can salmon
1 stick pie crust mix
Cucumber Sauce

Combine first 5 ingredients and ¼ teaspoon salt. Drain and flake fish; blend well into egg mixture. Pour into greased 8-inch pie plate. Prepare pie crust mix according to package directions. Roll to an 8-inch circle, ⅛ inch thick; trim edges. Cut circle in 6 wedges. Arrange atop fish mixture. Bake at 400° for 20 to 25 minutes. Serve with Cucumber Sauce. Makes 6 servings.

Cucumber Sauce: Cut 1 medium unpared cucumber in half lengthwise; scoop out seeds. Grate cucumber (about 1 cup); drain. Combine cucumber, ½ cup dairy sour cream, ¼ cup mayonnaise, 1 tablespoon snipped parsley, 1 teaspoon grated onion, 2 teaspoons white vinegar, and dash *each* salt and pepper; blend well. Makes 1½ cups sauce.

TUNA-SPAGHETTI BAKE

½ 7-ounce package spaghetti, broken, cooked, and drained
1 6½-, 7-, or 9¼-ounce can tuna, drained and flaked
¼ cup chopped canned pimiento
¼ cup slivered almonds (optional)
1 tablespoon butter or margarine (optional)
1 10½-ounce can condensed cream of mushroom soup
½ cup milk
4 ounces sharp process American cheese, shredded (1 cup)
½ cup crushed potato chips

Combine first 3 ingredients. In saucepan, brown nuts in butter, if desired; add soup, milk, and cheese. Heat and stir till cheese melts. Add to tuna mixture; mix well. Pour into 1½-quart casserole; sprinkle with chips. Bake at 350° for 30 minutes. Makes 4 servings.

SALMON WITH CRAB SAUCE

2 cups water
2 lemon slices
½ teaspoon salt
½ teaspoon dillseed
1 bay leaf
2 12-ounce packages frozen salmon steaks (6 steaks), partially thawed

. . .

1 cup chicken broth
4 teaspoons cornstarch
¼ cup dairy sour cream
2 tablespoons butter or margarine
Dash nutmeg
1 7½-ounce can crab meat, drained and flaked

In a large skillet, combine water, lemon slices, salt, dillseed, and bay leaf; heat to boiling. Add salmon steaks and return to boiling. Reduce heat; simmer 4 to 5 minutes or till salmon is done or flakes easily.

Meanwhile, prepare crab sauce by gradually stirring cold broth into cornstarch in saucepan. Cook quickly, stirring constantly, till mixture is thick and bubbly. Cook 1 minute more then remove from heat. Stir in sour cream, butter or margarine, and nutmeg; add crab meat. Heat through but do not boil.

Place salmon on warm serving platter. Serve with crab sauce. Makes 6 servings.

Salmon seasoned with dill and topped with a creamy sauce makes Salmon with Crab Sauce a double seafood special.

SEAFOOD TURNOVERS

1 10½-ounce can condensed cream of mushroom soup
1 7¾-ounce can salmon *or* 1 7-ounce can tuna, drained and flaked
¼ cup chopped celery
¼ teaspoon monosodium glutamate
2 sticks pie crust mix
2 tablespoons milk
Dash dried dillweed

Combine ½ cup of the soup, fish, celery, and monosodium glutamate. Prepare pie crust mix using package directions; roll into four 6-inch circles. Place ¼ of the filling on ½ of each circle; fold to form turnovers. Seal edges with fork; prick top. Bake on ungreased cookie sheet at 450° for 15 to 20 minutes. Combine remaining soup, milk, and dillweed; heat. Serve with turnovers. Serves 4.

COCKTAIL SAUCE

Combine ¾ cup chili sauce, 2 tablespoons lemon juice, 1 to 2 tablespoons prepared horseradish, 2 teaspoons Worcestershire sauce, ½ teaspoon grated onion, and few drops bottled hot pepper sauce. Season with salt to taste; chill. Makes 1¼ cups.

TARTAR SAUCE

Combine 1 cup mayonnaise or salad dressing, 3 tablespoons finely chopped dill pickle, 1 tablespoon snipped parsley, 2 teaspoons chopped canned pimiento, and 1 teaspoon grated onion; chill. Makes 1 cup sauce.

FROG LEGS WITH SAUCE

Dip 2 pounds frog legs in ½ cup milk, then ½ cup all-purpose flour. In skillet, brown frog legs in ½ cup butter, melted, for 10 to 15 minutes. If legs are large, cook, covered, 15 minutes longer; remove to warm platter. Season with salt and pepper. Add ¼ cup *each* butter and slivered almonds to skillet; brown lightly. Add 2 teaspoons lemon juice. Pour almond mixture over legs; top with ¼ cup snipped parsley. Makes 6 servings.

New ways with poultry

TURKEY WITH RICE

- 1 2½- to 3-pound rolled turkey roast
- 1 10½-ounce can condensed chicken broth
- 1 soup can water
- 1 cup uncooked long-grain rice
- ⅛ teaspoon powdered saffron
- 2 tablespoons snipped parsley
- 1 tablespoon chopped canned pimiento
- ⅓ cup toasted slivered almonds

Prepare turkey roast according to package directions. In saucepan, combine chicken broth and water; bring to boiling. Stir in rice and saffron. Cover and simmer about 25 minutes or till water is absorbed. Remove from heat. Stir in snipped parsley, chopped pimiento, and almonds. Serve with hot sliced turkey roast. Makes 6 to 8 servings.

TURKEY TIPS

Turkeys now come in forms which are geared for busy homemakers. *Boneless turkey roasts*, in 2 to 9 pound sizes, are oven ready. They are uncooked turkey meat, either all white or a light-dark combination. Sometimes they are covered with turkey skin, then tied. Some roasts come in foil pans and are not tied. *Boneless turkey rolls* are usually fully cooked and most often used for institutional cooking.

TWIN TURKEY ROASTS

Prepare two 2½- to 3-pound boneless turkey roasts using package directions. Allow about ⅓ pound turkey roast for each serving. If directions call for thawing turkey before roasting, insert meat thermometer in center of thawed roast. Frozen meat must be roasted for a time before the thermometer can be inserted. Turkey is done when thermometer registers 185°. Allow roast to stand about 10 minutes after removing from the oven for best slicing. Cover loosely and keep warm.

DEVILED DRUMSTICKS

- ¼ cup all-purpose flour
- ¼ teaspoon chili powder
- 4 turkey legs (about 2½ pounds)
- 3 tablespoons shortening
- ½ medium onion, sliced
- ⅓ cup catsup
- 3 tablespoons brown sugar
- ¼ cup butter or margarine
- 3 tablespoons vinegar
- 2 teaspoons prepared mustard
- 2 teaspoons Worcestershire sauce
  Dash cayenne
- 1 lemon slice

Combine flour, chili powder, ½ teaspoon salt, and ⅛ teaspoon pepper in paper or plastic bag. Add turkey legs, one at a time, and shake to coat. In skillet, brown legs in hot shortening on all sides. In saucepan, combine remaining ingredients, ⅓ cup water, ½ teaspoon salt, and dash pepper; simmer, uncovered, for 20 minutes. Pour over turkey. Cover and simmer 1½ to 2 hours, or till tender, basting turkey often with sauce. Makes 4 servings.

ROAST TURKEY HALVES

- 1 18- to 20-pound turkey, halved or quartered
  Salad oil

Season cut side of turkey with salt. Place turkey, skin side up, on rack in shallow roasting pan. Brush skin with salad oil. Cover loosely with foil. Roast in slow oven (325°) for 4½ to 5 hours for turkey quarters, 5 to 5½ hours for turkey halves, or till meat thermometer registers 185°. When turkey has cooked to within 45 minutes of total time, remove foil. Continue roasting, uncovered, till thick pieces are tender.

Convenience-style turkey

Treat the family to meaty Twin Turkey →
Roasts without the kitchen fuss. These roasts come from the store ready to cook.

POULTRY ROASTING CHART

General Roasting: Stuff, if desired, and truss. Place, breast side up, on rack in shallow roasting pan. Rub skin with salad oil. If meat thermometer is used, insert without touching bone in center of inside thigh muscle. Roast, uncovered, (unless specified) according to chart. When bird is ⅔ done, remove from oven and cut band of skin or string between legs and tail. Continue roasting till done. *Test for Doneness:* The thickest part of the drumstick should feel very soft when pressed between fingers protected with paper towels. The drumstick moves up and down and twists easily in socket. Meat thermometer should register 185°. Remove bird from oven; let stand 15 minutes before carving.

Poultry	Ready-To-Cook Weight	Oven Temp.	Roasting Time Stuffed and Unstuffed	Special Instructions
Chicken	1½-2 pounds 2-2½ pounds 2½-3 pounds 3-4 pounds	375° 375° 375° 375°	¾-1 hr. 1-1¼ hrs. 1¼-1½ hrs. 1½-2 hrs.	Brush dry areas of skin occasionally with pan drippings. Cover loosely with foil.
Capon	4-7 pounds	375°	1½-2 hrs.	Same as above.
Turkey	6-8 pounds 8-12 pounds 12-16 pounds 16-20 pounds 20-24 pounds	325° 325° 325° 325° 325°	3½-4 hrs. 4-4½ hrs. 4½-5½ hrs. 5½-6½ hrs. 6½-7½ hrs.	Top loosely with foil. Press lightly at end of drumsticks and neck, leaving air space between bird and foil. Last 45 minutes, cut band between legs and tail; continue roasting, uncovered, till done.
Foil-wrapped Turkey	8-10 pounds 10-12 pounds 14-16 pounds 18-20 pounds 22-24 pounds	450° 450° 450° 450° 450°	2¼-2½ hrs. 2½-3 hrs. 3-3¼ hrs. 3¼-3½ hrs. 3½-3¾ hrs.	Place trussed turkey, breast up, in center of greased, wide heavy foil. Bring ends of foil up over breast; overlap fold and press up against ends of turkey. Place bird in shallow pan (no rack). Open foil last 20 minutes to brown turkey.
Domestic Duck	3-5 pounds	375° then 425°	1½-2 hrs. 15 minutes	Prick skin well all over to allow fat to escape. Do not rub with oil.
Domestic Goose	4-6 pounds 6-8 pounds 8-10 pounds 10-12 pounds 12-14 pounds	325° 325° 325° 325° 325°	2¾-3 hrs. 3-3½ hrs. 3½-3¾ hrs. 3¾-4¼ hrs. 4¼-4¾ hrs.	Prick legs and wings with fork so fat will escape. During roasting, spoon off fat in pan. Do not rub with oil.
Cornish Game Hen	1-1½ pounds	375°	1½ hrs.	Roast, loosely covered, for 30 minutes, then 60 minutes uncovered or till done. If desired, occasionally baste with melted butter or glaze the last hour.
Guinea Hen	1½-2 pounds 2-2½ pounds	375° 375°	¾-1 hr. 1-1½ hrs.	Lay bacon over breast. Roast loosely covered. Uncover last 20 minutes.

HOW TO STUFF AND TRUSS

Stuff and truss bird just before roasting. Allow about ¾ cup stuffing per pound of ready-to-cook weight. Rinse bird and pat dry. Stuff wishbone cavity lightly; skewer neck skin to back. Sprinkle large cavity with salt. Lightly spoon in stuffing. If opening has band of skin across tail, push drumsticks under tail—no need to fasten opening. If not, close opening by placing skewers across it; lace shut with cord and tie drumstick to tail.

For unstuffed bird, rinse and pat dry. Sprinkle inside with salt; truss and roast.

HERB STUFFING

    8 slices bread
    1 cup chopped onion
    ¼ cup butter or margarine
    ½ cup chopped celery leaves
    ½ teaspoon dried basil, crushed
    ½ teaspoon dried thyme, crushed
    ½ teaspoon dried savory, crushed

Place bread on cooling racks. Let dry overnight; pull apart into small pieces, about 4 cups. In medium skillet, cook onion in butter till tender but not brown. Stir in bread crumbs, celery leaves, basil, thyme, savory, ½ teaspoon salt, dash pepper, and 3 to 4 tablespoons hot water. Makes enough stuffing for a 3- to 4-pound chicken.

GROUND BEEF STUFFING

    1 7-ounce package herb-seasoned
      stuffing croutons
    1 cup diced celery
    1 cup diced carrot
    ½ cup chopped onion
    3 tablespoons butter or margarine
    ½ pound ground beef
    2½ cups diced, pared apple

Combine stuffing mix, 1 cup water, and ½ teaspoon salt. Cook celery, carrot, and onion in butter till almost tender. Add meat and ½ teaspoon salt; brown meat breaking it into small pieces. Add to stuffing mix along with apples; toss to mix. Makes 8 cups or enough to stuff a 10- to 12-pound turkey.

CRACKER STUFFING

    1 cup chopped celery
    ¾ cup chopped onion
    ¼ cup butter or margarine
    2 cups coarsely crushed saltine
      cracker crumbs (44 crackers)
    ¾ cup milk
    1 slightly beaten egg
    1 tablespoon snipped parsley
    1 teaspoon dried sage, crushed
    ¼ teaspoon dried thyme, crushed
    ½ teaspoon salt
      Dash pepper

In medium skillet, cook celery and onion in butter till tender but not brown. Moisten crackers with milk; add onion mixture, egg, snipped parsley, dried sage, dried thyme, salt, and pepper. Makes 2⅔ cups or enough to stuff a 3- to 4-pound chicken.

BREAD STUFFING

    3 tablespoons chopped onion
    ¼ cup butter or margarine
    4 cups dry bread cubes (about 7
      slices cut in ½-inch cubes)
    ½ teaspoon poultry seasoning
    ½ teaspoon ground sage
    ¼ teaspoon salt
    ¼ teaspoon pepper
    2 to 4 tablespoons water *or*
      chicken broth

Cook onion in butter till tender. Combine with bread cubes, poultry seasoning, ground sage, salt, and pepper. Toss with enough liquid to moisten. Makes 3 cups stuffing or enough to stuff a 4- to 5-pound chicken.

HOW TO COOK GIBLETS

Place giblets, except liver, in saucepan. Add water just to cover giblets; salt lightly. Add a few celery leaves and onion slices to water, if desired. Cover; simmer for 1 to 2 hours for chicken giblets (2 hours for turkey giblets). Add the liver and continue to simmer for 5 to 10 minutes for chicken liver (20 to 30 minutes for turkey liver). Cool giblets in broth; remove and chop. Use broth and chopped giblets in gravy or stuffing.

HOW MUCH TO BUY FOR ONE SERVING

CHICKEN:	
Broiler-fryer	¼ to ½ bird
Capon, roaster, stewing	about ½ pound
Cornish game hens	1 bird
TURKEY:	
5 to 12 pounds	¾ to 1 pound
12 to 24 pounds	½ to ¾ pound
Uncooked boneless roast	⅓ pound
DUCK, domestic	about 1 pound
GOOSE, domestic	about 1 pound

CHICKEN GLOSSARY

Broiler-fryer or fryer—Young, tender bird weighing 1½- to 3½-pounds ready to cook. A broiler-fryer chicken may be roasted, simmered, baked, fried, grilled, or broiled.
Capon—Large 4- to 7-pound ready-to-cook bird with a large amount of tender and flavorful white meat. It is most often roasted.
Roaster—Tender bird weighing 3½- to 5-pounds ready to cook. It is roasted.
Stewing chicken—Mature, less tender bird weighing 2½- to 5-pounds with more fat than other birds. Cook this chicken in a large amount of liquid.
Cornish game hen—The smallest, youngest member of the chicken family weighing 1½ pounds or less. It may be roasted, broiled, or fried.

THAWING POULTRY

In refrigerator: Leave bird in original wrap; place on tray or drip pan. Thaw in refrigerator for 1 to 3 days. Once the bird has thawed, cook immediately.
In cold water: Use this method for faster defrosting. Leave poultry in original wrap or place in plastic bag. Place frozen bird in cold water. Change water frequently. Thawing will take 30 minutes to 1 hour for small chickens, and up to 6 to 8 hours for large turkeys. Never use warm or hot water. Once the bird is thawed, cook immediately.

ORANGE-SAUCED CHICKEN

    1   2½- to 3-pound ready-to-cook
        broiler-fryer chicken, cut up
    ⅓   cup all-purpose flour
    1   teaspoon grated orange peel
    1   teaspoon paprika
    ¼   cup shortening
        Orange Sauce

Coat chicken pieces with mixture of flour, orange peel, paprika, 1 teaspoon salt, and ⅛ teaspoon pepper; reserve remaining flour mixture. In skillet, slowly brown chicken on both sides in hot shortening till lightly browned, 15 to 20 minutes. Reduce heat; add 2 tablespoons water and cover. Cook 30 to 40 minutes or till tender. Uncover last 10 minutes of cooking. Remove chicken to platter reserving pan drippings. Serve with sauce.

Prepare *Orange Sauce:* Pour reserved pan juices and fat into large measuring cup. Skim off excess fat; return ¼ cup pan juices to skillet. Combine reserved flour mixture with additional flour to make ¼ cup; blend with ½ cup milk. Stir into drippings along with 1 cup milk, ½ cup orange juice, ¼ teaspoon ground ginger, and dash ground allspice. Cook and stir till thickened and bubbly; simmer 2 to 3 minutes. Season. Serves 4.

CHICKEN-STUFFED PEPPERS

    6   medium green peppers
   1⅓   cups packaged precooked rice
    2   cups cubed cooked chicken
    1   cup chopped celery
    ¼   cup finely chopped onion
    2   tablespoons chopped canned
        pimiento
    1   cup mayonnaise or salad dressing
    1   teaspoon curry powder

Remove tops and seeds from peppers; partially cook in small amount of boiling salted water, about 5 minutes; drain. Cook rice using package directions; add next 4 ingredients. Combine mayonnaise, curry, ½ teaspoon salt, and dash pepper; toss lightly with rice mixture. Fill peppers and place in greased 10x6x1½-inch baking dish; pour small amount of water around peppers. Bake at 350° about 30 minutes or till peppers are tender. Makes 6 to 8 servings.

CHICKEN POT PIE

    1 3-pound ready-to-cook stewing
       chicken, cut up
    1 medium onion, quartered
    3 celery leaves
    3 sprigs parsley
    1 bay leaf
   10 whole black peppercorns
    1 teaspoon monosodium glutamate
   ¼ teaspoon dried rosemary, crushed
    7 carrots, pared and cut up
   ¼ cup flour
   ½ cup milk
    1 10-ounce package frozen peas
       Plain Pastry (see Index)

In large kettle, combine first 8 ingredients. Add 2 quarts water and 2 teaspoons salt. Bring to boiling; simmer, covered, till chicken is tender, about 2 hours. Remove chicken. Strain stock. In 2 cups of the stock, cook carrots, covered, till tender. Remove chicken bones; cube. Turn into 2-quart casserole.

Blend flour, 1 teaspoon salt, and dash pepper with milk. Stir quickly into stock with carrots. Add thawed peas. Bring to boil, stirring constantly. Simmer till peas are tender. Pour over chicken in casserole; toss.

Roll pastry to fit top of casserole with ½-inch overhang. Turn edge under; seal and crimp. Slash vents in top. Bake at 425° for about 20 minutes. Makes 6 to 8 servings.

CHICKEN CHOW BAKE

    2 cups diced cooked chicken
    1 10½-ounce can condensed cream
       of mushroom soup
    1 8¾-ounce can (1 cup) pineapple
       tidbits, drained
    1 teaspoon soy sauce
    1 cup thinly sliced celery
    2 tablespoons chopped green onion
    1 3-ounce can (2½ cups) chow
       mein noodles

Combine chicken, soup, pineapple, soy sauce, celery, and onion; mix well. Gently fold in 1 *cup* of the noodles. Turn into 1½-quart casserole. Sprinkle with remaining noodles. Bake in moderate oven (350°) for 45 minutes or till hot. If desired, pass additional soy sauce. Makes 4 to 6 servings.

CHICKEN A LA KING

In saucepan, melt ¼ cup butter; blend in ⅓ cup all-purpose flour and ½ teaspoon salt. Add 1 cup *each* chicken broth and milk all at once. Cook and stir till sauce is thick and bubbly. Add 2 cups diced cooked chicken, one 3-ounce can sliced mushrooms, drained, and ¼ cup chopped canned pimiento; heat. Serve over toast points. Makes 5 servings.

ORANGE CHICKEN AND RICE

    1 2½- to 3-pound ready-to-cook
       broiler-fryer chicken, cut up
   ¼ cup frozen orange juice
       concentrate, thawed
    2 tablespoons butter or margarine
   ½ teaspoon ground ginger
       Raisin Rice

Sprinkle chicken with salt and pepper. Place pieces, skin side up and not touching, in foil-lined shallow baking pan. Bake in moderate oven (375°) for 40 minutes.

In saucepan, combine orange juice concentrate, butter, and ginger; heat. Spoon over chicken and bake 20 minutes longer or till tender. Stir pan drippings to blend. Serve over *Raisin Rice:* In saucepan, combine 1 cup water and 1 tablespoon frozen orange juice concentrate, thawed; bring to boiling. Add 1 cup packaged precooked rice, 2 tablespoons raisins, and ½ teaspoon salt; continue cooking according to directions on rice package. Sprinkle with 2 tablespoons toasted slivered blanched almonds. Makes 4 servings.

YORKSHIRE CHICKEN

Coat one 2½- to 3-pound ready-to-cook broiler-fryer chicken, cut up, with mixture of ¼ cup all-purpose flour, 1 teaspoon salt, 1 teaspoon ground sage, and dash pepper. Brown in ¼ cup hot shortening; drain. Place in 3-quart casserole. Sift together 1 cup sifted all-purpose flour, 1 teaspoon baking powder, and 1 teaspoon salt. Combine 3 well-beaten eggs, 1½ cups milk, ¼ cup butter or margarine, melted, and 2 tablespoons snipped parsley; add to flour mixture and beat till well blended. Pour over chicken. Bake at 350° for about 1 hour. Makes 4 servings.

HOW TO CUT UP CHICKEN

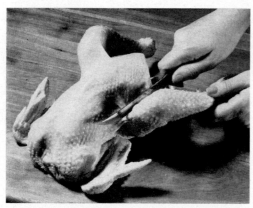

Cut the skin between thighs and body of chicken. Grasp one leg of chicken in each hand; lift till hips are free from body.

To remove the legs and thigh pieces from the chicken body, cut between hip joint and body close to bones in back of bird.

If desired, separate the thigh and leg. Locate knee joint by bending thigh and leg together. Cut through this joint.

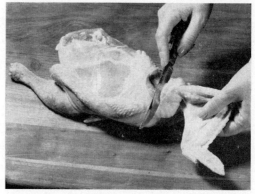

To remove the wings, pull wing away from body. Start cutting on inside of wing just over joint. Cut down through joint.

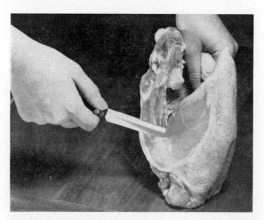

Separate breast and back section by cutting down along breast end of ribs to neck, through joints. Bend back in half to break at joint; cut through with knife.

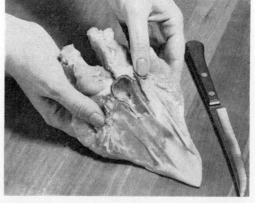

To bone breast, cut through cartilage at V of neck. Grasp small bones on either side of breast. Bend each side back; push up with fingers to snap out bone.

PERFECT FRIED CHICKEN

⅓ cup all-purpose flour
1 teaspoon paprika
1 2½- to 3-pound ready-to-cook
 broiler-fryer chicken, cut up
 Shortening for frying

Combine flour, paprika, 1 teaspoon salt, and ¼ teaspoon pepper in plastic bag; add chicken pieces and shake. Heat shortening (¼ inch deep in skillet) till drop of water sizzles.

Brown meaty pieces first; then add remaining pieces (don't crowd). Brown one side; turn with tongs. When lightly browned, 15 to 20 minutes, reduce heat; cover tightly. (If cover isn't tight, add 1 tablespoon water.) Cook till tender, 30 to 40 minutes. Uncover last 10 minutes of cooking. Makes 4 servings.

Note: Add ½ cup fine dry bread crumbs to flour for more crusty coating.

BASIC BROILED CHICKEN

Select 2 ready-to-cook broiler-fryer chickens (not over 2½ pounds each); split each in half lengthwise or quarter. Brush with salad oil. Season with salt, monosodium glutamate, and pepper. Place skin side down in broiler pan (no rack). Broil 5 to 7 inches from heat till lightly browned, about 20 minutes. Brush occasionally with oil. Turn; broil 20 minutes more. When drumstick moves easily, chicken is done. Makes 4 servings.

STEWED CHICKEN

1 5- to 6-pound ready-to-cook
 stewing chicken, cut up, *or*
 2 large broiler-fryer chickens,
 cut up
2 sprigs parsley
4 celery branches with leaves
1 carrot, pared and sliced
1 small onion, cut up

Place chicken pieces in Dutch oven with enough water to cover (about 2 quarts). Add remaining ingredients, 2 teaspoons salt, and ¼ teaspoon pepper. Cover; bring to boiling and cook over low heat about 2½ hours or till tender. Remove meat from bones. Makes about 5 cups diced cooked chicken.

POULTRY COATING TIPS

Combine flour and seasonings in paper or plastic bag; add 2 or 3 pieces of poultry at a time. Shake till well coated.

GARDEN CHICKEN BAKE

Melt 3 tablespoons butter or margarine; blend in 3 tablespoons all-purpose flour. Add 1½ cups chicken broth*; cook and stir till mixture thickens and bubbles. Add 2 cups diced cooked chicken, one 8-ounce can peas, drained, one 3-ounce can sliced mushrooms, drained, 2 medium carrots, cooked and sliced, ¼ cup chopped onion, 2 tablespoons chopped canned pimiento, and ¾ teaspoon salt; heat till bubbly. Pour into 1½-quart casserole. Snip 1 package refrigerated biscuits (6 biscuits) in quarters. Place rounded side down in ring atop chicken mixture. Bake at 425° for 8 to 10 minutes or till biscuits are done. Serves 5.

*Use canned broth or dissolve 2 chicken bouillon cubes in 1½ cups hot water.

CHICKEN ROMAINE

1 3-pound ready-to-cook broiler-
 fryer chicken, cut up
 Flour
3 tablespoons shortening
1 medium onion, sliced
1 large clove garlic, minced
1 teaspoon seasoned salt
½ teaspoon dried basil, crushed
 Dash bottled hot pepper sauce
1 10½-ounce can condensed tomato
 soup
½ cup diced celery
2 ounces natural Swiss cheese,
 shredded (½ cup)
 Hot buttered noodles

Coat chicken lightly with flour. In skillet, brown chicken in hot shortening. Combine onion, garlic, seasoned salt, basil, hot pepper sauce, tomato soup, and 1 cup water. Pour over chicken. Simmer, covered, 40 minutes; add celery and cook 10 to 15 minutes longer or till tender. Stir in ¼ *cup* of the cheese; sprinkle remaining atop. Serve with hot cooked noodles. Makes 4 servings.

CHICKEN BREASTS SUPREME

3 medium chicken breasts, cut in half lengthwise
¾ teaspoon seasoned salt
Paprika
1 chicken bouillon cube
1 cup boiling water
¼ cup sauterne
½ teaspoon instant minced onion
½ teaspoon curry powder
Dash pepper
Mushroom Sauce

Sprinkle chicken with seasoned salt and paprika; place in 11x7x1½-inch baking pan. Dissolve chicken bouillon cube in boiling water; add wine, instant minced onion, curry powder, and pepper. Pour over chicken. Cover with foil; bake at 350° for 30 minutes. Uncover and bake 45 minutes longer or till tender. Remove chicken to warm platter. Strain pan juices; reserve.

Prepare *Mushroom Sauce:* In saucepan, blend 2 tablespoons all-purpose flour with ¼ cup cold water; slowly stir in reserved pan juices. Cook and stir over low heat till sauce thickens and bubbles; boil 3 to 4 minutes longer. Add one 3-ounce can sliced mushrooms, drained (½ cup); heat through. Spoon sauce over chicken breasts. Garnish with watercress. Makes 6 servings.

CREAMY CHICKEN LIVERS

In skillet, cook, covered, one 8-ounce package frozen chicken livers, thawed and cut in large pieces, in 2 tablespoons butter or margarine till almost tender, about 10 minutes. Add one 6-ounce can sliced mushrooms, drained (1 cup), *or* 1 pint fresh mushrooms, sliced, and ¼ cup chopped green onion. Cook till onion and liver are tender. Combine ½ cup dairy sour cream, 1½ teaspoons soy sauce, 1½ teaspoons chili sauce, and dash pepper; add to liver mixture. Heat and stir just till sauce is hot; don't boil. Serve over toast points. Makes 4 servings.

A buffet special

← With a hint of curry and wine, Chicken Breasts Supreme are topped with a mushroom sauce and garnished with watercress.

CHICKEN ENCHILADAS

1½ cups chopped onion
2 tablespoons olive oil
2 16-ounce cans tomatoes, cut up
1 15-ounce can tomato sauce
2 cloves garlic, minced
2 to 3 teaspoons finely chopped
   canned green chilies
2 teaspoons sugar
1 teaspoon salt
2 to 3 teaspoons chili powder
2 cups chopped cooked chicken
½ cup sliced green onion
3 tablespoons chopped ripe olives
2 teaspoons chili powder
¾ teaspoon salt
12 frozen tortillas, thawed
6 ounces sharp process American
   cheese, shredded (1½ cups)
¼ cup sliced ripe olives

For sauce, cook chopped onion in oil till tender. Add tomatoes, tomato sauce, garlic, chilies, sugar, salt, and chili powder; simmer, uncovered, for 30 minutes.

For filling, combine chicken and next 4 ingredients. Soften tortillas according to package directions. Top each with 2 to 3 tablespoons filling and 1 tablespoon cheese; roll up. Arrange in 13x9x2-inch baking dish. Pour sauce over all. Sprinkle with remaining cheese and olive slices. Bake at 350° for 25 to 30 minutes or till heated. Serves 6.

STUFFED CORNISH HENS

1 6-ounce package long-grain and
   wild rice mix
½ cup diced celery
1 5-ounce can water chestnuts,
   sliced
1 3-ounce can chopped mushrooms,
   drained (½ cup)
¼ cup butter or margarine, melted
1 tablespoon soy sauce
4 1- to 1½-pound ready-to-cook
   Cornish game hens

Cook rice using package directions; cool. Add remaining ingredients except Cornish hens. Toss lightly to mix. Salt inside of birds and stuff and truss. Roast according to Poultry Roasting Chart (see Index) following directions for Cornish Game Hens. Serves 4.

CONTEMPORARY DUCKLING

2 5-pound ready-to-cook ducklings,
   quartered
1 envelope *dry* onion soup mix
½ cup rose wine

Place duckling quarters on rack in shallow roasting pan. Roast at 425° for about 30 minutes, or till browned. Remove from oven; remove ducks and rack. Drain fat from bottom of pan. Place duck quarters skin side up in pan. Sprinkle onion soup mix evenly over ducklings and baste with wine. Cover pan securely with heavy foil; bake at 325° for 1 hour and 15 minutes. Remove foil and bake an additional 20 minutes. Makes 8 servings.

NAVY BEAN STUFFED DUCK

1 cup dry small navy beans
1 quart water
2 chicken bouillon cubes
   • • •
½ pound bulk pork sausage,
   broken in bite-size pieces
1 medium tomato, peeled and
   chopped
½ cup finely chopped onion
¼ cup finely chopped celery
¼ cup snipped parsley
1 small clove garlic, minced
½ teaspoon dried thyme, crushed
1 small bay leaf
¼ teaspoon salt
   • • •
¼ cup sauterne
1 5- to 6-pound ready-to-cook
   duckling

In saucepan, combine beans, water, and chicken bouillon cubes; bring to boiling and boil gently for 2 minutes. Remove from heat; cover and let stand for 1 hour.

To the bean mixture, add sausage, tomato, onion, celery, parsley, garlic, thyme, bay leaf, and salt. Bring to boiling; cover and simmer 1 hour. Uncover and stir in wine. Boil gently, uncovered, for 30 minutes longer or till liquid is absorbed.

Salt inside of duckling; stuff lightly and truss. Roast according to Poultry Roasting Chart (see Index) following directions for Domestic Duck. Makes 4 servings.

VENISON

Venison is any meat of the deer family; the most common variety eaten is deer, followed by elk and moose. Venison from a freshly killed animal should be aged in a cool place for 1 to 2 weeks, according to taste. For best flavor, trim off all fat. Meat may be larded with salt pork or bacon for cooking.

Cook venison the same as beef. Tender cuts such as loin roast, rib chops, and loin chops are cooked by broiling or roasting. With these cooking methods, the meat may be cooked to your liking—rare, medium, or well-done. Before roasting or broiling, venison may be chilled overnight in a marinade turning occasionally to enhance the flavor.

Less tender cuts are cooked slowly by braising or cooking in liquid till meat is tender. For another variation, burgers, grind meat with a little salt pork.

OPOSSUM

Thoroughly wash one 1½- to 2-pound opossum and trim off excess fat. Season cavity with salt and pepper; add 1 to 2 bay leaves. Close with skewers and tie legs together. Place on rack in shallow roasting pan; add water to cover bottom of pan. Cover; cook at 350° for 1 hour or till tender. Uncover and cook till brown, 15 to 20 minutes more.

HASENPFEFFER

1 cup vinegar
1 medium onion, sliced
½ cup sugar
1 teaspoon mixed pickling spices
1 1- to 2-pound ready-to-cook rabbit, cut up
2 tablespoons all-purpose flour
2 tablespoons shortening

Mix 3 cups water, first 4 ingredients, 2 teaspoons salt, and ¼ teaspoon pepper. Add rabbit. Refrigerate 2 days. Remove meat from marinade, reserving 1 cup. Dry meat.

Coat rabbit with flour. Brown meat in hot shortening; slowly add marinade. Cover; simmer 45 to 60 minutes or till tender (add water, if necessary); remove meat. Thicken liquid for gravy, if desired. Serves 2 or 3.

FRIED RABBIT OR SQUIRREL

Coat one 1- to 1½-pound ready-to-cook young rabbit, cut up, *or* one 1-pound ready-to-cook young squirrel, cut up, with mixture of ¼ cup all-purpose flour, ¾ teaspoon salt, and dash pepper. In skillet, brown meat slowly in 2 tablespoons hot shortening. Reduce heat; add 2 or 3 tablespoons water. Cover; simmer for 30 minutes or till tender, adding more water if necessary. Serves 2.

WILD GEESE WITH FRUIT

1 cup dry bread cubes (about 2 slices cut in ½-inch cubes)
1 cup cooked prunes, pitted and quartered
4 small tart apples, pared, cored, and quartered
½ cup chopped celery
½ teaspoon salt
¼ teaspoon ground sage
¼ teaspoon dried rosemary, crushed
    Dash pepper
2 3-pound ready-to-cook wild geese

Toss together bread cubes, prunes, apples, celery, salt, sage, rosemary, and pepper. Stuff and truss wild geese. Roast according to Roasting Chart for Game Birds (see Index) using directions for wild goose. Serves 4 to 6.

PARTRIDGE IN RED WINE

2 1-pound ready-to-cook partridges, cut up
½ cup all-purpose flour
¼ cup butter or margarine
2 tablespoons finely chopped onion
1 10½-ounce can condensed beef broth
¾ cup claret or red Burgundy

Coat partridges with mixture of flour and 1 teaspoon salt. Brown birds in butter in Dutch oven. Add onion and broth. Cook, covered, over low heat for 50 to 60 minutes or till tender. Remove birds to serving dish. Add wine to Dutch oven; simmer 5 minutes, stirring up brown bits from bottom of pan. Pour sauce over partridges. Serves 2 or 3.

ROASTING CHART FOR GAME BIRDS

General Instructions: Salt the cavity of a ready-to-cook bird. Stuff, if desired. Truss the bird and place, with breast side up, on rack in a shallow roasting pan. Brush the game (except for wild duck) with salad oil, melted butter or margarine, or lay bacon slices over breast. Roast, uncovered, according to the roasting chart till tender. Baste meat occasionally with the drippings. When necessary, cap foil loosely over the top of the bird to prevent excess browning. Cooking times may vary with the age of the bird; a young bird is usually most suitable for roasting.

Game Birds	Ready-To-Cook Weight	Oven Temp.	Roasting Time	Amount per Serving	Special Instructions
Wild Duck	1-2 lbs.	400°	1-1½ hrs.	1-1½ lbs.	Stuff loosely with quartered onions and apples; discard stuffing before serving. Do not brush with oil.
Wild Goose	2-4 lbs. 4-6 lbs.	400° 400°	1½-3 hrs. 3-4 hrs.	1-1½ lbs.	Stuff loosely with quartered onions and apples; discard stuffing before serving. Baste often with drippings.
Partridge	½-1 lb.	450°	30-45 min.	½-1 lb.	Place bacon slices over breast.
Pheasant	1-3 lbs.	350°	1-2½ hrs.	1-1½ lbs.	Place bacon slices over breast.
Quail	4-6 oz.	400°	30-45 min.	½-1 lb.	Place bacon slices over breast.
Squab	12-14 oz.	400°	40-50 min.	12-14 oz.	Place bacon slices over breast.

PHEASANT WITH APPLES

Coat two 1½- to 3-pound ready-to-cook pheasants, cut up, with mixture of ¼ cup all-purpose flour, 1 teaspoon salt, and ¼ teaspoon pepper. In skillet, lightly brown pheasant pieces in 6 tablespoons butter or margarine. Add ¾ cup sauterne; simmer, covered, about 35 to 55 minutes or till tender. Remove pheasants, reserving pan drippings.

Beat ¾ cup light cream with 3 egg yolks. Slowly stir egg mixture into reserved pan drippings in skillet; cook and stir over medium heat just till smooth and thick. *Do not boil.* Pour sauce over pheasants. Garnish platter with *Sauteed Apples:* Add 2 apples, cored and sliced into wedges, to 3 tablespoons butter in skillet. Sprinkle with 1 teaspoon sugar and cook, turning often, till lightly browned. Makes 4 to 6 servings.

CANTONESE DUCK

Season two 1- to 2-pound ready-to-cook wild ducks inside and out with salt. Place in cavity of *each* bird ½ orange, cut in wedges, and a few celery leaves. Place birds, breast side up, on rack in a shallow roasting pan. Roast, uncovered, in hot oven (400°) for 1 hour or till tender. If necessary, cap with foil to prevent excess browning.

Meanwhile, prepare sauce by combining ½ cup apricot preserves, ¼ cup water, 1 tablespoon prepared mustard, 1 tablespoon soy sauce, 1 tablespoon lemon juice, and ½ teaspoon monosodium glutamate in a saucepan. Heat, stirring constantly. During the last 10 minutes of roasting, baste ducks occasionally with sauce. Remove meat from oven; discard stuffing. Serve ducks over hot cooked rice; pass remaining sauce. Serves 4.

Perfect gravy every time

PAN GRAVY

Remove roast to hot platter and keep warm. Leaving crusty bits in roasting pan, pour meat juices and fat into large measuring cup. Skim off fat reserving 3 to 4 tablespoons. For 2 cups gravy, return reserved fat to pan. Stir in ¼ cup all-purpose flour. Blend together fat and flour. Cook and stir over low heat till mixture is thickened and bubbly.

Remove pan from the heat. Add 2 cups liquid (meat juices plus water, milk, or giblet broth) all at once; blend. Season with salt, pepper, and monosodium glutamate. If desired, add a dash of dried thyme, crushed, and a few drops kitchen bouquet. Simmer and stir 2 to 3 minutes. Serves 6 to 8.

GIBLET GRAVY

Remove turkey to platter. Prepare Pan Gravy *except* add giblet broth (see Index, How To Cook Giblets) to make 2 cups liquid. Add chopped cooked giblets. Continue preparation of gravy using directions above.

POT ROAST GRAVY

Lift pot roast to hot platter. Skim most of fat from pan juices. Add water to juices to make 1½ cups. Put ½ cup cold water in shaker or small screw top jar. Add ¼ cup all-purpose flour; shake well. Stir into juices; cook, stirring constantly, till gravy is bubbly. Season with salt and pepper. Simmer 2 to 3 minutes; stir occasionally. Makes 2 cups.

CREAMY CHICKEN GRAVY

    1½ cups milk
     3 tablespoons all-purpose flour
     3 tablespoons chicken drippings*

In screw top jar, shake *half* the milk with flour, 1 teaspoon salt, and dash pepper till blended; stir into drippings in skillet. Add remaining milk. Cook and stir till thickened. Cook 2 to 3 minutes more. Makes 1½ cups.

*Fry chicken in half butter and half shortening. Make gravy in same skillet, leaving crusty bits in the skillet.

Leaving crusty bits in pan, pour meat juices and fat into a large measuring cup. Skim off fat that comes to the top.

Return some reserved fat to roasting pan. Stir in flour and blend well. Cook and stir over low heat till mixture bubbles.

Terms to know

Bake—To cook covered or uncovered in an oven or oven-type appliance. For meats cooked uncovered, it's called roasting except for ham, which is called baking.

Baste—To moisten meat during cooking with pan drippings, additional fat, or special sauce to add flavor and prevent drying.

Braise—To cook slowly with a small amount of water or other liquid in a tightly covered pan on top of the range or in the oven.

Broil—To cook by direct heat, usually in a broiler or over coals as in outdoor barbecuing.

Chop—To cut in pieces about the size of peas with knife, chopper, or blender.

Cube—To cut food in pieces of uniform size and shape, larger than diced.

Dice—To cut food in small cubes of uniform size and shape, larger than chopped.

Dredge—To sprinkle or coat with flour, cracker crumbs, or other fine substance.

Dry heat—To cook meat with no water or other liquid added by means of broiling, pan-broiling, panfrying, or roasting.

Flake—To break lightly into small pieces.

Fry—To cook in hot shortening. Panfrying is to cook in a small amount of shortening. Deep-fat frying is to cook immersed in a large amount of shortening.

Glaze—A mixture applied to food which adds flavor and a glossy appearance.

Marbling—Flecks of fat distributed within the lean muscle of meat.

Marinate—To allow meat to stand in a liquid to add flavor and/or to tenderize.

Mince—To cut or finely chop food into very small pieces, smaller than chopped.

Moist heat—To cook meat in a large amount of liquid or small amount as in braising.

Panbroil—To cook uncovered on hot surface, removing fat as it accumulates.

Panfry—To cook meat in skillet in small amount of hot shortening or hot salad oil.

Poach—To cook in hot liquid, being careful that food holds its shape while cooking.

Pound—To hit a less tender cut of meat with a meat mallet for flattening or tenderizing.

Roast—To cook uncovered without water added, usually in an oven.

Rotisserie—An appliance with a spit on which meat rotates in front of, under, or over the heat source and roasts the meat.

Sauté—To brown or cook meat in a small amount of hot shortening or hot salad oil.

Score—To cut narrow grooves or slits part way through the outer surface of food.

Sear—To brown the surface of meat very quickly by intense heat.

Simmer—To cook over low heat in liquid, just below the boiling point, at a temperature of 185° to 210°, where bubbles form at a slow rate and burst before reaching the surface.

Skewer—To fasten meat with metal or wooden pins to hold its shape while cooking; or the metal pins that hold pieces of food for kabobs.

Steam—To cook in steam with or without pressure. A small amount of boiling water is used, more water being added during steaming process if necessary.

Stew—To simmer meat slowly in small amount of liquid for long period of time.

Truss—To secure poultry or other meat with skewers to hold its shape during cooking.

102

MEAT SEASONING GUIDE							
Herbs and Spices	Beef	Veal	Ham	Lamb	Pork	Fish and Shellfish	Poultry
Allspice	*		*	*			
Basil	*	*		*	*	*	*
Bay Leaf	*	*		*		*	*
Caraway Seed	*			*	*		
Celery Seed	*					*	*
Chili Powder	*					*	*
Cloves			*		*		
Cumin	*					*	*
Curry	*	*		*		*	*
Dill				*		*	*
Garlic	*			*	*	*	*
Ginger	*	*	*	*	*		*
Mace	*	*					
Marjoram	*	*		*	*	*	*
Mint		*		*			
Mustard	*	*	*		*	*	*
Oregano	*	*		*	*	*	*
Rosemary	*	*		*	*	*	*
Saffron						*	*
Sage		*		*	*	*	*
Savory	*	*		*	*	*	*
Tarragon	*					*	*
Thyme	*	*		*	*	*	*

Use spices and herbs to perk up meats, fish, and poultry. Start with ¼ teaspoon dried herb for each 4 servings. Measure, then crush dried herbs if in leaf form. When substituting fresh herbs for dried, use 3 times more fresh herbs and snip rather than crush.

Spark meat with herbs

Marinated Pork Roast makes good use of →
herbs and spices. Garlic, mustard, thyme, and ginger give pork a special flavor. After measuring, crush dried leaf herbs.

Carving is the difference

Carving at the table can add glamour to the meal, but no matter whether the meat is carved at the table or in the kitchen, there are some important facts to keep in mind. Meat that is properly carved will be more tender and servings will be more attractive.

For successful carving, it is important that the meat be properly prepared at the market. Have the meatman saw the bones, especially the backbone, or remove them entirely. A boneless cut of meat is much easier to carve.

When preparing the meat, don't overcook it or the meat will fall apart when carving. Neither should it be cooked at too high a temperature or the outer crust will be difficult to cut. A roast should stand 10 to 20 minutes before carving to let the meat firm up. Cover it loosely with foil and keep warm during this time. Rare roasts need to stand a little longer than do medium and well-done pieces of meat. But it is not necessary to let steaks and chops stand. They should be served immediately after cooking.

Remove strings or skewers in the kitchen. For a rolled roast it might be easier to leave on one or two strings to avoid having the meat unroll when it is carved.

Preheat the platter and also individual dinner plates to keep servings piping hot. Rinse plates with hot water and dry just before using, or heat them in the oven at a very low temperature setting.

Don't over-garnish the carving platter and leave room for the slices cut off the roast. Give the carver elbowroom.

CUTLERY

Sharp knives are important for easy carving. Choose hollow-ground knives with sturdy, well-riveted handles. For large roasts—ham, sirloin, or rib roasts, choose a knife that is at least 11 inches long with a straight edge and narrow blade. It is usually rounded at the tip. A fork with wide tines, called the carver's helper, will help steady the meat as it is carved at the table or in the kitchen.

The standard carving set most often will include a knife with a curved blade that is 8 or 9 inches long. The fork has more narrow tines suitable for use with medium and smaller roasts, such as leg of lamb, pork roasts, and pot roasts. It also has a guard below the handle. The third piece of the carving set is the steel which is used to keep the knife cutting edge sharp for easier carving.

For steaks, chops, and poultry, choose a 6- or 7-inch curved-edge knife and a fork with narrow tines with no guard.

Proper storage is essential to keep knives in good condition. Keep them separated, either in a holder or on a magnetic knife rack. This will keep them from becoming blunted or knicked. To keep knives clean, wipe them with a wet cloth after each use and dry.

Keep knives sharp by using a steel or an electric or other type of sharpener. To use the steel, hold it firmly in the left hand with thumb on top of handle. Place heel edge of knife blade near the underneath tip of the steel making a 25° angle between knife and steel. Bring blade down along steel to the left with a swinging motion of the right wrist until the tip touches the bottom of the steel. Bring knife back to the starting position but with the blade on the opposite side of the steel as in first step making a 25° angle. Repeat stroking motion using alternating strokes. Don't scratch the upper side of the knife by touching it to the steel.

If the knife blade looks quite thick up to the cutting edge, it probably should be ground by a professional knife sharpener.

HINTS FOR CARVING MEAT

Carve on a cutting board when cuts are to be made against the platter to prevent dulling the knife or scratching the platter.

Anchor the meat firmly with a fork, then slice the meat across the grain. This produces shorter fibers and makes the slices more tender. If the piece of meat is thin, it is most often sliced diagonally across the grain. Cut uniformly thick slices. It's usually best to carve enough for everyone to have one serving, then start serving. Seconds can be carved later as they are needed.

On the following pages are drawings and suggested ways of carving the various cuts.

STANDING BEEF RIB ROAST

Carving is easier if the chine bone is removed and the rib bones are cut short by the meatman. Place rib roast on heated platter with the largest end down. This will form a solid base for carving.

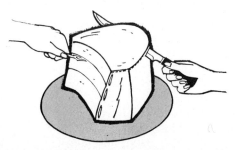

Insert carving fork between top two ribs. Starting on fat side of the piece of meat, slice across the grain to rib bone. For hearty eaters, serve the whole rib.

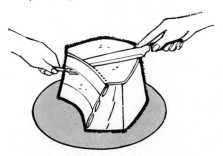

Use tip of knife to cut along rib bones to loosen each slice, if whole rib is not served. Keep as close to rib bones as possible, making the largest serving of meat.

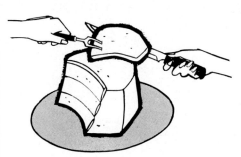

To lift slice off the roast, slide the knife under the slice and steady it with the fork on top. Arrange slices on carving platter or heated serving platter.

FLANK STEAK

Hold meat on board with carving fork; start cutting at narrow end. Hold knife blade at an angle parallel to board.

Cut remaining meat in very thin slices at same angle. Carving this way cuts with the grain of the meat.

BEEF BRISKET

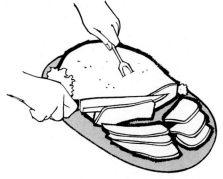

Slice brisket across the grain, ⅛ to ¼ inch thick. Carve from two sides since the grain goes in several directions.

WHOLE HAM

Place ham on a carving board with the shank end to the carver's right for ease of carving. (Roast leg of lamb is carved in the same way, for the shape and bone structure of the two cuts are similar.)

To make a stable base, remove several slices from the bottom of the ham. Turn ham on base and wedge cut slices underneath to keep ham from sliding.

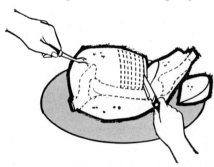

Starting at shank end of ham, cut out a small wedge and remove the piece of meat. Slices are then carved perpendicular to the long horizontal leg bone.

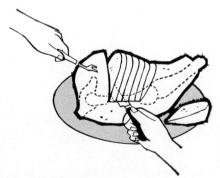

When desired number of slices is cut, release slices by running carving knife along leg bone, starting at the shank end. Turn ham to first position and slice.

CROWN ROAST

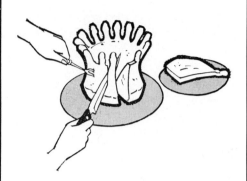

Remove any center stuffing before carving. Insert fork between ribs to steady. Start carving where ribs are tied together. Cut between ribs. Remove to plate.

PORK BLADE LOIN ROAST

For carving ease, have meatman loosen backbone from ribs without cutting into meaty portion. After roasting, place on board and remove backbone, leaving as much meat on roast as possible.

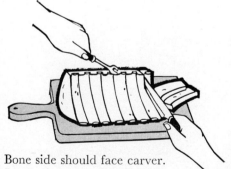

Bone side should face carver.
Insert fork in top of roast.
Carve by cutting close along each side of the rib bone. One slice will have the bone, the next slice will be boneless.

FILLETING COOKED FISH

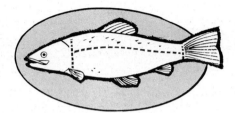

Remove head and tail. Using table knife, make a gentle lengthwise cut 1 inch from the upper edge, cutting into the fish just to the backbone.

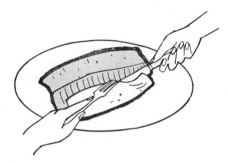

Slide knife along top of backbone gently lifting top section away from backbone. Place on plate; repeat for bottom fillet.

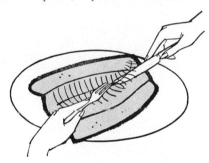

Carefully slide knife under the backbone lifting it away from bottom fillet. Use fork to assist. Discard the backbone.

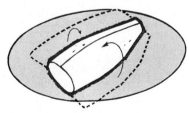

Gently replace the two pieces on the plate to their original position atop the fish. Head and tail may be replaced.

TURKEY

Pull leg out. Cut through meat between thigh and back. Disjoint leg from back.

For leg, slice meat parallel to bone and under some of the tendons, turning leg.

Make deep horizontal cut into breast close to wing before carving white meat. Note wing tips are folded behind back.

Cut slices from top down to horizontal cut. Repeat steps with other side of bird.

Brighten the budget with careful buying and storing

When purchasing meat, don't become baffled. Selecting a cut of meat which will be juicy, tender, and wholesome is a snap.

APPEARANCE OF THE CUT

Look for a moderate amount of marbling, flecks of fat distributed within the lean muscle. This enhances the quality by increasing the juiciness and flavor of the meat. A bright red color of the meat usually indicates high quality meat as well as freshness.

The flesh or meat of fresh fish should be firm and not separate from the bones. The eyes should be bright and transparent and protrude slightly. The gills are red and the skin has an iridescent color.

INSPECTION AND GRADING

All meat, meat products, and poultry are inspected by either federal meat inspectors from the U.S. Department of Agriculture's Consumer and Marketing Service or an equally effective state meat inspection program. Meat and poultry which are transported across state lines are required to be federally inspected.

Meat inspection is a shopper's assurance of wholesome meat. Four requirements must be met: The meat plant must be clean. Every part of the animal must be inspected before and after slaughter to assure that healthy animals are used. Each step in making meat products and all ingredients added to meat products must be continually checked. The label placed on the meat must be approved.

The grading of meat is an optional service conducted by the U.S. Department of Agriculture. It's requested and paid for by the meatpacker. As a result not all meat is graded. The grade indicates quality but is only put on meats that are inspected. Only whole carcasses or wholesale cuts are graded.

The grades for beef and veal most commonly sold, starting at the top grade, are prime, choice, and good. Common lamb grades, starting at the top, are prime and choice. Pork usually is not graded and smoked meat generally displays the meatpackers brand name.

SHAPE OF THE BONE

By identifying the bone, the location of the cut from the carcass can be made. This is very helpful in determining the tenderness of the cut and the cooking method to use.

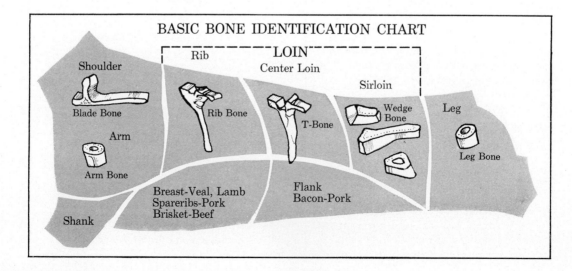

BASIC BONE IDENTIFICATION CHART

The round federal inspection mark is the assurance of wholesome meat. The mark may appear on large cuts of fresh meat and is harmless. It does not need to be trimmed off before eating.

The grade shield denotes the quality of beef, veal, and lamb. The grade is applied along the length of the carcass and may not be on each small cut.

The round federal inspection mark for poultry can be found on a wing tag, giblet wrapper, an insert, or on the outside wrapper. It is the assurance of wholesome poultry.

Chickens, turkeys, and ducks are federally graded. The shield can be found on the wing tag or on the outside wrapper. There are three grades, A, B, and C; but, grade A is sold most widely.

HOW MUCH MEAT TO SERVE

Meat	Servings per pound
Boneless meat (ground, stew, or variety meat)	4-5
Cuts with little bone (beef round or ham center cuts, lamb or veal cutlets)	3-4
Cuts with medium amount of bone (whole or end cuts of beef round, veal leg or shoulder, leg of lamb, bone-in ham; loin, rump, rib, or chuck roasts; steaks and chops)	2-3
Cuts with much bone (shank, ham hocks, brisket, plate, short ribs, spareribs, breast of veal or lamb)	1-2

The five basic bone shapes can be a guide to the method of cooking. When purchasing meat, keep in mind which bones indicate a tender cut of meat and which bones mean a less tender cut. The boneless cut is the same as the bone-in cut.

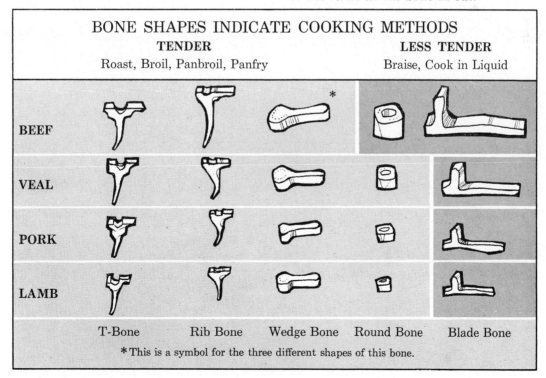

BONE SHAPES INDICATE COOKING METHODS

TENDER
Roast, Broil, Panbroil, Panfry

LESS TENDER
Braise, Cook in Liquid

BEEF   VEAL   PORK   LAMB

T-Bone   Rib Bone   Wedge Bone   Round Bone   Blade Bone

*This is a symbol for the three different shapes of this bone.

REFRIGERATOR STORAGE	
Refrigerator temperature 36° to 40°	
Meat Uncooked and Cooked	Time for Maximum Quality
BEEF	
Standing Rib Roast	5 to 8 days
Steaks	3 to 5 days
Pot Roast	5 to 6 days
Stew Meat	2 days
Ground Beef	2 days
VEAL	
Roasts	5 to 6 days
Chops	4 days
PORK	
Roasts	5 to 6 days
Chops	3 days
Spareribs	3 days
Bulk Pork Sausage	2 to 3 days
SMOKED MEAT	
Ham or Picnic Shoulder	
Whole or half	7 days
Slices	3 days
Bacon	5 to 7 days
Dried Beef	10 to 12 days
Corned Beef	5 to 7 days
LAMB	
Roasts	5 days
Chops	3 days
VARIETY MEATS	
Liver, sliced	2 days
Heart	2 days
Sweetbreads, cooked	2 days
Smoked Tongue	6 to 7 days
FISH	1 to 2 days
POULTRY	
Chicken, whole	2 days
Chicken, cut up	2 days
Turkey, whole	2 days
Ducklings, whole	2 days
COOKED MEATS	
Leftover Cooked Meats	4 days
Ham or Picnic Shoulder	7 days
Cooked Fish	3 to 4 days
Cooked Poultry	3 to 4 days
Poultry Gravy and Stuffing	3 to 4 days
Frankfurters	4 to 5 days
Sliced Luncheon Meats	3 days
Unsliced Bologna	4 to 6 days

STORING FRESH MEAT

Loosely wrap fresh meat and poultry and store in coldest part of the refrigerator. Fresh meat, prepackaged in moisture-vaporproof wrap, can be refrigerated, unopened, for 1 to 2 days. For longer storage, it should be opened at both ends to allow some air to circulate. Fresh meat paper wrapped from the meat-man should be rewrapped lightly in waxed paper. Remove giblets from poultry and wrap loosely. Cook as soon as possible.

Fresh fish should be placed in moisture-vaporproof bag or tightly covered containers; refrigerate immediately.

STORING COOKED MEAT

Cover and quickly cool cooked meat, meat dishes, poultry, and fish in the refrigerator. Or, allow foods to stand briefly in a cool room with good air circulation, then refrigerate. Large roasts may be cut in half to speed cooling. Remove meat from bones of cooked poultry, if desired. Refrigerate poultry, stuffing, and gravy in separate covered containers.

Refrigerate cured, smoked, and ready-to-serve meats in their original wrap. Canned beef, veal, and fish can be stored in a cool, dry place. After opening, refrigerate and use within a few days. Most canned hams and picnics also should be refrigerated (see label).

When preparing meat patties for freezing, separate patties with two pieces of waxed paper. Later, they'll separate with ease.

FREEZING MEAT AND FISH

Select high quality meat and fish for freezing. Remember, freezing cannot improve the quality of the products.

Do not freeze smoked meats for more than 1 month. The quality deteriorates rapidly.

Divide meat into family-size portions or individual servings before freezing.

Wrap meat in moisture-vaporproof materials such as moisture-proof cellophane, polyester and polyethylene films, clear plastic wrap, freezer-weight foil, or laminated wrap, according to directions below.

Keep packages small for rapid freezing. Place packages next to a refrigerated surface in freezer. Separate unfrozen foods from foods which have already been frozen.

Keep frozen foods at 0° or below as fluctuations above this temperature can cause loss of quality. Limit storage time for meat, poultry, fish, and shellfish following directions for Freezing Uncooked Meat (see Index).

Never attempt to refreeze foods.

Do not thaw commercially frozen stuffed poultry before cooking.

FREEZING COOKED MEAT

Don't oversalt or overseason. Some ingredients such as garlic, pepper, and celery intensify in flavor during freezing.

Don't overcook foods to be frozen. Undercook noodles, rice, macaroni, and spaghetti. Reheating finishes the cooking.

Use fat sparingly in sauces. It doesn't blend in well with other ingredients when reheated.

Add toppings like crushed potato chips, crumbs, and grated cheese at reheating time

Line casserole with heavy foil, leaving long ends. Fill. Fold ends of foil together to seal. When frozen remove container.

rather than before freezing to prevent them from becoming tough and soggy.

Cool cooked mixtures quickly before packaging. The best way is to set the pan of cooked food in a bowl, pan, or sink containing cold water with ice. When cooled to room temperature, spoon immediately into freezer containers and place in freezer.

Allow headspace when packing semiliquid foods to leave room for food to expand.

Use freezer containers with wide top openings so the food doesn't have to be completely thawed before it is removed.

It is better to reheat frozen cooked main dishes without thawing. If you prefer to thaw the food before heating, thaw in the refrigerator. Once thawed, use immediately.

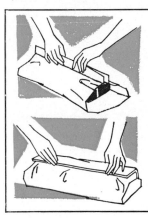

To wrap for freezer, use wrapping about 1½ times as long as needed to go around item. Put food in the center.

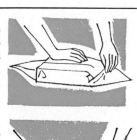

Crease ends into points. Press wrap to remove pockets of air. The coated side of paper should be next to the fold.

Bring sides of wrapper together at top. Fold edges down in a series of locked folds. Press wrapper against food.

Turn ends under. Secure with freezer tape. Label with contents and date. Freeze quickly for best end results.

FREEZING UNCOOKED MEAT

To thaw and cook: Frozen meat should be thawed in the refrigerator in its original wrap. Allow approximately 4 to 7 hours per pound for large roasts, 3 to 5 hours per pound for small roasts, and 12 to 14 hours for steaks cut 1 inch thick. Cold water thawing is recommended for meat that's to be cooked in liquid. Place meat, in its original wrap or plastic bag, in cold water changing water frequently as meat thaws. When thawed, cook according to directions for fresh meat.

To cook unthawed: Roast frozen meat according to directions for fresh meat. Allow for additional roasting time, approximately a third to a half again as long. For broiling thick steaks, chops, or ground meat patties, lower the distance from the heat to prevent over-browning on the surface before obtaining the desired degree of doneness. For panbroiling, use a hot skillet at first to quickly brown the surface. Reduce heat and continue cooking, turning meat often to prevent over-browning.

Meat	Storage time at 0°	Preparation for freezing
Beef		Select high quality meat. Trim off excess fat and avoid packing more bone than is necessary to save freezer space. Wrap meat tightly in moisture-vaporproof material. Seal, label package with name of contents, date, and amount. Freeze at 0° or below.
Roasts	8 to 12 months	
Steaks	8 to 12 months	
Lamb		
Roasts	8 to 12 months	
Chops	3 to 4 months	
Pork		
Roasts	4 to 8 months	
Chops	3 to 4 months	
Veal		
Roasts	4 to 8 months	
Chops	3 to 4 months	
Ground meat	2 to 3 months	
Poultry		Select high quality poultry. Wrap and freeze giblets separately. Disjoint and cut up bird or leave whole. Wrap bird or pieces in moisture-vaporproof material. Seal, label, and freeze packages. Never freeze stuffed poultry. Freeze stuffing separately.
Chicken	12 months	
Turkey	6 months	
Duck	6 months	
Goose	6 months	
Giblets	3 months	
Fish	6 to 9 months	Dress and wash fish as for cooking. Cut into steaks or fillets, if desired. Dip fish in solution of ⅔ cup salt to 1 gallon water for 30 seconds; remove. Wrap in moisture-vaporproof material. Seal, label with contents, amount, and date; freeze.
Shellfish		Wash and shuck. Pack in freezer containers leaving ½-inch headspace. Seal, label, and freeze. It's important to freeze immediately after shucking.
Oysters	3 months	
Clams	3 months	
Scallops	3 months	
Crabs	1 month	Cook crabs and lobsters as for eating; chill in refrigerator. Remove meat from shell. Wrap in moisture-vaporproof material. Seal, label with contents, amount, and date; freeze packages.
Lobsters	1 month	
Shrimp	3 months	Shrimp can be frozen either in the shells or with shells removed. Remove heads of shrimp. Wrap a small amount of shrimp in moisture-vaporproof material. Seal, label with contents, amount, and date, and freeze. Cook shrimp while still frozen.

FREEZING PREPARED FOODS			
Foods	Preparation for freezing	Storage	Thawing and cooking
Casseroles: Chicken, turkey, fish, or meat with vegetable and/or cereal product	Season lightly, adding more before serving if desired. Cool mixture quickly. Turn into freezer container or casserole. Cover tightly.	2 to 4 months	If frozen in oven-proof container, uncover. Bake at 400° for 1 hour for pints; 1¾ hours for quarts or till food is heated. Or, steam over hot water in top of double boiler.
Creamed dishes: Chicken, turkey, fish, or seafood	Cool quickly. Freeze any except those containing hard-cooked egg white. Don't overcook. Use fat sparingly when making sauce. This helps prevent separation of sauce when reheating. Cover tightly.	2 to 4 months	Heat in top of double boiler from the frozen state, stirring occasionally. If sauce separates, beat with fork or spoon during reheating. About 30 minutes is needed for thawing and heating 1 pint of a creamed mixture.
Meatballs with tomato sauce	Cook till done; cool quickly. Ladle into jars or freezer containers, allowing headspace. Freeze immediately.	3 months	Heat over low heat, stirring frequently, or in top of double boiler, stirring occasionally. Or, defrost overnight in refrigerator. Heat thoroughly in saucepan.
Meat pies and scallops	Cook meat till tender. Cook vegetables till almost tender. Cool quickly. Put in baking dish. Top with pastry, or freeze pastry separately. Wrap tightly and freeze.	2 to 3 months	Bake pies with pastry topper at 400° for 45 minutes for pints and 1 hour for quarts, or till hot and crust is lightly browned.
Roast beef, pork, other meats, poultry	Do not freeze fried meats or poultry. Prepare as for serving. Remove excess fat and bone. Cool quickly. Wrap tightly. Best to freeze small pieces or slices; cover with broth, gravy, or sauce. Wrap tightly, seal, and freeze.	2 to 4 months	Thaw large pieces of meat in the refrigerator before heating. Heat meat in sauce in top of double boiler.
Spaghetti sauce	Cool sauce quickly; ladle into jars or freezer containers, allowing headspace. Freeze.	2 to 3 months	Heat over low heat, stirring frequently, or in top of double boiler, stirring occasionally.
Stews and soups	Select vegetables that freeze well. Omit potatoes. Onions lose flavor. Green pepper and garlic become more intense in flavor. Omit salt and thickening if stew is to be kept longer than 2 months. Do not completely cook vegetables. Cool quickly, wrap tightly, freeze.	2 to 4 months	Heat quickly from frozen state. Do not overcook. Separate with fork as it thaws. Do not stir enough to make the mixture mushy.

MEALS
MADE WITH
EASE

When demands on time outside the home are great, a meal that requires little preparation time is a real boon to busy homemakers. These recipes feature sausages, frankfurters, and canned meats, as well as leftover and "planned-over" meats. Leftovers can be successfully disguised so that a gourmet cannot identify it the second time around. Some of the recipes have short cooking and preparation times. Others which need longer cooking are built around shopping shortcuts and a minimum of pot watching in the kitchen.

Franks, once thought of as only picnic or family fare, go fancy in Frank and Corn Crown. It's a meal-in-a-dish, making menu planning a snap.

Spark mealtimes with sausages and frankfurters

TOMATO POLENTA

½ cup finely chopped onion
1 clove garlic, minced
2 tablespoons salad oil
1 16-ounce can (2 cups) tomatoes, cut up
1 8-ounce can tomato sauce
1 3-ounce can chopped mushrooms, undrained
1 8-ounce package brown-and-serve sausage links, cut crosswise
½ teaspoon dried oregano, crushed
¼ teaspoon salt
½ cup grated Parmesan cheese
1 8-ounce package corn muffin mix
2 ounces sharp process American cheese, shredded (½ cup)

In skillet, cook onion and garlic in hot oil just till tender. Add next 6 ingredients and dash pepper; simmer, uncovered, 5 minutes. Add Parmesan cheese to muffin mix. Prepare according to package directions; spread in greased 8x8x2-inch baking dish. Top with tomato mixture. Bake at 400° 30 minutes. Sprinkle with American cheese. Serves 5 or 6.

SMOKY BEAN SKILLET

½ cup finely chopped onion
¼ cup chopped green pepper
2 tablespoons salad oil
1 12-ounce package (8) smoked sausage links, cut in 1-inch pieces
1 14-ounce can (2 cups) garbanzo beans, drained
1 31-ounce can (3½ cups) pork and beans in tomato sauce
¼ cup bottled barbecue sauce

Combine all ingredients in skillet. Cover and simmer 20 minutes, stirring occasionally. Uncover and simmer about 5 minutes, if necessary, to reduce liquid. Serves 5 or 6.

SAUSAGE-LIVER ROLLS

8 brown-and-serve sausage links
1 pound beef liver, ¼ inch thick, cut in 8 slices
1 tablespoon salad oil
1 8-ounce can tomato sauce with chopped onion

Lay a sausage link atop each piece of liver; roll liver around sausage; fasten with wooden pick. In 8-inch skillet, brown liver rolls slowly in hot oil; drain off excess fat. Combine tomato sauce with ⅓ cup water; pour over sausage-liver rolls. Cover tightly and simmer 20 minutes or till tender. Remove wooden pick before serving. Makes 6 servings.

BOLOGNA STICKS

1 pound piece bologna
¼ cup apricot preserves or marmalade
Lemon juice
⅛ teaspoon ground ginger

Slice bologna ½ inch thick; cut slices into sticks ¾ inch wide. In skillet, combine preserves with enough lemon juice, about 1 teaspoon, to make glaze; add ginger. Add bologna, turning to coat with glaze. Cook over low heat until heated through. Serves 4.

Sausage by the links

Keep a variety of sausages on hand for → fast, fast meals and snacks. Try these pleasing combinations. On plate upper left: Cervelat and Swiss Cheese on Rye; front left: a pair of Pfalzer with Sauerkraut and Potato Salad; front right: Assorted Cold Cuts and Cheese with Potato Salad, Beet Salad, and Cucumber Salad. For added zip, offer sweet or hot mustard. Serve with pickles and pretzels.

BOLOGNA BAKE

    ¾ cup mayonnaise
    1 tablespoon prepared mustard
    ¼ cup chopped onion
    1 tablespoon chopped canned
       pimiento
    1 ¾-pound piece bologna, diced
       (about 2 cups)
    1 cup sliced celery
    4 hard-cooked eggs, diced
    1 cup crushed potato chips

Combine mayonnaise, mustard, onion, and pimiento. Add bologna, celery, and hard-cooked eggs; toss gently. Turn into a 10x6x1½-inch baking dish; sprinkle crushed potato chips on top. Bake at 400° for 20 minutes, or till hot. Serves 4 or 5.

BOLOGNA BASKETS

    6 or 8 slices bologna
    2 tablespoons shortening
    1 16-ounce can German-style
       potato salad
       Paprika

In stacks of 2 slices each, heat bologna in hot shortening in skillet until meat forms cups. Heat potato salad. Fill bologna cups with potato salad. Sprinkle with paprika. Serve individually or as garnish. Serves 3 or 4.

ITALIAN SPAGHETTI TOSS

    4 ounces pepperoni, thinly sliced
    ½ cup chopped onion
    1 clove garlic, minced
    3 tablespoons salad oil
    1 10-ounce package frozen chopped
       broccoli
    6 ounces fine spaghetti
       Parmesan cheese

In medium skillet, cook pepperoni, onion, and garlic in oil till onion is tender but not brown. Cook broccoli according to package directions; drain. Add to pepperoni mixture. Meanwhile, cook spaghetti according to package directions; drain. Add pepperoni mixture to spaghetti; toss together lightly. Serve with Parmesan cheese. Makes 4 servings.

SNAPPERONI FRANKS

    6 frankfurters
    1 21-ounce can pork and beans in
       tomato sauce
    ½ cup diced pepperoni
    ¼ cup catsup
    2 tablespoons sweet pickle relish
    6 frankfurter buns, split and
       toasted

Heat frankfurters (see directions below). In saucepan, mash beans slightly with a fork. Blend in pepperoni, catsup, and pickle relish. Cook and stir until mixture is heated through. Place franks in buns; spoon pepperoni-bean mixture over franks. Makes 6 sandwiches.

TO HEAT FRANKFURTERS

In water: Cover frankfurters with cold water; bring to boiling. Simmer 5 minutes.

Panfry: Score frankfurters, making shallow (¼-inch) diagonal cuts 1 inch apart, if desired. Brown franks in 1 tablespoon hot butter for 5 minutes. Do not over-brown.

Broil: Frankfurters may be heated over hot coals or on rack of broiler pan in oven. Turn occasionally. Do not over-brown.

CONEY ISLANDS

Heat 10 frankfurters in water (see directions above). Place franks in 10 split and heated frankfurter buns; top with prepared mustard and chopped onion, if desired. Spoon the hot Coney Sauce atop. Serves 10.

Coney Sauce: Brown ½ pound ground beef slowly, breaking apart with fork. Add ¼ cup water, ¼ cup chopped onion, 1 clove garlic, minced, one 8-ounce can tomato sauce, and ½ teaspoon *each* chili powder, monosodium glutamate, and salt. Simmer, uncovered, 10 minutes. Makes 1⅓ cups.

Coney Tacos: Substitute tortillas (either canned or frozen) for buns. Prepare tortillas for taco shells following package directions. Place heated frank in each taco shell. Top with Coney Sauce and a little finely shredded lettuce; sprinkle with shredded cheese.

Quicky Coneys: Heat one 15-ounce can chili with beans; substitute for the Coney Sauce. Spoon over heated franks on buns.

SWEET AND SOUR FRANKS

- 1 8¾-ounce can pineapple tidbits
- 2 tablespoons butter or margarine
- ½ cup chopped onion
- 1 medium green pepper, cut in 1-inch strips
- 1 beef bouillon cube
- 2 tablespoons cornstarch
- 1 tablespoon brown sugar
- 2 tablespoons vinegar
- 1 tablespoon soy sauce
- ½ pound frankfurters (4 or 5), sliced crosswise
  Hot cooked rice

Drain pineapple, reserving syrup. In skillet, melt butter. Add onion and green pepper; cover and cook over low heat 5 minutes.

Dissolve bouillon cube in 1 cup boiling water. Mix cornstarch, sugar, and dash salt; add pineapple syrup, vinegar, soy, and bouillon. Pour over vegetables. Cook and stir till thickened and bubbly. Add franks and pineapple. Heat. Serve over rice. Serves 4.

FRANKS IN FOIL

- 2 cups finely chopped frankfurters
- ⅓ cup shredded sharp process American cheese
- 2 hard-cooked eggs, chopped
- 3 tablespoons chili sauce
- 2 tablespoons pickle relish
- 1 teaspoon prepared mustard
- ¼ teaspoon celery seed
- 8 frankfurter buns, split

Combine all ingredients except buns. Fill buns with frank mixture. Wrap each securely in foil. Place on baking sheet; bake at 400° for 15 to 18 minutes. Makes 8 sandwiches.

JIFFY CHEESY FRANKS

Split 8 to 10 frankfurters lengthwise, cutting ¾ of the way through. Spread cut surfaces with cheese food—nippy, garlic, smoky, or bacon flavored. Place franks in open buns in shallow baking pan. Sprinkle 1 cup crushed corn chips atop. Bake at 350° for 15 minutes, or till hot. Serves 8 to 10.

FRANK TRIANGLES

- 8 frankfurters
  Butter or margarine
- 8 slices bread, crusts removed
- ¼ cup grated Parmesan cheese
- 3 tablespoons prepared mustard
- 3 tablespoons finely chopped onion
- 16 pimiento-stuffed green olives

Place frankfurters in boiling water; cover, reduce heat, and simmer 5 minutes. Drain.

To make each triangle, butter bread. Dip slices in cheese, buttered side down. Spread other side of bread with mustard. Sprinkle each mustard spread side with about 1 teaspoon onion. Place a frank diagonally across each slice. Fasten two opposite corners of slice, cheese side out, with wooden picks. Place on side on broiler rack. Broil 3 inches from heat 2 to 3 minutes. Turn triangles over. Broil 2 to 3 minutes more. Trim with olives on wooden picks. Makes 8 servings.

RED HOTS ON KABOB

- ½ pound frankfurters (4 or 5), cut in 1-inch pieces
- ⅓ cup soy sauce
- ⅓ cup catsup
- ¼ cup salad oil
- 2 tablespoons vinegar
- 1 teaspoon dried thyme, crushed
- 1 teaspoon prepared mustard

• • •

- 16 small canned onions
- 16 canned pineapple chunks
- 1 green pepper, cut in 1-inch squares
- 8 slices bacon, cut in half crosswise

With sharp knife, score cut ends of frankfurter pieces. Combine soy sauce, catsup, oil, vinegar, thyme, and mustard for marinade. Pour marinade over franks, onions, pineapple, and green pepper. Chill 3 hours.

Partially cook bacon. Wrap bacon piece around each pineapple chunk. On 9- or 10-inch skewers, alternate the chunks of franks, vegetables, and bacon-wrapped pineapple. Broil 3 to 4 inches from heat about 12 minutes making a quarter turn every 3 minutes. Brush with glaze each turn. Serves 4 or 5.

SAUSAGE VARIETIES

Summer Sausage (*left*) was first made in northern Europe as a method of preserving meat to be eaten in the hot summer. Now it is the family name for an assortment of smoked, semidry sausages.

Frizzes (*right*) are dry sausages with an abundance of flavor, so slice thinly for best eating. Casing tied with blue string has sweet spices; red strings (being sliced on board) indicate hot spices.

Thuringer (*left*) is a semidry sausage either lightly or heavily smoked. This mildly seasoned summer sausage is popular for sandwiches and cold meat trays.

Bologna (*right*)—ring, stick, slices—is a mild blend of smoked and cooked beef and pork. It is the second most popular sausage and is big brother to the frank.

Dry Salami (*left*) is highly seasoned and packed in natural casings. It's not smoked, but is completely air dried. Because this garlic-flavored Italian-type sausage is chewy, it is great for snacking.

Cotto Salami (*right*) is identified by whole peppercorns. Mildly flavored with garlic, this cooked, smoked sausage is made of pork and beef. It originated in northern Italy as a summer sausage.

Pepperoni (*left*) is named after its peppery spicing. With this dry sausage, a thin slice goes a long way to add flavor and taste appeal to favorite dishes.

New England Style (*right*) is a cooked, smoked sausage made of cured lean pork. It has a delicate hamlike flavor and—good news for weight-watchers—a relatively low calorie count.

Genoa Salami and **Cervelatwurst** (*left*). Cervelatwurst, left, is a German specialty and is a mildly seasoned summer sausage. Genoa Salami, right, is an Italian dry sausage lightly flavored with garlic and sometimes wine is added.

Berliner (*right*) is a cooked and smoked sausage made primarily of coarsely ground cured pork, sometimes with a small amount of beef added.

SAUSAGE VARIETIES

Lebanon Bologna (*left*) originated in Lebanon, Pennsylvania, and is a semidry sausage made of lean beef. Long slow smoking gives it a wonderful tangy flavor that combines with hearty food.

Frankfurters, Wieners, Franks, or Hot Dogs (*right*) are the best-known and most popular sausage. They are a blend of ground beef and pork that is seasoned, smoked, and fully cooked.

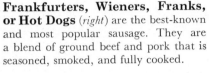

Liver Sausage (*left*) is a nutritious sausage of pork and livers that's seasoned. Available in an easy-to-slice firm loaf or a soft spread in a natural casing.

Franks (*right*) come in big dinner size or tiny cocktail size, skinless or with a natural casing. They are fully cooked and can be eaten as is but are best heated.

Braunschweiger (*left*) was originated in Brunswick, Germany, where the townspeople developed the art of smoking liver sausage. A seasoned, smoked sausage that's perfect for appetizers.

Smokies (*right*) come in regular and cocktail size and are in links in casings or skinless. The tang of these coarsely ground sausages comes from the heavy smoking. They are fully cooked.

Blood and Tongue (*left*) is a gourmet's choice. Cooked lamb and pork tongues are lengthwise in center of roll of blood sausage. Slice for sandwiches.

Knackwurst (Knoblauch) (*right*) is usually flavored with garlic. These beef and pork sausages are cooked and smoked and are similar to franks in seasonings. They come in natural casings or skinless.

Vienna Sausages (*left*) are tiny sausages that are mildly smoked and seasoned. They start out 80 feet long, but later are cut in 2-inch lengths, then canned.

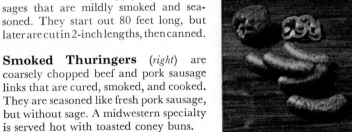

Smoked Thuringers (*right*) are coarsely chopped beef and pork sausage links that are cured, smoked, and cooked. They are seasoned like fresh pork sausage, but without sage. A midwestern specialty is served hot with toasted coney buns.

BARBECUED FRANKFURTERS

- ¼ cup chopped onion
- 1 tablespoon salad oil
- 1 cup catsup
- ½ cup chopped celery
- 2 tablespoons brown sugar
- 2 tablespoons Worcestershire sauce
- 1 tablespoon vinegar
- 1 tablespoon prepared mustard
- 1 pound (8 to 10) frankfurters
- 4 or 5 frankfurter buns, split

Cook onion in oil till tender; stir in next 6 ingredients, ½ cup water, and ½ teaspoon salt. Simmer, covered, 20 minutes. Score franks diagonally at 1-inch intervals; add to sauce. Simmer, covered, 15 minutes. Serve over toasted frankfurter buns. Makes 4 or 5 servings.

THREE-BEAN FRANK BAKE

In large bowl, combine 1 pound (8 to 10) frankfurters, sliced, one 16-ounce can pork and beans in tomato sauce, one 16-ounce can butter beans, drained, one 16-ounce can chili beans, ½ cup brown sugar, ½ cup chopped onion, 2 tablespoons wine vinegar, and ¼ teaspoon dried oregano, crushed. Turn into 2½-quart bean pot or casserole. Bake, uncovered, at 350° for 2 hours, stirring occasionally. Makes 8 to 10 servings.

FRANKS AND CABBAGE

- 4 cups coarsely shredded cabbage
- ½ pound (4 or 5) frankfurters, cut into 1-inch pieces
- 2 tablespoons butter or margarine
- 2 tablespoons all-purpose flour
- 1 cup milk
- 1 tablespoon prepared mustard

Cook cabbage, covered, in small amount of boiling salted water 5 to 6 minutes, or till barely tender; drain. Place in shallow 1-quart baking dish. Arrange franks on top. Melt butter; blend in flour and ½ teaspoon salt. Add milk all at once; cook and stir till sauce is thick and bubbly. Cook 1 minute longer. Stir in mustard. Pour sauce over franks. Heat in moderate oven (350°) for 20 to 25 minutes. Makes 3 or 4 servings.

SAUCY FRANK SUPPER

- 1 28-ounce can (3½ cups) tomatoes
- 1 cup chopped celery
- 1 cup water
- 1 1½-ounce envelope spaghetti sauce mix
- 1 tablespoon instant minced onion
- 1 teaspoon sugar

• • •

- ½ pound (4 or 5) frankfurters
- 2 tablespoons butter or margarine
- 4 ounces medium noodles
- 2 ounces sharp process American cheese, shredded (½ cup)

Combine tomatoes, celery, water, spaghetti sauce mix, onion, and sugar. Cut frankfurters in thirds diagonally. In large skillet, brown franks in butter or margarine. Add uncooked noodles and tomato mixture, stirring to moisten ingredients. Cover; cook over low heat 25 minutes, or till done, stirring occasionally. Stir in shredded cheese. Makes 4 servings.

FRANK-NOODLE BAKE

- 1 cup medium noodles
- ½ cup chopped onion
- 1 tablespoon butter or margarine
- ½ pound (4 or 5) frankfurters, thinly sliced
- 3 slightly beaten eggs
- 1 cup dairy sour cream
- ½ cup cream-style cottage cheese
- ½ teaspoon salt
  Dash pepper
- ½ cup cornflake crumbs
- 1 tablespoon butter or margarine, melted

Cook noodles according to package directions; drain. Cook onion in 1 tablespoon butter till tender but not brown. Set aside a few frankfurter slices for garnish. Combine remaining frankfurter slices, noodles, onion, eggs, sour cream, cottage cheese, salt, and pepper; pour into greased 9-inch pie plate.

Mix cornflake crumbs and 1 tablespoon melted butter; sprinkle over top of frankfurter mixture. Bake in moderate oven (375°) for 20 minutes; top with reserved frank slices. Bake 5 minutes more. Let stand 10 minutes; cut in wedges. Makes 4 to 6 servings.

FRANK AND CORN CROWN

 ½ cup chopped green pepper
 ¼ cup chopped onion
 ¼ cup butter or margarine
 2 cups soft bread crumbs (about
   3 slices)
 1 17-ounce can cream-style corn
 1 12-ounce can whole kernel corn,
   drained
 2 beaten eggs
 ¼ cup fine dry bread crumbs
 1 tablespoon butter, melted
 1 pound (8 to 10) frankfurters,
   cut in half crosswise

Cook green pepper and onion in ¼ cup butter till tender but not brown. Add next 4 ingredients and 1 teaspoon salt; mix lightly. Spoon into 8x1½-inch round baking dish.

Combine dry bread crumbs and melted butter; sprinkle over corn mixture. Bake, uncovered, at 350° for 30 minutes. Stand franks, cut end down, in crown around edge of stuffing. Bake 15 minutes longer. Serves 5 or 6.

CREOLE FRANKS

Cook 3 slices bacon, diced, till partially done. Add ⅓ cup chopped onion; cook till tender but not brown. Stir in ⅔ cup pineapple juice, ½ cup catsup, and dash chili powder. Score 1 pound (8 to 10) frankfurters diagonally at 1-inch intervals; add to sauce. Cover; bring to boiling. Add 2 tablespoons chopped green pepper; simmer 8 to 10 minutes. Serve over hot cooked rice. Serves 6.

GLAZED APPLES 'N FRANKS

 3 tablespoons butter or margarine
 2 tablespoons prepared mustard
 ¾ cup light corn syrup
 1 pound (8 to 10) frankfurters
 6 medium tart apples, cored and
   quartered

Melt butter in skillet; blend in mustard and corn syrup. Score franks at 1-inch intervals; add to sauce with apples. Cover; simmer slowly 10 to 15 minutes, turning apples and franks once. Arrange franks on serving platter; surround with apples. Pass syrup. Serves 4 or 5.

FRANK-POTATO PIE

 ½ pound (4 or 5) frankfurters
 ½ cup chopped onion
 2 tablespoons butter or margarine
 1 16-ounce can cut green beans,
   drained
 1 10¾-ounce can condensed
   tomato soup
   Potato Topper
 2 ounces sharp process American
   cheese, shredded (½ cup)

Cut franks in 1-inch pieces. Cook with onion in butter till franks are browned and onion is tender. Add beans and soup. Pour into 1½-quart casserole. Top with Potato Topper. Bake at 350° for 25 minutes; top with cheese. Heat 5 minutes. Makes 6 servings.

Potato Topper: Prepare packaged instant mashed potatoes (enough for 4 servings) according to package directions, *but reserve the milk.* Add 1 beaten egg; if needed, slowly add milk to make potatoes hold shape.

Spice up the family Sunday night supper with this new and easy frankfurter variation—Glazed Apples 'n Franks.

Meats ready to serve

FRUITED LUNCHEON LOAF

Using two 12-ounce cans luncheon meat, cut *each* loaf lengthwise in 8 slices to within 1 inch of bottom. Arrange one 11-ounce can mandarin oranges, drained, between meat slices. Place loaves in shallow baking pan; bake at 375° for 20 minutes. Heat one 22-ounce can raisin pie filling with 2 teaspoons vinegar. Serve with meat. Serves 8.

DRIED BEEF DINNER

Cook one 4-ounce package sliced dried beef (if quite salty, rinse with boiling water and drain), snipped, in 2 tablespoons butter or margarine for 4 or 5 minutes. Blend together 2 tablespoons all-purpose flour, dash pepper, and 1¼ cups milk; add to beef. Cook and stir till mixture thickens and bubbles; add ½ teaspoon Worcestershire sauce. Serve meat sauce over baked potatoes or toast. Serves 4.

Snip and measure smoked or dried beef in one step. Snip several slices at a time; separate into pieces before using.

MACARONI-MEAT SKILLET

Cook 1 cup chopped celery, ½ cup chopped onion, and 1 clove garlic, minced, in 2 tablespoons hot shortening till tender but not brown. Add one 12-ounce can luncheon meat, cut in sticks; brown lightly.

Stir in one 10¾-ounce can condensed tomato soup, half of a 7-ounce package macaroni, 1½ cups water, and ⅛ teaspoon pepper; bring to boil; reduce heat. Cover. Cook 25 minutes; stir occasionally. Serves 4 to 6.

SPEEDY KABOBS

    1 13½-ounce can pineapple chunks
    1 12-ounce can luncheon meat
    1 green pepper, cut in 12 squares
       Kabob Sauce
    2 medium tomatoes, quartered

Drain pineapple reserving syrup. Cut meat in 12 cubes. On four 9-inch skewers, thread pineapple, meat, and green pepper; brush with Kabob Sauce. Broil 5 to 6 inches from heat 8 to 9 minutes, or till brown. Turn; add tomatoes to skewers. Brush all with sauce; broil 4 to 5 minutes more. Serves 4.

Kabob Sauce: In saucepan, combine one 8-ounce can tomato sauce, ½ cup reserved syrup, ¼ cup finely chopped green onion, ¼ cup butter, and 1 teaspoon *each* monosodium glutamate and Worcestershire sauce. Simmer 15 minutes or till thick. Makes 1 cup sauce.

SAUSAGE IN BISCUITS

Using one 8-ounce package refrigerated biscuits (10 biscuits), pat out *seven* biscuits lengthwise; spread lightly with prepared mustard. Using one 4-ounce can Vienna sausages, roll each sausage in a biscuit; seal edges with fingers. Place seam side down on small baking sheet; bake at 425° about 10 minutes.

Prepare one 10-ounce package frozen peas in cream sauce following package directions. Spoon peas over biscuits. Makes 7 sausage rolls. If desired, bake remaining biscuits.

CORNED BEEF PIE

1 16-ounce can corned beef hash
¼ cup catsup
1 slightly beaten egg
1 10-ounce package frozen baby limas
2 ounces process American cheese, shredded (½ cup)
2 tablespoons milk

Combine hash, catsup, and egg; spread mixture on bottom and sides of greased 8-inch pie plate. Bake at 350° about 30 minutes.

Meanwhile, cook limas according to package directions; drain. Fill crust with limas. Heat shredded cheese and milk over *very low heat*, stirring constantly till cheese melts. Pour over limas. Makes 4 or 5 servings.

CORNED BEEF WITH NOODLES

1 5¾-ounce package noodles with sour cream-cheese sauce mix
1 12-ounce can corned beef, cubed
1 10-ounce package frozen peas, thawed
1 tablespoon prepared horseradish
1 teaspoon prepared mustard

In 2-quart saucepan, cook noodles from mix according to package directions; drain. Stir in butter, sauce mix, and ⅔ *cup milk* following package directions. Add cubed corned beef, peas, horseradish, and mustard; bring just to boiling. Makes 4 servings.

JIFFY MEXICAN DINNER

¼ cup chopped onion
¼ cup chopped green pepper
1 tablespoon shortening
1 15-ounce can chili with beans
1 15-ounce can tamales in sauce
2 ounces sharp process American cheese, shredded (½ cup)

In a 10-inch skillet, cook onion and green pepper in shortening till tender. Add chili. Remove shucks from tamales; arrange spoke-fashion on top. Cook, uncovered, over low heat, 10 to 15 minutes. Sprinkle with cheese and serve. Makes 4 servings.

PEPPER CUPS

Remove tops, seeds, and membranes from 6 large green peppers. Precook in boiling, salted water 5 minutes; drain. Cook ½ cup chopped onion in 2 tablespoons butter till tender; add 2 cups cooked long-grain rice, one 10½-ounce can condensed cream of celery soup, ½ teaspoon salt, and few drops bottled hot pepper sauce. Spoon into peppers.

In each pepper, form a well in rice mixture. Divide one 4½-ounce can deviled ham to fill wells. Stand peppers upright in shallow baking dish; add water just to cover bottom of dish. Bake at 350° about 30 minutes. Serves 6.

FILLED HAM-SCHNITZEL

1 6-ounce can chopped mushrooms, drained, and finely chopped
3 tablespoons butter or margarine
2 tablespoons snipped parsley
1 tablespoon all-purpose flour
6 slices boiled ham
1 slightly beaten egg
½ cup all-purpose flour
½ cup fine dry bread crumbs
3 tablespoons shortening

Brown mushrooms in butter with parsley. Add 1 tablespoon flour; cook and stir for 2 minutes. Cool. Spread mixture on one half of each slice of ham. Fold other half over; press to secure. Dip schnitzel in egg, then in ½ cup flour, back into egg, and then in crumbs. Brown on both sides in hot shortening. Serves 4.

HAM-PLATTER MEAL

Cut one 2-pound canned ham into 6 slices; center on broiler pan rack. Drain one 17-ounce jar spiced peaches (whole), reserving ¼ cup syrup; halve and pit peaches. Arrange peaches and one 18-ounce can vacuum-packed sweet potatoes, drained, around ham.

Blend reserved syrup with ¼ cup brown sugar; brush *half* of glaze over ham and peaches. Brush potatoes with *half* of 2 tablespoons butter, melted. Broil 4 to 6 inches from heat for 7 minutes. Turn; repeat brushing. Broil 5 to 7 minutes more. Arrange on platter with one 10-ounce package frozen peas, cooked, drained, and buttered. Serves 6.

Color menus with planned-overs

TURKEY PAPRIKA

- 1 medium onion, sliced
- 3 tablespoons butter or margarine
- 2 tablespoons all-purpose flour
- 2 teaspoons paprika
- 1 cup turkey *or* chicken broth
- 2 slightly beaten egg yolks
- 1 cup dairy sour cream
- 2 cups diced cooked turkey
- 1 3-ounce can sliced mushrooms, drained (½ cup)
  Poppy Seed Noodles

In saucepan, cook onion in butter till tender. Blend in flour, paprika, and ½ teaspoon salt; add broth. Cook and stir till mixture thickens and bubbles; cook 1 minute more. Stir a small amount of hot mixture into egg yolks; return to hot mixture. Cook over low heat for 1 minute more. Stir in sour cream till blended. Add turkey and mushrooms. Heat slowly just till hot. Serve over noodles.

Poppy Seed Noodles: Cook 4 ounces medium noodles in large amount of boiling salted water about 10 minutes, or till tender; drain. Stir in 2 tablespoons melted butter or margarine and 1 teaspoon poppy seed. Season to taste with salt. Makes 4 or 5 servings.

CHEDDAR TURKEY BAKE

Prepare 1 cup packaged precooked rice according to package directions, adding 2 tablespoons instant minced onion to rice in boiling water. Combine half 10-ounce package (1 cup) frozen peas, thawed and broken apart, 2 cups diced cooked turkey, one 10¾-ounce can condensed Cheddar cheese soup, 1 soup can milk, 1 teaspoon prepared mustard, and ½ teaspoon salt. Place in 10x6x1½-inch baking dish. Combine ½ cup finely crushed rich round crackers with 2 tablespoons butter or margarine, melted. Sprinkle atop casserole. Bake at 350° for 35 minutes or till heated through. Makes 4 to 6 servings.

BOMBAY TURKEY

- 4 tablespoons butter or margarine
- 2 to 3 teaspoons curry powder
- ½ cup chopped onion
- 3 tablespoons all-purpose flour
- ¼ teaspoon salt
  Dash pepper
- 1½ cups chicken broth
- 2 cups diced cooked turkey
- 1 teaspoon shredded lemon peel
- ⅔ cup long-grain rice
- ¼ cup chopped cashew nuts
- 2 tablespoons chopped canned pimiento

In medium skillet, melt butter. Add curry and heat 2 to 3 minutes. Stir in onion and cook till tender but not brown. Blend in flour, salt, and pepper, stirring well. Add chicken broth all at once. Cook and stir till boiling; cook 2 minutes longer. Add cooked turkey and shredded lemon peel; heat mixture to boiling.

Cook rice according to package directions. Stir in cashew nuts and pimiento. Serve turkey mixture over rice. Makes 4 to 6 servings.

QUICK CURRIED HAM

In skillet, melt 1 tablespoon butter. Add ¼ to ½ teaspoon curry powder and heat. Stir in 1 tablespoon chopped green pepper and 1 tablespoon chopped onion and cook till tender but not brown. Stir in one 10½-ounce can condensed cream of celery soup, ¾ cup milk, and ⅓ cup mayonnaise or salad dressing. Add 2 cups cubed cooked ham, and one 3-ounce can sliced mushrooms, drained (½ cup). Cook and stir till heated through. Serve over fluffy hot cooked rice. Makes 6 servings.

Leftovers go special

In Bombay Turkey the combination of→ curry and lemon peel enhances the flavor of cooked turkey. Serve it over fluffy rice.

HAM AND RICE CROQUETTES

1 10½-ounce can condensed cream
   of celery soup
1 pound ground cooked ham (3 cups)
1 cup cooked rice
1 tablespoon finely chopped onion
1 tablespoon finely chopped green
   pepper
1 to 2 tablespoons prepared
   mustard

      •   •   •

1 beaten egg
1 cup fine dry bread crumbs
   Shortening
2 8-ounce packages frozen peas in
   cream sauce

Blend together first 6 ingredients; chill. Shape mixture into croquettes, using about ¼ cup per croquette. Drip croquettes in egg, then in bread crumbs; let stand a few minutes. Fry 2 or 3 at a time in deep hot fat (365°) for 3 to 5 minutes or till brown; drain. Prepare peas in cream sauce according to package directions; serve over croquettes. Makes 8 to 10 servings.

To cube meat, cut sticks of uniform width from thick slices of meat. Place several sticks together; cut pieces the same size.

KETTLE-OF-BEAN STEW

In Dutch oven, bring 1½ cups dried navy beans and 4½ cups water to boil; reduce heat, simmer 2 minutes. Remove from heat; let stand 1 hour. Drain beans, reserving liquid. Add enough water to reserved liquid to make 3½ cups. In Dutch oven, combine beans, 1 medium onion, sliced, 1 meaty ham bone *or* 2 cups small pieces cooked ham, ½ teaspoon salt, dash pepper, 1 bay leaf (optional), and reserved liquid. Heat to boiling; reduce heat. Cover and simmer 2¼ hours. (If using ham bone, remove; cut off any meat, returning meat to stew.) Uncover; continue cooking 15 minutes more. Makes 4 servings.

SNAPPY BEEF STEW

1 envelope *dry* onion soup mix
2 medium potatoes, pared and cubed
1 10-ounce package frozen mixed
   vegetables
1 tablespoon all-purpose flour
2 cups cubed cooked beef
2 ounces sharp process American
   cheese, shredded (½ cup)

Add soup mix, potatoes, and frozen vegetables to 2¾ cups boiling water; cover and cook 10 to 12 minutes or till vegetables are tender. Mix together flour and ¼ cup cold water; stir into vegetables. Cook and stir till slightly thickened and bubbly. Add meat; heat. Sprinkle cheese atop. Serves 4 or 5.

ORIENTAL HASH

2 tablespoons salad oil
   Dash garlic powder
1½ cups cubed cooked pork
2 cups cooked rice
3 tablespoons soy sauce
2 well-beaten eggs
2 cups shredded lettuce

Heat oil in skillet. Add garlic powder and pork; cook till meat is lightly browned. Add cooked rice and soy sauce. Cook 10 minutes, stirring occasionally. Mix in eggs and cook 1 minute longer, stirring frequently. Remove from heat. Add shredded lettuce; toss together. Serve immediately. Makes 6 servings.

PORK OR BEEF PIE

- ½ cup chopped onion
- 6 tablespoons butter or margarine
- ½ cup all-purpose flour
- 3 beef bouillon cubes
- 3 cups cubed cooked pork *or* beef
- 1 10-ounce package frozen peas and carrots, cooked and drained
- ¼ cup snipped parsley
  Plain Pastry (see Index)
  Milk

In saucepan, cook onion in butter till tender. Blend in flour and 1 teaspoon salt. Dissolve bouillon cubes in 3 cups boiling water. Stir into flour mixture all at once; cook and stir till thick and bubbly. Add next 3 ingredients; heat through. Pour meat mixture into 2-quart casserole. Prepare pastry; roll ½ to 1 inch larger than casserole. Place atop *hot* meat mixture. Cut slits in top. Turn under edge and flute. Brush with milk. Bake at 450° for 20 to 25 minutes. Serves 6 to 8.

Note: To use leftover gravy, omit flour, salt, boiling water, and beef bouillon cubes.

SPANISH LAMB

- ½ cup finely chopped onion
- 1 clove garlic, minced
- 2 tablespoons salad oil
- 1 20-ounce can tomatoes, cut up
- 1 8-ounce can tomato sauce
- 1 3-ounce can broiled whole mushroom crowns, undrained
- 1 bay leaf
- 2 cups diced cooked lamb
- ¼ cup sliced pimiento-stuffed green olives
- 12 ounces spaghetti
  Grated Parmesan cheese

In medium saucepan, cook onion and garlic in hot oil till tender but not brown. Stir in tomatoes, tomato sauce, mushrooms with liquid, and bay leaf. Simmer, covered, for 1 hour; uncover and simmer 30 minutes more, stirring occasionally. Stir in lamb and olives; simmer 10 minutes more. Remove bay leaf. Cook spaghetti according to package directions; drain. Pour sauce over spaghetti; sprinkle with Parmesan cheese. Serves 4.

Put a snap in the meal by planning a menu around Spanish Lamb. It's a good way to feature lamb the second time around. Serve over cooked spaghetti.

Plan ahead when buying

BUYING TIPS

A beef roast—an all-time favorite—can fit into any family spending plan, depending on which cut is purchased. For a penny-wise purchase that tastes extravagantly good, select a blade pot roast, sometimes called a seven-bone roast because of the shape of the bone. It's an even better buy if the beef roast is on "special." Choose a 4- to 5-pound beef blade pot roast to divide for the two main dishes shown at right. The sketch below shows how to divide the roast.

Have meatman cut the pot roast crosswise at the tip of the blade bone. This gives a large, bone-in piece and a smaller, boneless piece. Use the bone-in piece to prepare Mushroom Pot Roast (top, right) or use in a favorite pot roast recipe. If the family is small, divide the bone-in piece before cooking. Cut through the center of the roast, along the natural "seam," to form two smaller roasts. One portion can be used for pot roasting and the other for Swiss steak.

Ask meatman to grind the boneless piece. Use to prepare a variation of the popular meat pie—Cheeseburger Pie (bottom, right). Another time, cut the boneless piece of meat into cubes or strips instead of grinding; use in a favorite stew, casserole, main-dish salad, or a variation of beef stroganoff.

Divide beef blade pot roast. Use bone-in piece (left) for pot roast; grind boneless piece (right) for ground meat dishes.

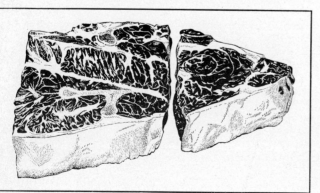

MUSHROOM POT ROAST

Trim excess fat from one 3½- to 4-pound beef blade pot roast. Coat meat with all-purpose flour. In Dutch oven, brown meat on both sides in 2 tablespoons hot shortening. Season with salt and pepper; add 2 cups sliced onion. Combine ¼ cup *each* water and catsup, ⅓ cup dry sherry, 1 clove garlic, minced, ¼ teaspoon *each* dry mustard, dried marjoram, crushed, dried rosemary, crushed, and dried thyme, crushed, and 1 medium bay leaf; add to meat. Simmer, covered, for 2 hours or till tender. Remove meat to platter.

Discard bay leaf. Skim excess fat from pan juices. Add one 6-ounce can sliced mushrooms, drained, to juices. Blend ¼ cup cold water with 2 tablespoons all-purpose flour; stir into juices. Cook and stir till thickened and bubbly. Drizzle a little gravy over roast; pass remaining gravy. Serves 6 to 8.

CHEESEBURGER PIE

- 1 pound ground beef
- ½ cup evaporated milk
- ½ cup catsup
- ⅓ cup fine dry bread crumbs
- ¼ cup chopped onion
- ½ teaspoon dried oregano, crushed
  Plain Pastry (see Index)
- 4 ounces process American cheese, shredded (1 cup)
- 1 teaspoon Worcestershire sauce

Combine first 6 ingredients, ¾ teaspoon salt, and ⅛ teaspoon pepper. Prepare pastry to line one 8-inch pie plate. Fill with meat mixture. Bake at 350° for 35 to 40 minutes. Toss cheese with Worcestershire sauce; sprinkle atop pie. Bake 10 minutes more. Remove from oven; let stand 10 minutes before serving. Trim with pickle slices, if desired. Serves 6.

Flavor on a budget

Tempting Mushroom Pot Roast and→ hearty Cheeseburger Pie score for flavorful eating that's economical.

SALADS
AND
SANDWICHES

Make meat salads and sandwiches the focal point of the meal. A casual occasion calls for casual food, and pizza is just that. It's sure to make a hit at any informal party or gathering. Or, what about fancy hot or cold sandwiches? They're perfect for luncheons or family suppers. When a lighter meal is the order for the day, plan the menu around a hearty salad. No matter whether it's made with meat, seafood, or poultry, it's a team that is hard to beat when served with freshly baked rolls or muffins hot from the oven and a dessert.

King-size is the word for this salad sandwich— Dilly Beef Cartwheel. Roast beef, rolled around dill pickles, is perched atop crisp salad greens.

Imagination makes for savory sandwiches

DILLY BEEF CARTWHEEL

- 1 cup dairy sour cream
- 4 teaspoons *dry* onion soup mix
- 1 tablespoon prepared horseradish
- 4 slices large round rye bread
- 1½ cups shredded lettuce
- 1½ cups shredded endive *or* spinach
- 1 medium tomato, sliced
- 6 thin slices roast beef
- 6 dill pickle strips
- 1 medium tomato, cut in wedges
  Milk
  Pitted ripe olives

Combine first 3 ingredients and dash freshly ground pepper. Arrange *2 slices* of the bread, bottom to bottom, to form large circle; spread with a *third* of the sour cream mixture. Toss together lettuce and endive; place *two-thirds* atop bread. Top with tomato slices. Place remaining bread atop lettuce mixture; spread with *half* of remaining sour cream mixture. Top with remaining lettuce mixture.

Make 6 cornucopias of beef with pickle in center of each; arrange with tomato wedges atop sandwich. Thin remaining sour cream mixture slightly with a little milk; drizzle over top. Garnish with olives. With thin, sharp knife, cut in wedges to serve. Serves 6.

CHOW MEIN BURGERS

In medium skillet, combine 1 pound ground beef with ½ cup chopped onion; cook till meat is lightly browned and onion is tender. Add one 16-ounce can chop suey vegetables, drained. Stir ⅓ cup cold water and 3 tablespoons soy sauce into 2 tablespoons cornstarch; stir into beef mixture. Cook 1 to 2 minutes till thick and bubbly, stirring to coat vegetables and meat. Split, toast, and butter 8 hamburger buns; spoon mixture on bottom halves. Crumble one 3-ounce can (2¼ cups) chow mein noodles over sandwiches; cover with top halves of buns. Makes 8 sandwiches.

PIZZA BY THE YARD

- 1 loaf French bread, about 18 inches long
- 1 pound ground beef
- 1 6-ounce can (⅔ cup) tomato paste
- ⅓ cup grated Parmesan cheese
- ¼ cup finely chopped onion
- ¼ cup chopped pitted ripe olives
- ½ teaspoon dried oregano, crushed
- 3 tomatoes peeled and sliced
- 6 slices sharp process American cheese *or* mozzarella cheese, halved diagonally

Cut bread lengthwise in half. Combine next 6 ingredients and ½ teaspoon salt. Spread evenly on each half loaf. Broil about 5 inches from heat 12 minutes or till meat is done.

Overlap tomato and cheese slices on top of loaves. Broil 1 to 2 minutes more or just till cheese slices begin to melt. Cut each half loaf in 4 or 5 slices. Makes 4 or 5 servings.

PIZZA PRONTO

With palms of hands, flatten biscuits from two 8-ounce packages refrigerated biscuits into 4½x2-inch ovals. On greased baking sheet, stagger 10 biscuits in 2 rows so narrow ends fit between space left between biscuits in other row. Press adjoining ends together securely. Repeat with remaining biscuits.

Combine one 8-ounce can tomato sauce, 1 teaspoon instant minced onion, and ¼ teaspoon *each* ground oregano and garlic salt; spread evenly over biscuits to within ½ inch of edges. Sprinkle with one 4-ounce package (1 cup) shredded sharp Cheddar cheese; top with 2 slices mozzarella cheese torn in pieces. Arrange one 6-ounce can mushroom crowns, drained (1 cup), atop cheese.

Bake in very hot oven (450°) for 8 to 10 minutes, or till edges of crusts are brown. If desired, garnish with ½ cup pitted ripe olives, halved lengthwise. Makes 2 pizzas.

Watch guests turn their heads when you serve this salami-olive "wheel" atop Duo Sausage Pizza. Package mix adds an extra appeal for the busy hostess.

DUO SAUSAGE PIZZA

Using one package cheese pizza mix (for 1 pizza), prepare pizza crust according to package directions. Roll or pat out to fit 12-inch pizza pan. Crimp edges with fork; brush dough with 2 teaspoons olive oil. Shake on *half* the grated cheese from package mix; cover with pizza sauce. Using one 6-ounce package sliced mozzarella cheese, cut in thirds, overlap pieces in a circle atop pizza; sprinkle with remaining grated cheese. Place one 4-ounce package sliced pepperoni in a ring around outer edge. Bake at 425° for 15 to 20 minutes or till crust is done.

Using 6 slices Cotto salami and 6 stuffed green olives, make 6 cornucopias of salami using an olive in center of each. Arrange spoke fashion, in center of pizza, seam side down. Place sprig of parsley in center of salami "wheel." Makes one 12-inch pizza.

JIFFY PIZZA CRUST

Prepare one 13¾-ounce package hot roll mix according to package directions, but using *1 cup warm water* (110°) and *no egg. Omit rising*. Cut in half. With oiled hands, pat each into 12-inch circle on greased baking sheet. Clip edge at 1-inch intervals; press so it stands up. Brush with salad oil. Fill. Bake at 450° for 15 to 20 minutes or till crust is done. Makes two 12-inch crusts.

PIZZA TOPPERS

For creative cooking with a jiffy flair, start with packaged pizza mix. For salami pizza, top with small pieces of salami; shake grated Parmesan cheese atop. Try anchovy pizza with wedges of mozzarella cheese. Season pepperoni pizza with anise seed.

HAM WAFFLEWICHES

Combine ½ pound finely chopped cooked ham (1½ cups), one 3-ounce can chopped mushrooms, drained, ⅓ cup mayonnaise, ¼ cup chopped celery, and 1 tablespoon chopped onion. Using one 9-ounce package frozen waffles (12 waffles), spread mixture on 6 waffles; top with remaining waffles. Bake at 425° for 12 to 15 minutes or till crisp. In saucepan, melt 2 tablespoons butter; blend in 2 tablespoons all-purpose flour, 4 teaspoons prepared mustard, and ½ teaspoon salt. Add 1½ cups milk; cook and stir till thickened and bubbly. Serve over sandwiches. Serves 6.

DEVILED HAM AND TUNA

Combine one 6½- or 7-ounce can tuna, drained and flaked, one 4½-ounce can deviled ham, 3 hard-cooked eggs, chopped, ¼ cup finely chopped celery, 2 tablespoons chopped dill pickle, and ½ teaspoon grated onion; blend in ⅓ cup mayonnaise. Chill. Spread 16 slices white bread with softened butter; spread 8 of the slices with tuna mixture. Top each with lettuce leaf, then bread. Serves 8.

Serve Hot Crab Open-facers for lunch, or spread the filling on toast points, broil, and serve as an hors d'oeuvre.

FRIED SALMON SANDWICH

1   7¾-ounce can salmon
2   well-beaten eggs
⅓   cup milk
    Dash ground nutmeg
¼   cup finely chopped celery
¼   cup dairy sour cream
1   teaspoon prepared horseradish
1   teaspoon prepared mustard
½   teaspoon finely chopped green onion
¼   teaspoon dried tarragon, crushed
¼   teaspoon salt
8   slices white bread
    Sesame seed
¼   cup shortening

Drain salmon, reserving liquid. Remove bones and skin from salmon; flake into bowl. In shallow dish, combine salmon liquid, eggs, milk, and nutmeg. Blend together salmon, celery, sour cream, horseradish, mustard, onion, tarragon, salt, and dash pepper. Spread mixture evenly on 4 slices bread; top with remaining 4 slices. Dip each sandwich into egg mixture; sprinkle with sesame seed. Fry in shortening on griddle till brown on both sides. Makes 4 sandwiches.

HOT CRAB OPEN-FACERS

1   7½-ounce can crab meat, drained, flaked, and cartilage removed
¼   cup mayonnaise or salad dressing
1   3-ounce package cream cheese, softened
1   egg yolk
1   teaspoon finely chopped onion
¼   teaspoon prepared mustard
3   English muffins, split and toasted
2   tablespoons butter or margarine, softened

Stir together crab meat and mayonnaise; set aside. Beat together cream cheese, egg yolk, onion, mustard, and dash salt till smooth and creamy. Spread toasted muffin halves with butter or margarine, then with crab mixture. Top with cream cheese mixture. Place on baking sheet; broil 5 to 6 inches from heat for 2 to 3 minutes, till top is bubbly and golden. Makes 6 sandwiches.

SHRIMP SANDWICHES

1 3-ounce package cream cheese,
  softened
2 tablespoons mayonnaise
1 tablespoon catsup
1 teaspoon prepared mustard
  Dash garlic powder
1 cup chopped, cooked, cleaned
  shrimp
¼ cup finely chopped celery
1 teaspoon finely chopped onion
8 to 10 slices lightly buttered
  white bread

Blend cheese with mayonnaise; mix in catsup,
mustard, and garlic powder. Stir in shrimp,
celery, and onion. Spread mixture between
bread slices. For tea sandwiches, use 10 slices;
for luncheon size, use 8 slices. Trim crusts,
if desired. Cut each tea sandwich diagonally
in 4 triangles; cut luncheon size in half.
Makes 4 luncheon or 20 tea sandwiches.

SHRIMP BOAT

3 cups cooked, cleaned shrimp
4 hard-cooked eggs, chopped
¾ cup diced celery
¼ cup sliced green onions
¼ cup chopped dill pickle
2 tablespoons drained capers
  (optional)
1 cup mayonnaise or salad dressing
2 tablespoons chili sauce
2 teaspoons prepared horseradish
1 unsliced loaf Vienna bread,
    about 11x5 inches
  Leaf lettuce
  Lemon slices and wedges

Reserve a few large shrimp for garnish; cut
up remainder. Combine cut-up shrimp and
next 5 ingredients. Blend mayonnaise, chili
sauce, horseradish, and ½ teaspoon salt. Add
to shrimp mixture; toss lightly. Chill. Cut a
wide deep wedge, lengthwise, out of bread.
Brush cut surfaces with 3 tablespoons butter,
melted. Place loaf on ungreased baking sheet;
toast at 350° for 15 minutes. Cool.

  Line bread "boat" with lettuce; mound
with salad. Trim with shrimp and lemon
slices. Pass lemon wedges. Slice loaf at table
and serve on dinner plates. Serves 6 to 8.

HOT TURKEY SANDWICHES

2 cups diced cooked turkey
½ cup finely chopped celery
⅔ cup cranberry-orange relish
½ cup mayonnaise or salad dressing
4 hamburger buns split,
  toasted, and buttered

Combine turkey, celery, ⅓ *cup* of the relish,
mayonnaise, ½ teaspoon salt, and dash pepper. Spread on buns. Top with rest of relish.
Bake at 350° about 10 minutes. Serves 8.

CHICKEN SWISS-WICHES

  Combine 1½ cups diced cooked chicken,
⅓ cup mayonnaise, ¼ cup diced celery, and
¼ cup diced process Swiss cheese. Spread
filling on 4 slices bread. Arrange one 14½-
ounce can asparagus spears, drained, atop
filling; top with 4 more slices bread. Melt ½
cup butter on griddle or in skillet; use to
brush on outside of sandwich. Coat sandwiches with one 2⅜-ounce package seasoned
coating mix for chicken. Brown sandwiches
on both sides in remaining butter. Serves 4.

Packaged seasoned coating mix adds
crunch to Chicken Swiss-wiches which
team chicken, asparagus, and cheese.

Plan a meal around hearty salads

TUNA IN PEPPER CUPS

    6 medium green peppers
    ¾ cup packaged precooked rice
    1 6½- or 7-ounce can tuna, drained
    ½ cup chopped celery
    2 tablespoons finely chopped onion
    2 tablespoons finely chopped
      canned pimiento
    ¾ cup mayonnaise or salad dressing
    ⅓ cup finely crushed potato chips

Cut peppers in half lengthwise; remove tops and seeds. Cook peppers in small amount boiling salted water 5 minutes; drain; lightly sprinkle insides with salt. Prepare rice according to package directions. Combine with tuna, celery, onion, and pimiento. Blend mayonnaise with ½ teaspoon salt and dash pepper; add to rice mixture and toss lightly. Spoon salad mixture into green pepper halves; sprinkle with potato chips. Place peppers in 10x6x1½-inch baking dish; pour about ⅓ cup water around peppers. Bake at 350° about 35 minutes. Makes 6 servings.

CREAMY TUNA RING

Soften ½ envelope (1½ teaspoons) unflavored gelatin in ⅓ cup cold water; stir over low heat till gelatin is dissolved. Beat one 12-ounce carton (1½ cups) cream-style cottage cheese slightly; stir in dissolved gelatin, ¼ cup chopped green pepper, 1 tablespoon finely chopped green onion, and ¼ teaspoon salt. Pour into a 5-cup ring mold. Chill till almost set.

Meanwhile, soften ½ envelope unflavored gelatin in 2 tablespoons cold water; dissolve gelatin over hot water.

Mix two 6½- or 7-ounce cans tuna, drained and flaked, ½ cup chopped celery, ¾ cup mayonnaise or salad dressing, and 1 tablespoon lemon juice; stir in dissolved gelatin. Spoon over cheese layer. Chill till firm. Unmold. Makes 6 servings.

TUNA SOUFFLE MOLD

    2 envelopes (2 tablespoons)
      unflavored gelatin
    2 cups cold water
    1 cup mayonnaise or salad dressing
    ½ cup chili sauce
    2 tablespoons lemon juice
    ¼ teaspoon salt
    2 6½- or 7-ounce cans tuna,
      drained and flaked
    1 cup chopped celery

Soften gelatin in *1 cup* of the cold water; stir over low heat till gelatin dissolves. Stir in remaining cold water. Combine mayonnaise, chili sauce, lemon juice, and salt. Stir in gelatin and beat till smooth with rotary beater. Chill till partially set.

Stir in tuna and celery. Pour into 6-cup mold; chill till firm. Unmold on crisp lettuce on platter. Serve with hard-cooked egg wedges, if desired. Makes 8 to 10 servings.

MEAT AND POTATO SALAD

    1 cup mayonnaise or salad dressing
    2 tablespoons vinegar
    2 teaspoons prepared mustard
    ½ teaspoon salt
      Dash pepper
    1 12-ounce can luncheon meat,
      chilled, cut in julienne strips
    4 cups cubed cooked potatoes
    1½ cups sliced celery
    ¼ cup chopped green onions
    ¼ cup thinly sliced radishes
    2 tablespoons snipped parsley
    3 hard-cooked eggs, cut in wedges

Combine mayonnaise, vinegar, mustard, salt, and pepper. Reserve small amount of meat strips for garnish. Add rest of meat and remaining ingredients, except eggs, to mayonnaise; toss lightly. Chill. Trim with egg wedges and reserved meat. Serves 6 to 8.

TUNA-BEAN SALAD

Rinse 1 cup dry navy beans; add to 3 cups cold water and soak overnight. Add 1 teaspoon salt to beans and soaking water. Cover and bring to a boil; reduce heat and simmer until tender, about 1 hour. Drain and chill.

In jar, combine ¼ cup olive oil, ¼ cup white wine vinegar, ½ teaspoon dry mustard, ½ teaspoon salt, and dash pepper; cover and shake well. Chill; shake thoroughly again just before using.

Combine chilled beans, one 6½-, 7-, or 9¼-ounce can tuna, drained and chilled, and 1 small red onion, thinly sliced and separated in rings. Drizzle with dressing; toss lightly. Sprinkle with 1 tablespoon snipped parsley. Makes 4 servings.

SAN MARINO BEEF SALAD

```
4  to 5 pounds beef short ribs
⅓  cup chopped carrot
⅓  cup chopped onion
¼  cup olive oil
¼  cup red wine vinegar
½  teaspoon dry mustard
½  teaspoon salt
   Dash cayenne
1  medium red onion
½  sweet red pepper
3  medium carrots
3  branches celery
2  tablespoons cut celery leaves
```

In large saucepan, cover first 3 ingredients with salted water. Bring to a boil. Cover and simmer till tender, about 1½ to 2 hours. Strip meat from bone and trim off fat. Cut meat in julienne strips (3 cups); chill.

In a jar, combine olive oil, wine vinegar, mustard, salt, and cayenne. Shake well; chill. Shake again before using. Slice onion and separate in rings. Cut pepper, carrots, and celery branches into julienne strips.

To serve, combine beef strips, onion rings, and the pepper, carrot, and celery strips. Toss with dressing. Sprinkle with cut celery leaves. Makes 4 servings.

Serve a salad meal

Tuna-bean Salad doubles as main dish or an appetizer. Below, strips of meat and vegetables make San Marino Beef Salad.

CHICKEN-CRANBERRY MOLD

1 envelope (1 tablespoon)
  unflavored gelatin
1 16-ounce can (2 cups) whole
  cranberry sauce
1 8¾-ounce can crushed
  pineapple, undrained
1 tablespoon lemon juice

. . .

1 envelope (1 tablespoon)
  unflavored gelatin
1½ cups chicken broth
1 cup mayonnaise or salad dressing
1 tablespoon lemon juice
¼ teaspoon salt
1½ cups diced cooked chicken
½ cup diced celery
2 tablespoons snipped parsley

To prepare cranberry layer, soften 1 envelope gelatin in ½ cup cold water; heat and stir over low heat till dissolved. Combine cranberry sauce, pineapple, and 1 tablespoon lemon juice. Add dissolved gelatin; mix well. Pour into 10x6x1½-inch baking dish; chill cranberry layer till almost firm.

Meanwhile, prepare chicken layer. Soften gelatin in chicken broth; heat and stir over low heat till gelatin is dissolved. Gradually stir into mayonnaise. Add lemon juice and salt. Chill till slightly thickened. Add remaining ingredients. Pour over cranberry layer; chill till firm. Cut in 6 to 8 squares; invert on lettuce. Garnish each with dollop of mayonnaise and walnut half, if desired.

FRUITED CHICKEN SALAD

3 cups cubed cooked chicken
1 cup diced celery
1 11-ounce can mandarin oranges,
  drained
1 8¾-ounce can pineapple
  tidbits, drained
½ cup toasted slivered almonds
¾ cup mayonnaise or salad dressing
½ teaspoon salt
⅛ teaspoon ground marjoram

Combine first 5 ingredients. Chill thoroughly. Blend together mayonnaise, salt, and marjoram. Add to chicken mixture. Toss together lightly to coat all ingredients. Serves 6.

GOLDEN CHICKEN SALAD

Cook, covered, 1 pound fresh asparagus in small amount boiling salted water till tender *or* cook one 10-ounce package frozen asparagus spears according to package directions; drain. Marinate in ¼ cup Italian salad dressing 2 hours in refrigerator, turning once. Combine ½ cup mayonnaise, 1 teaspoon lemon juice, ½ teaspoon ground turmeric, and 1 tablespoon snipped chives; set aside.

Mix 1½ cups diced cooked chicken, 2 hard-cooked eggs, chopped, ½ cup diced celery, and ½ teaspoon salt. Add mayonnaise mixture; toss lightly. Chill.

Arrange drained asparagus on individual lettuce leaves; top with chicken salad. Dash with paprika. Makes 4 servings.

CHICKEN SALAD

In mixing bowl, combine 2 cups cubed cooked chicken, 2 hard-cooked eggs, chopped, ½ cup finely diced celery, 3 tablespoons chopped sweet pickle, 2 tablespoons chopped canned pimiento, ½ cup mayonnaise or salad dressing, 2 tablespoons lemon juice, and ¼ teaspoon salt. Toss gently to blend. Serve on lettuce. Makes 4 or 5 servings.

TOKYO TURKEY TOSS

2 cups diced cooked turkey
1 16-ounce can (2 cups) bean
  sprouts, drained
1 cup cooked rice
1 cup chopped celery
1 cup coarsely shredded carrot
2 tablespoons chopped green pepper
¼ cup French salad dressing
2 tablespoons soy sauce
¼ teaspoon salt
½ cup mayonnaise or salad dressing
½ cup toasted slivered almonds

In large bowl, combine turkey, bean sprouts, cooked rice, celery, carrot, green pepper, French dressing, soy sauce, salt, and a dash pepper; mix well and chill. Just before serving, add mayonnaise and almonds; toss together lightly. Serve in lettuce cups; sprinkle each serving with additional toasted almonds, if desired. Makes 6 servings.

KING CRAB CROWN

1 envelope (1 tablespoon)
  unflavored gelatin
3 tablespoons cold water
2 tablespoons mayonnaise or salad
  dressing

. . .

¼ cup lemon juice
2 tablespoons finely snipped
  parsley
4 teaspoons finely snipped chives
1 tablespoon prepared mustard
¼ teaspoon salt
  Dash pepper
1 7½-ounce can crab meat,
  drained, flaked, and cartilage
  removed
1 cup whipping cream
  Unpeeled cucumber slices cut
    ¼-inch thick (optional)
  Lemon slices

Soften gelatin in cold water; dissolve over
hot water. Stir gelatin into mayonnaise.
Blend in lemon juice, parsley, chives, mustard, salt, and pepper. Fold in crab meat.
Whip cream; fold into salad. Turn salad into
3-cup mold. Chill till firm, at least 2 hours.
Unmold on chilled platter; garnish with
cucumber and lemon slices. Makes 6 servings.

SALMON-SALAD LOAF

1 3-ounce package lemon-flavored
  gelatin
1 cup boiling water
½ cup cold water
3 tablespoons vinegar
½ cup mayonnaise or salad dressing
¼ teaspoon salt

. . .

1 16-ounce can (2 cups) salmon,
  drained and coarsely flaked
1 cup diced celery
¼ cup snipped parsley
2 tablespoons finely chopped onion

Dissolve gelatin in boiling water. Add cold
water, vinegar, mayonnaise or salad dressing,
and salt. Beat well; chill till partially set.
Beat till fluffy; fold in salmon, celery, parsley,
and onion. Pour into 8½x4½x2½-inch loaf
dish. Chill till set; unmold. Makes 6 servings.

LOBSTER SALAD

1 5-ounce can lobster, drained and
  flaked
2 tablespoons lemon juice
¾ cup sliced celery
⅓ cup mayonnaise or salad dressing
¼ teaspoon salt
2 avocados, peeled and halved
  Lemon juice

Sprinkle lobster with 2 tablespoons lemon
juice. Add celery, mayonnaise, salt, and dash
pepper. Mix lightly; chill thoroughly. Brush
avocados with lemon juice; mound lobster
salad atop avocados. Makes 4 servings.

SHRIMP-AVOCADO BOWLS

Among 6 individual salad bowls, divide 1
small head lettuce, torn in bite-size pieces
(4 cups) and ½ head curly endive, torn in
bite-size pieces (4 cups). Hard cook 6 eggs;
peel and slice. Divide among the salad bowls
3 cups cooked, cleaned shrimp, hard-cooked
eggs, and 2 avocados, sliced. Pass clear or
creamy French salad dressing. Serves 6.

SHRIMP-CUCUMBER RING

2 envelopes (2 tablespoons)
  unflavored gelatin
½ cup cold water
3 vegetable bouillon cubes
2 cups boiling water
¾ cup mayonnaise or salad dressing
2 tablespoons lemon juice

. . .

1½ cups cooked, cleaned shrimp,
  sliced
¾ cup shredded cucumber
¼ cup sliced green onion
1 cup whipping cream, whipped

Soften gelatin in cold water; dissolve gelatin and bouillon cubes in boiling water.
Blend in mayonnaise and lemon juice. Chill
till partially set; then whip till light and
fluffy. Fold in shrimp, cucumber, green onion,
and whipped cream. Turn gelatin mixture
into 6½-cup ring mold; chill till firm.

Unmold on large plate; garnish with watercress and whole shrimp, if desired. Serves 8.

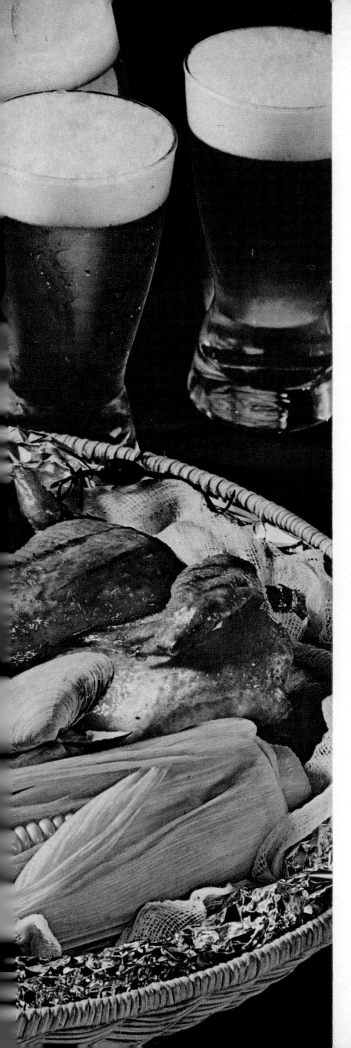

FOOD FUN
WITH
ACTION-MEALS

Be inventive when planning a party and let everyone join in the food preparation. Keep guests active and they'll long remember the party as a fun-filled event. Serve outdoors, weather permitting, if that is where the food is prepared. It can be near a bubbling stream where fresh fish are caught and fried over a campfire. Try a clambake on the beach or stay right in the backyard for a barbecue or chuck wagon dinner. Move indoors, if desired, to serve an appetizer buffet or Hawaiian luau. Keep table and area decorations simple.

Individual Clambake features a heaping plate of lobster, clams in shells, chicken half, and corn on the cob. Plan cold, juicy watermelon for dessert.

Clambake for everyone

OLD-FASHIONED CLAMBAKE

The traditional New England clambake is cooked in a pit on the beach. A roaring fire, built onto rocks which line the shallow pit, is allowed to burn till the rocks are red hot. Then the ashes are raked to the sides and a layer of wet rockweed, about 4 inches thick, is tossed atop the hot rocks. When this is done, the pit is ready for the long, slow cooking.

Place clams and lobsters on the steaming mass of rockweed. Precooked chicken and corn in husks, both wrapped in foil, can then be placed atop the seafood. A thicker layer of rockweed is placed on top of the food to create steam for flavor. This is all covered with wet burlap bags or canvas. To hold in the heat, sand is shoveled on top of the bags. Allow several hours for the clambake to steam and be ready to eat; meanwhile, enjoy the party.

MODERN CLAMBAKE

With the fast modern pace, several new methods have replaced the old-fashioned clambake. The fastest and easiest method is to cook each food separately; however, the steamed flavor of the rockweed is thus lost. To obtain this flavor, another way is to layer the food in one large container similar to the layering of the food for the old-fashioned clambake. For small crowds this is a fun and different method for preparing a clambake.

PARTY ATMOSPHERE

Whichever method you choose, the purpose of the party is a social gathering. Plenty of story-swapping, group singing, and general conversation should be the rule. Make the party informal with plenty of food available. Set the table using only paper service. Plan on 4 plastic-coated paper plates for each person, for with this quantity of food each item should have a plate. Large paper napkins, too, will be needed, for much of the eating will be done with the fingers. Use paper cups —hot cups for clam broth and melted butter, cold cups for beverage. Then relax and have fun at the clambake.

❊MENU❊

INLAND-STYLE CLAMBAKE
Steamed Clams   *Clam Liquor*
Whole Lobster   *Melted Butter*
Grilled Chicken
Corn in Husks
Watermelon
Coffee   *Beer*

Preparation tips

If a beach is not within immediate reach, do not despair. An outdoor-inland clambake on the grill can be just as much fun, whether the food is cooked individually on the grill, or lobster, clams, chicken, and corn are wrapped together in foil for an Individual Clambake.

When purchasing clams for a clambake, order small soft-shell clams in the shells, usually called steamers. They are sold by the dozen or by the pound. Make sure they are alive when purchased. A gaping shell that does not close or contract when the clam is touched indicates that the clam is dead.

To eat cooked clams, remove clam from shell which has opened during cooking. Pull off black neck cover. Dip clams into clam liquor (the water in which the clams were steamed) to remove any sand that might be present. Then dip clams into melted butter and enjoy good eating. When serving individual clambakes, the clams are soaked in salted water to remove sand before cooking.

Individual clambakes wrapped in foil and flavored with rockweed are great for guests who have the excitement and fun of opening a steaming package full of delicious morsels. If this doesn't appeal, cook the traditional clams, lobsters, chickens, and corn over the fire and let each guest sample a little of each. (For Steamed Clams, see Index.) The food will be enjoyed by all.

INDIVIDUAL CLAMBAKE

        48 soft-shelled clams, in shells
        8 live whole lobsters
        4 2- to 2½-pound ready-to-cook
           broiler-fryer chickens, halved
        ½ cup butter or margarine, melted
        8 whole ears of corn
           Rockweed
        1 pound butter, melted

Thoroughly wash clams in shells. Cover with salt water (⅓ cup salt to 1 gallon water); let stand 15 minutes. Rinse; repeat twice. Rinse off lobsters with salt water. For chickens, break joints of drumstick, hip, and wing so birds will stay flat. Brush chickens with ½ cup melted butter; broil over *hot* coals, skin side down for about 5 minutes. Turn back husks of corn and strip off silk with a stiff brush. Lay husks back in position.

Tear off 3-foot lengths of 18-inch wide heavy foil. Place 1 sheet crosswise over another sheet. Repeat making total of 8 individual packages. Lay a handful of rockweed in center of each package. Cut eight 18-inch squares cheesecloth; place 1 square atop rockweed in each package.

For each package arrange the following: 6 live clams in shells, 1 live lobster, 1 precooked chicken half, and 1 ear of corn. Securely tie cheesecloth, opposite ends together. Seal the foil, opposite ends together, using the drugstore wrap. Place on grill, seam side up, over *hot* coals and cook for 45 minutes. To test for doneness, the chicken drumstick should move up and down easily in socket. When the chicken is done, the clambake is ready. Serve with individual cups of hot melted butter. Serves 8.

GRILLED CHICKEN

Cut four 2- to 2½-pound ready-to-cook broiler-fryer chickens in half lengthwise. Break joints of drumstick, hip, and wings so birds will stay flat during cooking. Brush chickens with ½ cup melted butter or salad oil. Season with salt and pepper. Broil over *slow* coals, bone side down, for 20 to 30 minutes. Turn and cook 20 to 30 minutes longer, brushing with butter occasionally.

To test for doneness, the drumstick should move up and down and twist easily in socket. The thickest parts should feel very soft.

LOBSTER OVER-THE-COALS

        8 frozen lobster tails (about 6
           ounces each), thawed
        4 lemons, halved crosswise
           Melted butter

With scissors, cut away thin underside membrane of lobster tails by cutting down each side. Remove thin membrane. Thread lobster tails lengthwise on skewers alternately with lemon halves. Brush lobster meat with some of the melted butter. Broil, meat side up, over *hot* coals for 10 minutes, brushing occasionally with more butter. Turn and broil about 20 minutes longer, or till lobster is cooked through. Brush occasionally with remaining butter. Remove lobster and lemon from skewers; serve with hot lemon halves. Serves 8.

FRESH CORN ON THE COB

Remove husks from fresh corn. With a stiff brush, remove silk. Place each ear on a piece of foil. Spread corn liberally with softened butter or margarine and sprinkle generously with salt and pepper.

Wrap foil securely around each ear of corn —don't seal seam, but fold or twist foil around ends (that way corn will roast instead of steam). Place corn on grill and roast over *hot* coals 15 to 20 minutes or till corn is tender, turning ears frequently. Serve with softened butter, salt, and freshly ground pepper; or, pass Herb Butter (see recipe below).

GRILLED CORN ON THE COB

Turn back husks and strip off silk. Lay husks back in position. Place ears on grill over *hot* coals; roast, turning frequently, for 15 to 20 minutes or till husks are dry and browned. (A longer roasting time will give sweeter, more caramelized corn.) Serve with butter.

HERB BUTTER

To ½ cup softened butter or margarine, add ½ teaspoon dried rosemary, crushed, and ½ teaspoon dried marjoram, crushed. Blend herbs into butter till light and fluffy. Serve with corn on the cob. Makes ½ cup.

Barbecue is hot coals and sizzling juices

Preparing the coals

• A foil-lined firebox or ashpit reflects heat to speed cooking, catches fat and drippings, and keeps barbecue unit looking new.
• A bed of coarse gravel 1 inch deep helps prevent the firebox from burning out and aids even air and heat distribution.
• The amount of charcoal needed varies with food being cooked and equipment used. Heap charcoal in a pyramid in the firebox.
• Soak charcoal with liquid lighter (do not use gasoline or kerosene) and let stand a few minutes before lighting.
• Allow 45 minutes for coals to burn down. Cooking coals look ash-gray by day and have a red glow after dark. *No flames.* Don't start cooking too soon. A too hot fire dries out meat.
• To estimate heat, hold *palm* of hand over coals at height food will be cooking. Count "one thousand one, one thousand two," and so on. The number of seconds the hand can comfortably be held over the fire will indicate how hot the fire is. "One thousand one" or "two" is a relatively hot fire, good for steaks, burgers, and kabobs. "One thousand three" or "four" is a moderate fire for roasts, and "one thousand five" or "six" is a slow fire for pork chops and spareribs.

Kabobs

Select quick-cooking foods such as lamb, tender steak, fully-cooked ham, franks, green pepper squares, mushrooms, tiny tomatoes, canned potatoes, canned onions, fresh or canned pineapple. For cuts of meat that are not tender, use marinades or meat tenderizer.

When different kinds of food share the same skewer, choose only those that cook in the same length of time. Leave space between pieces so heat reaches all surfaces. Brush vegetables with melted butter during cooking. Baste meats often with marinades. Sauces go on near end of cooking. Cook kabobs over *hot* coals so food stays moist, yet browns well.

❊MENU❊

PATIO DINNER
Lamb Kabobs
Fluffy Rice
Western Salad   French Dressing
Homemade Bread   Butter
Chocolate Cake
Rosé Wine
Coffee

LAMB KABOBS

In mixing bowl, combine 1 cup rosé wine, $\frac{1}{2}$ cup orange juice, $\frac{1}{2}$ cup finely chopped onion, $\frac{1}{4}$ cup chili sauce, $\frac{1}{4}$ cup salad oil, 1 clove garlic, minced, 1 tablespoon brown sugar, 1 teaspoon salt, 1 teaspoon dried oregano, crushed, and $\frac{1}{4}$ teaspoon pepper. Place 2 pounds boneless lamb, cut in 2-inch cubes, in a bowl. Pour wine mixture over lamb. Cover; marinate lamb for 2 hours at room temperature or overnight in refrigerator. Drain lamb, reserving marinade.

In small saucepan, pour boiling water over 12 fresh whole mushrooms (5-ounce carton); let mushrooms stand for 2 minutes. Drain. Cut 2 green peppers into $1\frac{1}{2}$-inch squares. Thread lamb cubes, green pepper squares, and mushrooms alternately on skewers. Broil 4 to 6 inches from heat for 25 to 30 minutes, turning skewers frequently and brushing with reserved marinade. Makes 6 servings.

On the patio

Appetites build as Lamb Kabobs cook on —) the grill. Serve with Western Salad—lettuce, avocado, melon balls, and bacon.

CUTS TO BARBECUE

In general, all roasts and steaks which are tender enough for oven roasting or broiling may be cooked over charcoal too. Cuts usually classified as less tender barbecue satisfactorily when marinades or meat tenderizers are used properly. In some areas of the country, the availability of pre-tendered beef increases the number of cuts for barbecuing.

Steaks and chops should be cut at least 1-inch thick for cooking directly over the coals. Thinner cuts may be "panbroiled" on heavy foil. To test doneness, cut a small slit in the meat and check the color inside.

Hamburgers, frankfurters, smoked sausage links, and fully-cooked specialty sausages are good for grilling. Chicken halves or quarters are also popular for the grill.

Roasts for the rotisserie are usually boneless, but a bone-in rib of beef, lamb, or pork and loin roasts can be balanced on a spit. A well-tied canned ham or piece of Canadian-style bacon are easy to barbecue. Chickens and small turkeys are rotisserie favorites.

GOURMET HAMBURGERS

¼ pound liver sausage or braunschweiger (½ cup)
1 beaten egg
1 pound ground beef
¼ cup fine dry bread crumbs
¼ cup catsup
2 tablespoons *dry* onion soup mix

Blend liver sausage and egg. Add remaining ingredients; mix till blended. Shape mixture into 4 patties about ½ inch thick. Broil over *medium* coals 5 minutes. Turn and broil 5 minutes longer. Makes 4 servings.

SMOKED LINKBURGERS

Combine 1 pound ground beef, 1 tablespoon brown sugar, 1 tablespoon finely chopped onion, 1 tablespoon lemon juice, ½ teaspoon salt, and dash pepper and mix thoroughly. Divide into 8 portions. Using one 12-ounce package (8) smoked sausage links, mold ground meat around each link. Grill over *medium* coals for 18 to 20 minutes, turning frequently. Makes 8 servings.

COUNTRY-STYLE RIBS

4 pounds country-style pork ribs, cut in serving-size pieces
1 tablespoon butter or margarine
1 clove garlic, crushed
• • •
½ cup catsup
⅓ cup chili sauce
2 tablespoons brown sugar
2 tablespoons chopped onion
1 tablespoon Worcestershire sauce
1 tablespoon prepared mustard
1 teaspoon celery seed
¼ teaspoon salt
   Dash bottled hot pepper sauce
3 thin lemon slices

Simmer ribs, covered, in salted water to cover, about 1 hour. In saucepan, melt butter; add garlic and cook 5 minutes. Add catsup, chili sauce, brown sugar, onion, Worcestershire sauce, mustard, celery seed, salt, bottled hot pepper sauce, and lemon slices. Bring to boil. Drain ribs. Grill over *medium* coals about 10 minutes on each side, brushing often with sauce till well coated. (If ribs are chilled before grilling, cook 15 to 18 minutes on each side.) Makes 6 to 8 servings.

GRILLED HAM SLICE

½   cup grape jelly
2   tablespoons prepared mustard
1½ teaspoons lemon juice
⅛   teaspoon ground cinnamon
• • •
1   fully-cooked center-cut ham slice, cut 1 inch thick (about 1½ pounds)

In a saucepan, combine jelly, mustard, lemon juice, and cinnamon. Heat till jelly melts.

Slash fat edge of ham slice. Pour sauce over ham in a shallow dish. Refrigerate overnight or let stand at room temperature for 2 hours, spooning sauce over ham several times. Remove ham, reserving marinade.

Broil ham over *low* coals 5 minutes on each side. Brush one side of ham with marinade; turn. Broil brushed side 3 minutes. Repeat with other side, broiling 3 minutes longer. Heat remaining marinade on edge of grill. Serve with ham. Makes 6 servings.

BASIC BARBECUE SAUCE

Combine one 12-ounce bottle extra-hot catsup, 3 tablespoons vinegar, 2 teaspoons celery seed, and 1 clove garlic, halved. Chill. Remove garlic before using. Makes 1¼ cups.

BURGUNDY SAUCE

Combine ½ cup *each* salad oil and Burgundy *or* claret, 2 tablespoons *each* catsup, molasses, and finely snipped candied ginger, 1 large clove garlic, minced, and ½ teaspoon *each* curry powder, salt, and pepper. Use as marinade and basting sauce. Makes 1 cup.

ARMENIAN MARINADE

Combine ½ cup *each* salad oil and chopped onion, ¼ cup *each* snipped parsley and lemon juice, 1 teaspoon *each* dried marjoram, crushed, dried thyme, crushed, and salt, ½ teaspoon pepper, and 1 clove garlic, minced. Use for marinade and basting. Makes 1 cup.

MARINADE ITALIANO

Thoroughly combine ½ cup Italian salad dressing, ¼ cup lemon juice, 1 teaspoon dried oregano, crushed, ¼ teaspoon salt, and ⅛ teaspoon pepper. Use as marinade and basting sauce. Makes about ¾ cup.

CORNED BEEF 'N CABBAGE

    8 cups shredded cabbage (1
      medium head)
    2 cups shredded carrot (4 medium
      carrots)
    ¼ cup *dry* onion soup mix
    2 tablespoons butter or margarine
    1 12-ounce can corned beef, cut
      in 4 slices

Toss together cabbage, carrot, and soup mix. Divide into 4 portions. Center each portion on 12-inch square of heavy foil. Dot with butter. Top each with slice of corned beef. Close foil and seal well, allowing room for steam. Grill over *medium* coals for about 10 minutes; turn foil packages once. Serves 4.

ROTISSERIE ROASTS

Slip one of the holding forks onto spit rod. Push rod through center of roast, inserting tines of fork firmly into meat. Push in second holding fork; fasten. Test balance of roast by cradling ends of rod in upturned hands and rotating roast. If it twirls evenly, it balances; if not, meat is off center—remount and test again or add counterbalances to adjust weight. Tighten fork screws with pliers. Insert meat thermometer so tip is in center of roast, not touching fat, bone, or metal spit.

Arrange hot coals at back of firebox and place drip pan in front, under roast. Knock gray ash from coals. Attach spit, turn on motor and cook till meat is desired doneness. See Index for meat (beef, veal, pork, or lamb) roasting charts. A meat thermometer is the only trusty guide to doneness of rotisserie cooked roasts because roasting time will vary with diameter of roast and heat of coals.

Meat may be basted with marinade or favorite herbs mixed with 2 tablespoons salad oil. (See Index for Meat Seasoning Guide.) Very sweet or tomato barbecue sauces should be brushed on roast only during last 30 minutes cooking time. They turn dark with prolonged heating making them less desirable.

BARBECUED CHUCK ROAST

    1 3-pound chuck roast, 1½ to 2
      inches thick
    1 teaspoon monosodium glutamate
    ⅓ cup wine vinegar
    ¼ cup catsup
    2 tablespoons salad oil
    2 tablespoons soy sauce
    1 tablespoon Worcestershire sauce
    1 teaspoon prepared mustard
    1 teaspoon salt
    ¼ teaspoon pepper
    ¼ teaspoon garlic powder

Sprinkle both sides of roast with monosodium glutamate. Place roast in a shallow baking dish. Thoroughly combine remaining ingredients. Pour barbecue mixture over roast and marinate 2 to 3 hours, turning twice. Place meat on grill about 6 inches from heat. Turn and baste with marinade every 10 to 15 minutes. Grill over *medium* coals about 35 to 45 minutes for medium-rare roast. Serves 6 to 8.

Fish fry over a blazing campfire

FROM STREAM TO SKILLET

Seeing the day's catch sizzling in the skillet over the blazing campfire is the pride of the true fisherman. Outdoor cooking presents the star of the catch at the peak of freshness. One can hardly find a faster, more direct route for food than from mountain stream to skillet. And it's not possible to find fish that taste better or that create greater excitement.

MOUNTAIN RAINBOW TROUT

    ⅔ cup yellow cornmeal
    ¼ cup all-purpose flour
    ½ teaspoon paprika
    6 large fresh or frozen trout
      Shortening

Combine cornmeal, flour, 2 teaspoons salt, and paprika; use to coat fish. In skillet, heat a little shortening over hot coals until both skillet and shortening are hot. Cook fish till lightly browned, about 4 minutes on each side. Fish is done when it flakes easily with fork. (Do not overcook.) Makes 6 servings.

SESAME RAINBOW TROUT

    6 whole rainbow trout
      Salt and pepper
    ½ cup salad oil
    ¼ cup sesame seed, toasted
    ¼ cup lemon juice
    3 lemons

Season inside of fish. Combine oil, sesame seed, lemon juice, 1 teaspoon salt, and dash pepper; mix well. Place fish in well-greased, hinged wire basket. Brush fish inside and out with sauce; close basket. Cook over *medium hot coals* for 5 to 8 minutes. Repeat brushing. Turn; cook 5 to 8 minutes longer or till fish flakes easily when tested with a fork. Serve with lemon wedges. Makes 6 servings.

❋MENU❋

FISHERMAN'S CATCH
Mountain Rainbow Trout
Baked Potatoes   *Butter*
Grill-top Tomatoes
Relish Tray
Fresh Fruit   *Brownies*
Coffee

Preparation tips

The best guarantee of happy camp cooking is "common sense" planning in advance. *Be a list maker.* Make a list for food and a list for utensils. Check each item off as you pack.

Pack extras of disposable items such as napkins, paper toweling, plastic wrap, and foil.

Use clear plastic bags to hold pre-measured ingredients for individual recipes. Attach recipe to outside of each bag. When mealtime arrives, just hand every family member a bag with instructions attached.

Use moistureproof containers to store food. Place food in cooler or ice chest. Avoid having to store leftovers.

Add an outdoor flavor to vegetables by heating over hot coals. Try brushing cut surfaces of tomato halves with Italian salad dressing, then season. Heat on foil over coals.

Bake-ahead cookies served with fresh fruit will double as a dessert and a snack.

Outdoor fish fare

Mountain Rainbow Trout sizzling over fire will tempt outdoor fans. Serve with foil-wrapped potatoes cooked over coals.

Chuck wagon full of western favorites

PLAN EASY TO SERVE FOODS

"Yippee-yi-yay"—it's chuck wagon fare for downright good eating served either in the backyard or out by a roaring campfire. Table setting takes care of itself as hungry family members arrive. Keep accompaniments simple. Toss salad with dressing at the last minute. Serve corn bread either hot or cold. Pack hot foods separately from cold foods.

TEXAS-STYLE BEANS

      2 cups pinto beans
    ¼ pound salt pork, diced (1 cup)
      1 cup chopped onion
      1 clove garlic, minced
      2 teaspoons salt
        Dash pepper
      2 16-ounce cans tomatoes, cut up
    ¾ cup diced green pepper
      1 tablespoon sugar
      6 drops bottled hot pepper sauce

In 2-quart bean pot or casserole, cover beans with water; soak overnight. *Do not drain.* Add salt pork, onion, garlic, salt, and pepper. Simmer beans, covered, for 2 hours. Add tomatoes, diced green pepper, sugar, and bottled hot pepper sauce; simmer, covered, for 3 hours more. Serve beans atop corn bread squares. Makes 8 to 10 servings.

CORN BREAD

In mixing bowl, sift together 1 cup sifted all-purpose flour, ¼ cup sugar, 4 teaspoons baking powder, and ¾ teaspoon salt; stir in 1 cup yellow corn meal. Add 1 cup milk, 2 eggs, and ¼ cup shortening; beat with rotary or electric beater just till smooth, about 1 minute. (Do not overbeat.) Pour into greased 9x9x2-inch pan. Bake in hot oven (425°) for 20 to 25 minutes. Cut in squares to serve. Makes 8 to 10 servings.

❊MENU❊

COWBOYS' SPECIAL
Ranch Round Steak
Texas-style Beans
Crisp Tossed Salad   Vinegar and Oil
Corn Bread   Butter
Apple Pie with Ice Cream
Coffee

RANCH ROUND STEAK

      3 pounds beef round steak, ½ inch
        thick, cut in serving-size pieces
    ¼ cup all-purpose flour
      2 teaspoons dry mustard
    ¼ cup salad oil
      1 tablespoon Worcestershire sauce

Trim excess fat from meat; slash edges to prevent curling. Combine flour, dry mustard, 1½ teaspoons salt, and ⅛ teaspoon pepper; use to coat meat. Reserve remaining mixture.

In skillet, brown meat, half at a time, on both sides in hot oil. Push meat to one side. Stir in reserved flour mixture. Combine ½ cup water and Worcestershire sauce; stir into skillet. Cook and stir till thickened and bubbly; reduce heat. Simmer meat in gravy, covered, for 1 to 1¼ hours or till tender. Remove meat to warm serving platter. Skim excess fat from gravy; drizzle gravy over meat or, if desired, pass with meat. Makes 8 servings.

Hearty outdoor eating

Round up hungry appetites for a savory →
chuck wagon meal of Ranch Round Steak with Texas-style Beans and Corn Bread.

American-style luau

SETTING THE SCENE

Bring the Islands to the mainland and have a Hawaiian luau. It's a fun way to entertain and creates an informal atmosphere. Since the food and decorations will be informal, have the guests dress informally. For the women (wahines), it's muumuus or sarongs; for the men (kanes), it's brightly printed sport shirts. Have flowers to put in the ladies' hair, and welcome each guest with a lei to go around his neck. Make your own leis out of fresh or paper flowers, or buy inexpensive paper leis. Use available flowers from the garden or florist if the Hawaiian hibiscus, plumeria, and orchids are not available.

Plan the party to be outdoors on the patio (indoors if weather does not cooperate). Set the scene by draping fishnet (badminton or tennis nets can be used) around the area on walls. Scatter seashells or coral pieces on the net. Travel posters and maps of Hawaii also make good backgrounds. If the feast is outdoors, stick torches in the lawn and use candles or hurricane lamps on the table.

The table itself can be as elaborate or as simple as desired. The Hawaiian way would be to spread straw mats on the ground or floor and let guests sit on cushions or mats around the "table." This is for the young and agile. It may be more comfortable for guests to sit around a large table that has been covered with fishnet, matting, rough-textured fabric, or paper that resembles "tapa" cloth. Straw or bamboo mats or individual place mats made from ferns will also do.

Use wooden bowls and platters, hollowed-out coconut shells, or seashells for serving dishes. Straw baskets are also handy. Decorate food platters with fresh flowers and greens. Typically, food is eaten with the fingers off the ti leaves, but guests will probably feel more comfortable with plates and flatware.

Seashells and flowers or potted plants can be combined with fresh tropical fruits—pineapples, bananas, papayas, mangoes, coconuts, limes, etc.—for the table centerpiece.

Play Hawaiian records for background music during the party and guests will think they've visited the Islands at evening's end.

❈MENU❈

HAWAIIAN PARTY
Tropical Fruit Cocktail
Roast Pork Loin   *Pineapple Sauce*
Sweet Potatoes   *Green Beans*
Honey-baked Bananas
Coconut Cake with Ice Cream
Fruit Punch   *Coffee*

Preparation tips

Typically, a whole roast suckling pig is served at a luau. It is cooked in an *imu* (underground oven). The Hawaiian way is to fill the pig with hot rocks, then place it in a large pit, cover with hot rocks, and surround with wet leaves, burlap, and canvas (tapa cloth originally was used). It is then covered with dirt and allowed to steam and smoke for many hours. The Roast Pork Loin may be substituted for the pig. It is a much easier version and still keeps pork in the menu. A fish dish, such as lomilomi salmon, also can be served.

Decorate the fruit punch and punch table with fresh or waxed flowers and fresh fruit.

Accompany the pork roast with baked sweet potatoes. To prepare, scrub sweet potatoes; bake at 325° for 1¼ to 1½ hours. Pass butter.

To give the luau an authentic touch, serve small bowls of poi to guests with the main course. It's made from taro root and is allowed to ferment. Buy it by the jar; it's to be eaten with the fingers.

The coconut cake for dessert can be a white cake iced with Seven-minute Frosting and topped with freshly shredded coconut. If desired, use lemon filling between layers.

If finger foods are included in the menu, it's a nice idea to have finger bowls and float a fresh flower along with a lemon slice in each bowl. Remember also to have plenty of paper napkins on hand.

To make the Hawaiian luau easy and relaxed, serve
the food buffet-style. Arrange Honey-baked Bananas
on ti leaves around fruit-topped Roast Pork Loin.

FRUIT PUNCH

1   46-ounce can (about 6 cups) red
    Hawaiian fruit punch
1   6-ounce can frozen pink
    lemonade concentrate, thawed
1   6-ounce can frozen orange juice
    concentrate, thawed
1   6-ounce can frozen pineapple
    juice concentrate, thawed
6   cups cold water
              .   .   .
1   1-pint 12-ounce bottle (3½ cups)
    ginger ale, chilled

Combine Hawaiian fruit punch, fruit juice
concentrates, and water. Pour over ice in a
large punch bowl. Resting bottle on rim of
bowl, carefully pour ginger ale down side.
Mix gently with up-and-down motion. Trim
with fresh fruit slices. Makes 30 servings.

ROAST PORK LOIN

Place a pork loin on rack in shallow roasting pan. Roast, uncovered, at 325° till meat
thermometer registers 170°. Plan on 2½ to 3
hours for a 3- to 5-pound roast; 3½ to 4¼
hours for a 5- to 7-pound roast.

Heat together one 12-ounce jar pineapple
preserves and ⅓ cup horseradish mustard.
Brush small amount on roast during last 15
minutes of roasting. Pass remaining sauce.
Allow 3 to 4 servings per pound of meat.

HONEY-BAKED BANANAS

Peel 6 bananas, halve, and place in shallow
baking dish. Mix 2 tablespoons *each* butter,
melted, and lemon juice; add ¼ cup honey.
Brush on bananas; bake at 325° for 15 minutes, turning occasionally. Makes 12 servings.

Evening appetizer buffet

PARTY TIPS

An appetizer buffet is a perfect way to get the evening off to a good start. Set up a large, easily accessible table with a seasonal centerpiece. Choose some hot and some cold appetizers, and some that are crisp and some that are soft. Keep foods hot over candle warmers or on hot trays. Have small plates and cocktail-size napkins on hand.

FANCY FRANKS

In small skillet or saucepan, combine ½ cup chili sauce, ½ cup currant jelly, 1½ tablespoons lemon juice, and 1½ teaspoons prepared mustard. Add two 7-ounce packages cocktail franks and one 13½-ounce can pineapple chunks, drained. Simmer together 15 minutes. Serve warm with cocktail picks.

DEVILED DIP

1 5-ounce jar process cheese spread with pimiento
1 4½-ounce can deviled ham
½ cup mayonnaise or salad dressing
2 tablespoons snipped parsley
1 tablespoon minced onion
4 drops bottled hot pepper sauce

With electric or rotary beater, thoroughly combine cheese spread, deviled ham, mayonnaise, parsley, onion, and bottled hot pepper sauce. Chill. Serve with assorted crackers or potato chips. Makes about 1¾ cups.

ARTICHOKE-HAM BITES

Drain one 15-ounce can artichoke hearts. Cut hearts in half. Marinate in ½ cup garlic Italian salad dressing several hours; drain. Cut one 6-ounce package fully-cooked smoked sliced ham in 1½-inch strips. Wrap 1 strip around each artichoke half. Spear with cocktail pick. Bake in slow oven (300°) for about 10 minutes, or till heated through.

MENU

SERVE-YOURSELF APPETIZERS
Meat Appetizers
Chips with Dips
Cheese and Crackers
Crisp Vegetable Nibblers
Beverages

CLAM COCKTAIL DUNK

2 3-ounce packages cream cheese, softened
2 teaspoons lemon juice
3 drops onion juice
1 teaspoon Worcestershire sauce
3 drops bottled hot pepper sauce
1 7½-ounce can minced clams, chilled and drained
1 tablespoon snipped parsley

With electric or rotary beater, combine first 5 ingredients and ¼ teaspoon salt. Beat till fluffy. Stir in clams and snipped parsley. Serve with assorted crackers or crisp relishes. Makes 1¼ cups.

POLKA-DOT PINWHEELS

Have bakery cut 1 loaf unsliced white bread into lengthwise slices about ¼ inch thick. Trim off crusts from 4 slices bread*. Spread with softened butter or margarine. Combine one 4¾-ounce can chicken spread, 2 tablespoons mashed pimiento, and ¼ teaspoon curry powder. Spread each slice of buttered bread with about 3 tablespoons filling. Place 5 thin green pepper strips, equal distance apart, on filling, crosswise on each slice.

Roll up, beginning at narrow end. Wrap in foil or clear plastic wrap; chill. Slice into ⅜-inch pinwheels. Makes about 20.

*To use whole loaf bread, double filling.

SPICY BEEF DIP

1 pound ground beef
½ cup chopped onion
1 clove garlic, minced
1 8-ounce can (1 cup) tomato
  sauce
¼ cup catsup
1 teaspoon sugar
¾ teaspoon dried oregano, crushed
1 8-ounce package cream cheese,
  softened
⅓ cup grated Parmesan cheese

Cook first 3 ingredients in skillet till meat is lightly browned and onion is tender. Stir in next 4 ingredients. Cover; simmer gently for 10 minutes. Spoon off excess fat. Remove from heat. Add cheeses. Heat and stir till cream cheese is melted and well combined. Keep warm in chafing dish or buffet server and serve with crackers. Makes 3 cups.

SHRIMP IN JACKETS

Thaw 1 pound frozen medium, shelled shrimp. Sprinkle with ½ teaspoon garlic *or* onion salt. Cut ¾ pound bacon (about 15 slices) in thirds. Wrap each shrimp in ⅓ slice bacon. Arrange on broiler rack. Broil 3 to 4 inches from heat just till bacon is crisp and browned, 8 to 10 minutes; turn occasionally. Serve on cocktail picks. Makes about 40.

SPICED CRANBERRY DRINK

6 whole cloves
6 inches stick cinnamon
4 whole cardamom, shelled
4 cups cranberry juice cocktail
1 cup light raisins
¼ cup sugar
2 cups port wine

Tie spices in cheesecloth bag; place in saucepan. Add *2 cups* of the cranberry cocktail, raisins, and sugar; bring to boiling. Simmer, uncovered, for 10 minutes. Remove spice bag. Before serving, add remaining cranberry cocktail and wine. Heat almost to boiling. Pour into heat-proof serving pitcher or bowl. Serve in mugs or punch cups, adding a few of the raisins to each. Makes about 6 cups.

EDAM SAGE SPREAD

1 whole Edam cheese, about 8
  ounces
1 cup dairy sour cream
1 teaspoon ground sage
  Dash onion powder

Have cheese at room temperature. Using a sawtooth cut, remove top of whole Edam cheese. Carefully scoop out cheese, leaving a thin shell. Finely chop cheese; mix with sour cream, sage, and onion powder. Spoon into cheese shell; chill thoroughly. Arrange on tray with assorted crackers. Makes about 2 cups Edam cheese spread.

An appetizer buffet features Spicy Beef Dip and Shrimp in Jackets with Edam Sage Spread and Spiced Cranberry Drink.

INDEX

A-B

Amber Skillet Dinner, 40
Appetizer Buffet,
  Evening, 156-157
Appetizers, 156-157
Apple-beef Patties, 66
Au Jus, 6
Bacon, 37
  Canadian-style, 37
  Liver Bake, and, 72
  -macaroni Bake, 37
Bananas, Honey-
  baked, 155
Barbecue, 146-149
Barbecue, Cuts to, 148
Barbecue Pork Chops, 40
Barbecued
  Chuck Roast, 149
  Frankfurters, 122
  Lamb Riblets, 58
  Short Ribs, 16
  Spareribs, 42
  Veal, 30
Basic Bone Identification
  Chart, 108
Beans, Texas-style, 152
Beef
  Bones, Deviled, 23
  Brown Meat, To, 21
  Cartwheel, Dilly, 134
  Chateaubriand, 6
  Cuts, 8-10
  Fondue, 12
  Ground
    Cabbage Rolls,
      Savory, 70
    Cheeseburger Pie, 130
    Chili-burger Stack-
      ups, 71
    Chow Mein
      Burgers, 134
    Dip, Spicy, 157
    Gourmet
      Hamburgers, 148
    Hamburger
      Skillet, 70
    Hamburgers, 66
    Linkburgers,
      Smoked, 148
    Meat Loaf
      Supreme, 62
    Meat Loaves,
      Target, 62
    Meatballs, Quick
      Swedish, 64
    Meatballs, Saucy
      Italian, 64
    Patties, Apple-, 66

Beef, Ground, *continued*
    Sausage and Muffin
      Bake, 69
    Skilletburgers, 66
    Sour Cream
      Burgers, 68
    Spanish Rice
      Skillet, 70
    Stuffed Hamburger
      Roll, 62
    Stuffingburgers, 68
    Teriyaki Burgers, 68
  Kidney Pie, and, 74
  Minute Steak, 16
    Bean Pot, and, 17
    Skillet Pizza, 17
    Sukiyaki, 17
  Pie, 129
  Pot Roast, 19
    Beer, in, 19
    Cranberry, 19
    Fruited, 21
    Mushroom, 130
    Polynesian, 19
    Rump, Hawaiian, 17
    Rump, Spicy, 17
    Snowcap, 21
  Rib Supreme, 6
  Roast
    Chuck,
      Barbecued, 149
    Rib, Rolled, Au
      Jus, 6
    Rib, Standing, 6
    Rib Supreme, 6
    Rump, Rolled, Au
      Jus, 6
    Sirloin Tip, 7
  Roasting Chart, 7
  Round Steak
    Burgundy, 18
    Cooking, 15
    Dinner, 18
    Italian Stuffed, 16
    Onions, and, 18
    Ranch, 152
    Roll-ups, 15
    Savory Pepper
      Steak, 15
  Salad, San
    Marino, 139
  Sauerbraten, 19
  Shanks, Simmered, 22
  Short Ribs
    Barbecued, 16
    Braised, 16
    Stew, 16
  Steak
    Broiled, 11
    Broiling Chart, 11
    Diane, 13

Beef, Steak, *continued*
    Flank Rolls,
      Deviled, 12
    Flank, Stuffed, 12
    Identification, 10
    London Broil, 12
    Panbroiled, 11
    Planked, 11
    Tenderized, 11
  Stew
    Bake, 22
    Chinese, 23
    Snappy, 128
    Sprouts, and, 23
    Stroganoff, 13
    Swiss Steak, 18
    Swiss Steak, Pizza, 18
    Tenderloin Deluxe, 7
    Tenderloin, Roast, 6
    Tenderloin Tips,
      Saucy, 13
    Teriyaki, 13
  Bologna
    Bake, 118
    Baskets, 118
    Sticks, 116
  Bone Shapes, 108-109
  Brains, Deep-fried, 77
  Brains, Scrambled, 77
  Broiling Chart
    Ham Slice, 48
    Lamb Chop, 52
    Steak, 11
  Butter, Basil, 12
  Butter, Herb, 145
  Buying, 108-109
    Beef, Tips, 66, 130
    Fish, Guide, 85
    Poultry, Guide, 92
    Shrimp, Guide, 80

C-E

Cabbage Rolls, Savory, 70
Canadian-style
  Bacon, 37
Carving, 104-107
Chateaubriand, 6
Cheese Noodle
  Casserole, 41
Cheeseburger Pie, 130
Chicken
  a la King, 93
  and Rice, Orange, 93
  Bake, Garden, 95
  Breasts Supreme, 96
  Broiled, Basic, 95
  Chow Bake, 93
  -cranberry Mold, 140
  Enchiladas, 97
  Fried, Perfect, 95

Chicken, *continued*
  Glossary, 92
  Gravy, Creamy, 100
  Grilled, 145
  How to Cut Up, 94
  Livers, Creamy, 96
  Orange-sauced, 92
  Pinwheels, Polka-
    dot, 156
  Pot Pie, 93
  Romaine, 95
  Salad, 140
  Salad, Fruited, 140
  Salad, Golden, 140
  Stewed, 95
  -stuffed Peppers, 92
  Swiss-wiches, 137
  Yorkshire, 93
Chili-burger Stack-
  ups, 71
Chops, *see Lamb, Pork,
  and Veal*
Chuck Wagon, 152-153
City Chicken, 30
Clam Cocktail Dunk, 156
Clam-mushroom Bake, 81
Clambake, 144-145
Clams, Steamed, 81
Coney Islands, 118
Cooking Terms, 101
Corn
  Bread, 152
  on the Cob, Fresh, 145
  on the Cob,
    Grilled, 145
Corned Beef
  and Apples, 23
  Cabbage, 'n, 149
  Dinner, 22
  Noodles, with, 125
  Pie, 125
Cornish Hens, Stuffed, 97
Crab
  -artichoke Bake, 83
  Crown, King, 141
  Jambalaya, 83
  Meat Newburg, 83
  Open-facers, Hot, 136
  Sauce, Salmon with, 87
Cranberry
  Drink, Spiced, 157
  Ham, Topped, 44
  Mold, Chicken-, 140
  Pot Roast, 19
Croquettes, Ham and
  Rice, 128
Curried
  Ham, Quick, 126
  Lamb, 59
  Lamb Chops, 52
Curry Sauce, 12

Cutlets, *see Veal*
Deviled Ham
  Dip, Deviled, 156
  Pepper Cups, 125
  Tuna, and, 136
Dilly Beef
  Cartwheel, 134
Dried Beef Dinner, 124
Drugstore Wrap, 111
Duck
  Cantonese, 99
  Contemporary
    Duckling, 97
  Navy Bean Stuffed, 97
Dumplings, Veal with, 30
Edam Sage Spread, 157
Enchiladas, Chicken, 97

F-I

Fish, *see also Salmon
  and Tuna*
  Buying Guide, 85
  Fillet Roll-ups,
    Stuffed, 84
  Fillets, Baked, 85
  Fried, 85
  Fry, 150-151
  Halibut Royale, 84
  Lemon-stuffed, 85
  Trout, Mountain
    Rainbow, 150
  Trout, Sesame
    Rainbow, 150
Fondue, Beef, 12
Frank and Corn
  Crown, 123
Frankfurters
  Bake, Three-bean, 122
  Barbecued, 122
  Cabbage, and, 122
  Cheesy, Jiffy, 119
  Coney Islands, 118
  Coney Sauce, 118
  Coney Tacos, 118
  Coneys, Quicky, 118
  Corn Crown, and, 123
  Creole, 123
  Fancy, 156
  Foil, in, 119
  Glazed Apples 'n, 123
  Heat, To, 118
  -noodle Bake, 122
  -potato Pie, 123
  Red Hots on Kabob, 119
  Snapperoni, 118
  Supper, Saucy, 122
  Sweet and Sour, 119
  Triangles, 119
Freezing, 111-113
Frog Legs with Sauce, 87

Game Birds, Roasting
  Chart for, 99
Game, Wild, 98-99
Geese with Fruit,
  Wild, 98
Giblet Gravy, 100
Giblets, How to Cook, 91
Glaze, Apricot-honey, 48
Glaze, Jewel, 48
Gravy, 100
Ground Meat, *see indi-
  vidual meats, ground*
Ham
  Bites, Artichoke-, 156
  Broiling Chart, 48
  Cheddar Rice, and, 44
  Cook, How to, 48
  Cranberry Topped, 44
  Creamed, 50
  Curried, Quick, 126
  Cuts, 46-47, 51
  Glazes, 48
  Ground
    and Rice Croquettes,
    128
    Glazed Ham-raisin
      Balls, 65
    Glazed Ham Ring, 62
    Pork-apricot
      Loaf, 64
  Nectarines, with, 44
  Panfrying Chart, 48
  -platter Meal, 125
  Potato Scallop,
    and, 50
  Roasting Chart, 48
  -schnitzel, Filled, 125
  Slice, Grilled, 148
  Stew, Kettle-of-
    bean, 128
  Stew, and Vegetable, 50
  Sweet-sour, over
    Rice, 50
  Tropicale, 49
  Wafflewiches, 136
Hamburger Skillet, 70
Hamburgers, 66-68, *see
  also Beef, Ground*
Hasenpfeffer, 98
Hash, Oriental, 128
Heart, Chicken-fried, 75
Heart, Stuffed Beef, 75
How Much to Serve, 109
How to Cook Giblets, 91
Individual Clambake, 145

K-O

Kabobs, 146
Kidney, 74
Lamb, 146

Kabobs, *continued*
  Lamb, Garlic, 58
  Liver, 73
  Red Hots on, 119
  Speedy, 124
Kidney
  Kabobs, 74
  Pie, Beef and, 74
  Wine Sauce, in, 74
Kraut-pork Pinwheel, 64
Lamb
  Broiler Dinner, 68
  Chops
    Broiling Chart, 52
    Curried, 52
    Orange, 52
    Oriental, 52
    Tangy, 52
  Curried, 59
  Cuts, 54-56
  Kabobs, 146
  Kabobs, Garlic, 58
  Leg of, Fruited, 57
  Pinwheels, 71
  Riblets,
    Barbecued, 58
  Roast
    Honey-lime, 58
    Plum Sauce, with, 57
    Roll, Savory, 57
    Shoulder,
      Stuffed, 57
  Roasting Chart, 57
  Shanks, Herbed, 61
  Shanks, Zippy, 61
  Spanish, 129
  Stew, Dilled, 59
  Stew, Shepherd's, 59
  Vegetables, with, 58
Liver, 72
  Bake, Bacon and, 72
  Creamy, over Rice, 72
  Kabobs, 73
  Loaf, 73
  Rolls, Sausage-, 116
  Tomato Skillet,
    and, 72
Livers, Chicken,
  Creamy, 96
Lobster, 82
  Newberg, 83
  Over-the-coals, 145
  Salad, 141
  -shrimp Chowder, 83
  Tails, Rock, 82
London Broil, 12
Luau, American-
  style, 154-155
Luncheon Meat
  Kabobs, Speedy, 124
  Loaf, Fruited, 124

Luncheon Meat, *continued*
  Potato Salad, and, 138
Macaroni-meat
  Skillet, 124
Marinade, Armenian, 149
Marinade Italiano, 149
Marinated Pork Roast, 33
Meat Loaves, 62, 64, 73
Meat Seasoning
  Guide, 102
Meatballs, 64, 65
Mexican Dinner,
  Jiffy, 125
Opossum, 98
Oxtail Stew, Old-
  time, 75
Oysters
  Fried, 81
  Scalloped, 80
  Stew, 80

P-R

Pan Gravy, 100
Parmigiano, Veal, 31
Partridge in Red
  Wine, 98
Pastry, Plain, 83
Pea Soup, Old-
  fashioned, 44
Pepper Steak, Savory, 15
Pepperpot Soup, 77
Pheasant with Apples, 99
Pizza
  by the Yard, 134
  Crust, Jiffy, 135
  Pronto, 134
  Sausage, Duo, 135
  Toppers, 135
Plain Pastry, 83
Pork, *see also Bacon, Ham,
  and Sausage*
  Cheese Noodle
    Casserole, 41
  Chops
    Amber Skillet
      Dinner, 40
    Barbecue, 40
    Braised, 38
    Gourmet, 38
    Orange-glazed, 38
    Risotto Bake, 40
    Sour Cream, in, 40
    Stuffed, 38
    Supreme, 40
  Cuts, 34-35
  Cuts, Smoked, 36
  Ground
    -apricot Loaf, 64
    Cabbage Rolls,
      Savory, 70

Pork, Ground, *continued*
  Chopped Meat
    Suey, 70
  Ham-raisin Balls,
    Glazed, 65
  Ham Ring, Glazed, 62
  Meat Loaf Supreme,
    62
  -pork Pinwheel,
    Kraut, 64
Hash, Oriental, 128
Hocks and Kraut, 41
Pie, 129
Ribs, Country-
  style, 148
Ribs, Plum-glazed, 42
Roast
  Boston Shoulder,
    Glazed, 32
  Crown, Gingery, 37
  Loin, 155
  Loin, Cherry-
    sauced, 32
  Marinated, 33
  Shoulder Butt,
    Glazed, 37
  Sirloin, Gingered, 32
  Stuffing, with, 33
  Veal and, 24
Roasting Chart, Fresh
  and Smoked, 32
Sausage, Bulk, 69
Saute, Chinese, 41
Spareribs
  Barbecued, 42
  Onion Sauce, with, 42
  Sweet-sour, 42
Sweet-sour, 41
Tenderloin, Breaded, 41
Tenderloin, Roast, 33
Pot Roast, *see Beef*
Pot Roast Gravy, 100
Potatoes, Duchess, 11
Poultry, *see also Chicken,*
  Duck, and Turkey
  Coating Tips, 95
  Roasting Chart, 90
  Thawing, 92
Punch, Fruit, 155
Rabbit, Fried, 98
Ribs, *see also Beef*
  Short Ribs and Pork
  Spareribs
  Country-style, 148
  Plum-glazed, 42
Roast, *see Beef, Lamb,*
  Pork, and Veal
Roasting Charts, *see*
  individual meats
Rotisserie Roasts, 149
Round Steak, *see Beef*

S

Salads, 138-141
Salmon
  Crab Sauce, with, 87
  Pastry-topped Fish
    Bake, 86
  -salad Loaf, 141
  Sandwich, Fried, 136
  Seafood Turnovers, 87
Sandwiches, 134-137
Sauce
  Barbecue, Basic, 149
  Barbecue, Burgundy, 149
  Bearnaise, 6
  Cocktail, 87
  Curry, 12
  Mint
    Fresh, 58
    In-a-hurry, 58
    Tangy, 58
  Mustard, 49
  Mustard, Hot, 12
  Raisin, 49
  Tartar, 87
  Tomato, 12
Sauerbraten, 19
Sausage
  Biscuits, in, 124
  Linkburgers,
    Smoked, 148
  -liver Rolls, 116
  Mostaccioli, and, 69
  Muffin Bake, and, 69
  Smoky Bean Skillet, 116
  Tomato Polenta, 116
  Varieties, 120-121
  -zucchini Boats, 69
Scallopini, Veal, 31
Scallops, Fried, 81
Seafood, *see Clams, Crab,*
  Lobster, Scallops,
  Shrimp, and Oysters
Seasoning Guide,
  Meat, 102
Sesame Topper, 11
Shanks, Herbed Lamb, 61
Shanks, Simmered Beef, 22
Shanks, Zippy Lamb, 61
Shepherd's Lamb Stew, 59
Shrimp
  -avocado Bowls, 141
  Boat, 137
  Buffet Casserole, 80
  Buying Guide, 80
  Chowder, Lobster-, 83
  -cucumber Ring, 141
  Foo Yong, 78
  French Fried, 78
  Fresh Cooked, 78
  Jackets, in, 157

Shrimp, *continued*
  Newburg, 83
  Quiche, 78
  Sandwiches, 137
  Skillet, Jiffy, 80
Skilletburgers, 66
Soup
  Lobster-shrimp
    Chowder, 83
  Oyster Stew, 80
  Pea, Old-fashioned, 44
  Pepperpot, 77
Sour Cream Burgers, 68
Spaghetti
  Bake, Tuna-, 86
  Meatballs, Saucy
    Italian, 64
  Toss, Italian, 118
Spanish Rice Skillet, 70
Spareribs, *see Pork*
Squirrel, Fried, 98
Steak, *see Beef Steak*
Steak Diane, 13
Steamed Clams, 81
Stew
  Beef and Sprouts, 23
  Beef, Bake, 22
  Beef, Snappy, 128
  Chinese, 23
  Ham and Vegetable, 50
  Kettle-of-bean, 128
  Lamb, Dilled, 59
  Lamb, Shepherd's, 59
  Oxtail, Old-time, 75
  Short Rib, 16
  Veal, 29
Storing, 110 *see also*
  Freezing
Stroganoff, Beef, 13
Stuffed Pork Chops, 38
Stuffing
  Bread, 91
  Cracker, 91
  Ground Beef, 91
  Herb, 91
  How to Stuff and
    Truss, 91
Stuffingburgers, 68
Sukiyaki, Minute
  Steak, 17
Swedish Meatballs,
  Quick, 64
Sweetbread Bake, 76
Sweetbreads, Creamed, 77
Swiss Steak, 18
Swiss Steak, Pizza, 18

T-W

Teriyaki, Beef, 13
Teriyaki Burgers, 68

Terms to Know, 101
Tomato Polenta, 116
Tongue
  Bean Skillet, 'n, 76
  on Rice, Cheesy, 76
  Spiced, 76
  Stuffed Peppers, 76
Trout, 150
Tuna
  -bean Salad, 139
  Company, Bake, 86
  Deviled Ham and, 136
  Pastry-topped, Bake, 86
  Pepper Cups, in, 138
  Ring, Creamy, 138
  Seafood Turnovers, 87
  Souffle Mold, 138
  -spaghetti Bake, 86
  Tetrazzini, 86
Turkey
  Bake, Cheddar, 126
  Bombay, 126
  Drumsticks, Deviled, 88
  Paprika, 126
  Rice, with, 88
  Roast, Halves, 88
  Roasts, Twin, 88
  Sandwiches, Hot, 137
  Tips, 88
  Toss, Tokyo, 140
Variety Meats, 72-77
Veal
  Barbecued, 30
  Birds, 29
  Chops, 29
  Chops, Italian, 29
  City Chicken, 30
  Cutlets
    Breaded, 28
    Parmigiano, 31
    Roll-ups, 28
    Scallopini, 31
    Wiener Schnitzel, 28
    Wiener Schnitzel a la
      Holstein, 28
  Cuts, 26-27
  Ground
    Patties, 68
    Skillet, 71
    Special, Dilled, 65
  Pork Roast, and, 24
  Roast, 24
  Roasting Chart, 24
  Spinach-stuffed, 24
  Stew, 29
  Sweet-sour, 30
  with Dumplings, 30
Venison, 98
Wiener Schnitzel, 28
Wiener Schnitzel a la
  Holstein, 28